"This comprehensive workbook deserves to be in the library of every active therapist, but it shouldn't be left on the shelf! Once again, the authors have empowered the reader with straightforward instructions on every major approach to stress management known. From worry to chronic headaches to information overload, here is your one-stop guide to recovery."

> —R. Reid Wilson, Ph.D., author of *Don't Panic: Taking Control of Anxiety Attacks*

"This text remains, after twenty years, the clearest, best-organized, and most readable book on stress management. It has achieved the status of the 'classic' self-help reference in the field."

> —Edmund J. Bourne, Ph.D., author of *The Anxiety and Phobia Workbook, Coping with Anxiety,* and *Beyond Anxiety and Phobia*

"An exemplary book on stress. It is lucidly written, rationally ordered, and comprehensive, and each section is densely packed with instructions and exercises which make the workbook easy to practice."

> —*Somatics Magazine: Journal of the Mind/Body Arts and Sciences*

The Relaxation & Stress Reduction WORKBOOK

SIXTH EDITION

Martha Davis, PhD

Elizabeth Robbins Eshelman, MSW

Matthew McKay, PhD

New Harbinger Publications, Inc.

Publisher's Note

This publication is designed to provide accurate and authoritative information in regard to the subject matter covered. It is sold with the understanding that the publisher is not engaged in rendering psychological, financial, legal, or other professional services. If expert assistance or counseling is needed, the services of a competent professional should be sought.

The material in chapter 13 that is based upon the work of Michelle G. Craske and David H. Barlow's *Master Your Anxiety and Worry*, 2nd ed. (2006) pages 99–109 is used by permission of Oxford University Press.

Distributed in Canada by Raincoast Books

Copyright © 2008 by Martha Davis, Elizabeth Robbins Eshelman, and Matthew McKay
New Harbinger Publications, Inc.
5674 Shattuck Avenue
Oakland, CA 94609
www.newharbinger.com

Acquired by Tesilya Hanauer; Cover design by Amy Shoup;
Edited by Kayla Sussell

Library of Congress Cataloging-in-Publication Data

Davis, Martha, 1947-
  The relaxation and stress reduction workbook / Martha Davis, Elizabeth Robbins Eshelman, and Matthew McKay. -- 6th ed.
      p. cm.
  Includes bibliographical references and index.
  ISBN-13: 978-1-57224-549-5 (pbk. : alk. paper)
  ISBN-10: 1-57224-549-2 (pbk. : alk. paper) 1. Stress management. 2. Relaxation.
I. Eshelman, Elizabeth Robbins. II. McKay, Matthew. III. Title.
RA785.D374 2008
616.9'8--dc22

                                2008003637

15   14   13

20   19   18   17   16   15   14   13   12

We would like to dedicate this book to our families.

Thank you, Bill and Amanda, Don, Judy, Rebekah and Jordan.

Contents

Preface to the Sixth Edition

Today, we are inundated with all kinds of information, including a lot of information about stress and stress management. What is unique about this book is that it immediately zeros in on what is relevant to you; that is, the specific stressors in your life and how you react to them. Once you've identified the sources of your stress, your most disturbing symptoms, and how you typically cope with them, you are directed to the techniques that will help you in your particular situation. In short, you don't have to waste your time reading material that isn't relevant to your specific needs; instead you can focus on simple step-by-step instructions that will teach you how to feel better now.

This workbook is based on more than twenty-five years of clinical experience working with clients who came to us with symptoms of tension and stress like insomnia, worry, high blood pressure, headaches, indigestion, depression, and road rage. When they seek help, many of these people report they are experiencing some kind of a transition, such as a loss, a promotion, or a move. This isn't surprising, since stress can be defined as any change to which you must adapt. Most clients describe feeling worn down by everyday hassles such as dealing with inconsiderate or rude people, commuting long distances, caretaking children and elderly relatives, and managing tons of paperwork. One client referred to this "wearing down" process as a "death by a thousand cuts." Indeed, unmanaged stress can have an accumulative effect that may lead to major psychological and physical illnesses. Clients also tell us about some of their less successful stress-management strategies: working harder and faster; numbing their pain and soothing themselves with drugs, alcohol, and food; worrying about their problems; procrastinating; and taking their frustrations out on others.

To date, more than 700,000 people have purchased this book to learn how to relax their bodies, calm their minds, turn around their self-defeating behavior, and take control of their hectic lives. About every five years we update this workbook, adding new strategies that the latest research and our clinical experience have shown to be effective. We eliminate techniques we've learned are not especially helpful, and we simplify and shorten some techniques to save you time. This allows us to keep this workbook as an up-to-date, relevant resource for professionals, a solid source of information for individuals who want to learn to manage their stress on their own, and a popular textbook in classes and workshops on stress management and relaxation.

Recent research supports the commonsense notion that it is better to face your troubles than to run away from them. Although escaping painful feelings like anxiety, depression, and anger may make you feel better in the short run, in the long run, avoidance prevents you from having positive corrective experiences associated with facing these painful feelings. For example, dropping a speech class because you are worried about blowing a talk in front of a group of strangers may alleviate your anxiety immediately, but you don't get the experience of surviving giving the talk and the confidence that comes from learning that you can do it, albeit imperfectly. Instead, you continue to live in fear of public speaking, and the next time you are faced with giving a talk in front of a group, you are still terrified.

With this in mind, we've added some techniques to strengthen your ability to tolerate distressing feelings as well as build up your self-confidence so you can accomplish your goals more effectively. We've replaced the chapter called Thought Stopping with the new chapter Focusing. This chapter will teach you to explore the feelings in your body and understand what they mean. Rather than trying to suppress your feelings, you are invited to move toward accepting them and learning from them, using a simple but profound technique called "Focusing." Typically, this lessens or eliminates the power of distressing feelings in your life.

We've revised the Worry Control chapter (now called Facing Worry and Anxiety) with an emphasis on facing your fear of uncertainty, using Michelle G. Craske's and David H. Barlow's new model of exposure. The Coping Skills Training chapter has been divided into two chapters: Coping Skills Training for Fears and a new chapter called Anger Inoculation.

Whether you want to make just a few changes in your lifestyle or you need a major life overhaul, this workbook shows you how to get started and stick with a program that is tailored just for you. Based on the feedback we've received from our clients and readers who've used these techniques, your efforts will be amply rewarded.

Acknowledgments

The authors wish to acknowledge the following contributors to the sixth edition of this book. Their expertise, experience, and collaboration have made this a more valuable edition.

Caryl Fairfull, RD, is a registered dietitian and has held leadership positions in the American Dietetic Association. She is a graduate of the University of California at Santa Barbara and completed her dietetic internship at the Bronx VA Hospital in the Bronx, New York. Ms. Fairfull managed the Department of Nutrition Services for Kaiser Permanente's Santa Clara Medical Center in northern California. She has developed nutrition care guidelines and provided individual and group nutrition counseling. She currently works at Sierra Nevada Memorial Hospital in Grass Valley, California, providing clinical nutrition services. Ms. Fairfull wrote chapter 19, Nutrition and Stress.

Cheryl Pierson-Carey, PT, MS, is a rehabilitation specialist at Kaiser Permanente in Fremont, California, and an associate clinical professor in the UCSF/SFSU Graduate Program in Physical Therapy. She holds degrees from Indiana University, Purdue University, and Samuel Merritt College. She is a member of the American Physical Therapy Association. Ms. Pierson-Carey wrote chapter 20, Exercise.

The authors would like to thank Albert Ellis, PhD for volunteering to review and give feedback on the Refuting Irrational Ideas chapter. Dr. Ellis developed Rational Emotive Behavior Therapy upon which this chapter is based.

We would also like to express our appreciation to Patricia Eaton LMFT for suggesting the case study in the Focusing chapter. Ms. Eaton is a therapist in the Psychiatry Department at Kaiser-Permanente Medical Center in Santa Clara.

How to Get the Most Out of This Workbook

This workbook teaches you clinically proven stress-management and relaxation techniques. Each technique is presented with concise background information followed by step-by-step exercises. As you practice these techniques, you will gain new insight into your personal stress response and learn how to reestablish balance and a sense of well-being in your life.

Use this workbook as a guide. Read chapters 1 and 2 first. They are the foundation upon which all of the other chapters are built. Then you will know enough about stress and your personal reactions to stress to decide which chapters will be most helpful for you to read next.

Chapters 3 through 10 teach techniques for relaxation. Chapters 11 through 15 will help you with your stressful thoughts and feelings. Chapter 16 assists you in managing your time more effectively so that you can free up time to relax and do more of what is most important to you. From chapter 17 you can learn to communicate more assertively and chapter 18 gives you many options to deal with environmental and interpersonal stress at work. Chapters 19 and 20 teach the basics of nutrition and exercise. Chapter 21 gives you some suggestions on how to increase motivation, deal with problems that come up along the way, and stick to your plan.

Stress and tension are present in your life every day. Stress management and relaxation can be effective only if you make them a daily part of your lifestyle. As you are learning the skills in this book that are pertinent to you, practice them repeatedly to ensure that you will be able to carry them out anytime you need to, without having to refer to written materials. Regular conscious practice can lead to habits of regular relaxation and stress reduction at an unconscious level.

Here are some suggestions that will help you relax on a regular basis:

- Make an agreement with yourself to set aside a specific time each day dedicated to relaxation. If finding the time to do the exercises in this book is an issue, read chapter 16 on time management.

- The length of time required each day to practice the relaxation techniques in this workbook varies. Start small. Doing a relaxation exercise for five minutes on a regular basis is better than doing it only once for an hour. Aim for twenty to thirty minutes of relaxation time once or twice a day. Note that some people prefer to take more frequent, shorter relaxation breaks.

- You decide when is the best time to relax based on your schedule by answering these two questions: When do you need to relax most? When can you realistically break away from external demands to take some time for yourself? Here are some examples of what clients in our stress-management and relaxation classes have found most helpful and doable:

  - Beginning the day with a relaxation exercise makes people more focused and proactive in dealing with the stressful demands of their day.

  - Taking a relaxation break during the day can reverse growing tension that would otherwise culminate in painful symptoms such as a headache or indigestion.

  - Relaxing before leaving work or upon arriving at home allows a person to let go of and decompress from the tensions of his or her busy day and to become calm and revitalized enough to enjoy personal time at home.

  - Using a relaxation exercise to go to sleep quickly and then sleep soundly can result in waking up refreshed.

- Choose a quiet place where you will not be interrupted to learn the techniques. Once mastered, many of the relaxation techniques presented in this workbook can be done in stressful situations.

- Since this is a new activity for you, it is a good idea to let people around you know what you are doing. Ask them to help out by leaving you alone without distracting you. Family members, fellow office workers, and friends are usually very supportive of these exercises once they understand what you are doing and why.

- It's best not to practice a relaxation exercise right after eating a big meal or when very tired, unless your purpose is to fall asleep.

- You will enjoy your experience more if you choose a comfortable position in a location that has a comfortable temperature, wear loose clothing, and remove your contacts or glasses.

See your health care provider before beginning the work in this book if any of the following circumstances are relevant to you:

- If you are over thirty or if your reaction to stress involves physical symptoms, such as frequent headaches, stomach problems, or high blood pressure, your doctor should perform a physical examination to rule out possible physical problems that may need medical attention.

- If, after starting your stress-management program, you experience any prolonged negative physical effects.

- If you have been taking medication that you may no longer need once your stress-related symptoms go away with regular practice of these exercises.

Your health care provider can be a supportive partner in your efforts to live a healthier life.

How You React to Stress

Stress is an everyday fact of life. You can't avoid it. *Stress* results from any change you must adapt to, ranging from the negative extreme of actual physical danger to the exhilaration of falling in love or achieving some long-desired success. In between, day-to-day living confronts even the most well-managed life with a continuous stream of potentially stressful experiences. Not all stress is bad. In fact, stress is not only desirable it is also essential to life. Whether the stress you experience is the result of major life changes or the cumulative effect of minor everyday hassles, it is how you respond to these events that determines the impact that stress will have on your life.

SOURCES OF STRESS

You experience stress from four basic sources:

1. Your environment bombards you with demands to adjust. You must endure weather, pollens, noise, traffic, and air pollution.

2. You also must cope with social stressors such as demands for your time and attention, job interviews, deadlines and competing priorities, work presentations, interpersonal conflicts, financial problems, and the loss of loved ones.

3. A third source of stress is physiological. The rapid growth of adolescence; the changes menopause causes in women; lack of exercise, poor nutrition, and inadequate sleep; illness, injuries, and aging all tax the body. Your physiological reaction to environmental and social threats and changes also can result in stressful symptoms such as muscle tension, headaches, stomach upset, anxiety, and depression.

4. The fourth source of stress is your thoughts. Your brain interprets complex changes in your environment and body and determines when to turn on the "stress response." How you interpret and label your present experience and what you predict for your future can serve either to relax or to stress you. For example, interpreting a sour look from your boss to mean that you are doing an inadequate job is likely to be very anxiety-provoking. Interpreting the same look as tiredness or preoccupation with personal problems will not be as frightening.

Stress researchers Lazarus and Folkman (1984) have argued that stress begins with your appraisal of a situation. You first ask how dangerous or difficult the situation is and what resources you have to help you cope with it. Anxious, stressed people often decide that (1) an event is dangerous, difficult, or painful and (2) they don't have the resources to cope.

FIGHT-OR-FLIGHT RESPONSE

Walter B. Cannon, a physiologist, laid the groundwork for the modern meaning of "stress" at Harvard in the beginning of the twentieth century. He was the first to describe the "fight-or-flight response" as a series of biochemical changes that prepare you to deal with threat or danger. Primitive people needed quick bursts of energy to fight or flee predators like saber-toothed tigers. You can thank this response for enabling your ancestors to survive long enough to pass on their genetic heritage to you. Think of occasions in your life when the fight-or-flight response served you well, such as when you had to respond quickly to a car that cut in front of you on the freeway or when you had to deal with an overly aggressive panhandler. These days, however, when social custom prevents you from either fighting or running away, this "emergency" or "stress response" is rarely useful.

Hans Selye (1978), the first major researcher on stress, was able to trace what happens in the body during the fight-or-flight response. He found that any problem, imagined or real, can cause the cerebral cortex (the thinking part of the brain) to send an alarm to the hypothalamus (the main switch for the stress response, located in the midbrain). The hypothalamus then stimulates the sympathetic nervous system to make a series of changes in the body. These changes include the following: The heart rate, breathing rate, muscle tension, metabolism, and blood pressure all increase. The hands and feet become cold as blood is directed away from the extremities and digestive system into the larger muscles that can help to fight or run. Some people experience butterflies in their stomachs. The diaphragm and anus lock. The pupils dilate to sharpen vision and hearing becomes more acute.

Regrettably, during times of chronic stress when the fight-or-flight physiological responses continue unchecked, something else happens that can have long-term negative effects. The adrenal glands secrete *corticoids* (adrenaline or epinephrine, and norepinephrine), which inhibit digestion, reproduction, growth, tissue repair, and the responses of the immune and inflammatory systems. In other words, some very important functions that keep the body healthy begin to shut down.

Fortunately, the same mechanism that turns the stress response on can turn it off. This is called the *relaxation response*. As soon as you decide that a situation is no longer dangerous, your brain stops sending emergency signals to your brain stem, which in turn ceases to send panic messages to your nervous system. Three minutes after you shut off the danger signals, the fight-or-flight response burns out. Your metabolism, heart rate, breathing rate, muscle tension, and blood pressure all return to their normal levels. Herbert Benson (2000) suggests that you can use your mind to change your physiology for the better, improving your health and perhaps reducing your need for medication in the process. He coined the term "the relaxation response" to refer to this natural restorative response.

CHRONIC STRESS AND DISEASE

Chronic or persistent stress can occur when life stressors are unrelenting, as they are, for example, during a major reorganization or downsizing at work, while undergoing a messy divorce, or coping with chronic pain or disease or a life-threatening illness. Chronic stress also takes place when small stressors accumulate and you are unable to recuperate from any one of them. As long as the mind perceives a threat, the body remains aroused. If your stress response remains turned on, your chances of getting a stress-related disease may be increasing.

Researchers have been looking at the relationship between stress and disease for over a hundred years. They have observed that people suffering from stress-related disorders tend to show hyperactivity in a particular "preferred system," or "stress-prone system," such as the skeletomuscular, cardiovascular, or gastrointestinal system. For example, chronic stress can result in muscle tension and fatigue for some people. For others, it can contribute to stress hypertension (high blood pressure), migraine headaches, ulcers, or chronic diarrhea.

Almost every system in the body can be damaged by stress. When an increase in corticoids suppresses the reproduction system, this can cause amenorrhea (cessation of menstruation) and failure to ovulate in women, impotency in men, and loss of libido in both. Stress-triggered changes in the lungs increase the symptoms of asthma, bronchitis, and other respiratory conditions. Loss of insulin during the stress response may be a factor in the onset of adult diabetes. Stress suspends tissue repair and remodeling, which, in turn, causes decalcification of the bones, osteoporosis, and susceptibility to fractures. The inhibition of immune and inflammatory systems makes you more susceptible to colds and flu and can exacerbate some specific diseases such as cancer and AIDS. In addition, a prolonged stress response can worsen conditions such as arthritis, chronic pain, and diabetes. There are also some indications that the continued release and depletion of norepinephrine during a state of chronic stress can contribute to depression and anxiety.

The relationship between chronic stress, disease, and aging is another area of research. Experts in aging are looking at the changing patterns of disease and the emergence of degenerative disorders. Over just a few generations, the threat of infectious diseases such as typhoid, pneumonia, and polio has been replaced with such "modern plagues" as cardiovascular disease, cancer, arthritis, respiratory disorders like asthma and emphysema, and a pervasive incidence of depression. As you age normally, you expect a natural slowing down of your body's functioning. But many of these mid- to late-life disorders are stress-sensitive diseases. Currently, researchers and clinicians are asking how stress accelerates the aging process and what can be done to counteract this process.

SCHEDULE OF RECENT EXPERIENCE

Thomas Holmes, MD, and his research associates at the University of Washington found that people are more likely to develop illnesses or clinical symptoms after experiencing a period of time when they've had to adapt to many life-changing events (1981).

Dr. Holmes and his associates developed the Schedule of Recent Experience, which allows you to quantify how many changes you've experienced in the past year and consider how these stressful events may have increased your vulnerability to illness. The main purpose of this scale, however, is to increase your awareness of stressful events and their potential impact on your health so that you can take the necessary steps to reduce the level of stress in your life.

Instructions: Think about each possible life event listed below and decide how many times, if at all, each has happened to you within the last year. Write that number in the Number of Times column. (Note that if an event happened more than four times, you would still give it a 4 in that column.)

Event	Number of Times	x	Mean Value	=	Your Score
1. A lot more or a lot less trouble with the boss.		x	23	=	
2. A major change in sleeping habits (sleeping a lot more or a lot less or a change in time of day when you sleep).		x	16	=	
3. A major change in eating habits (eating a lot more or a lot less or very different meal hours or surroundings).		x	15	=	
4. A revision of personal habits (dress, manners, associations, and so on).		x	24	=	
5. A major change in your usual type or amount of recreation.		x	19	=	
6. A major change in your social activities (e.g., clubs, dancing, movies, visiting, and so on).		x	18	=	
7. A major change in church activities (attending a lot more or a lot less than usual).		x	19	=	

8. A major change in the number of family get-togethers (a lot more or a lot fewer than usual).		x	15	=	
9. A major change in your financial state (a lot worse off or a lot better off).		x	38	=	
10. Trouble with in-laws.		x	29	=	
11. A major change in the number of arguments with spouse (a lot more or a lot fewer than usual regarding child rearing, personal habits, and so on).		x	35	=	
12. Sexual difficulties.		x	39	=	
13. Major personal injury or illness.		x	53	=	
14. Death of a close family member (other than spouse).		x	63	=	
15. Death of spouse.		x	100	=	
16. Death of a close friend.		x	37	=	
17. Gaining a new family member (through birth, adoption, oldster moving in, and so on).		x	39	=	
18. Major change in the health or behavior of a family.		x	44	=	
19. Change in residence.		x	20	=	
20. Detention in jail or other institution.		x	63	=	
21. Minor violations of the law (traffic tickets, jaywalking, disturbing the peace, and so on).		x	11	=	
22. Major business readjustment (merger, reorganization, bankruptcy, and so on).		x	39	=	
23. Marriage.		x	50	=	
24. Divorce.		x	73	=	
25. Marital separation from spouse.		x	65	=	
26. Outstanding personal achievement.		x	28	=	
27. Son or daughter leaving home (marriage, attending college, and so on).		x	29	=	
28. Retirement from work.		x	45	=	
29. Major change in working hours or conditions.		x	20	=	
30. Major change in responsibilities at work (promotion, demotion, lateral transfer).		x	29	=	

31. Being fired from work.		x	47	=
32. Major change in living conditions (building a new home or remodeling, deterioration of home or neighborhood).		x	25	=
33. Spouse beginning or ceasing to work outside the home.		x	26	=
34. Taking out a mortgage or loan for a major purchase (purchasing a home or business and so on).		x	31	=
35. Taking out a loan for a lesser purchase (a car, TV, freezer, and so on).		x	17	=
36. Foreclosure on a mortgage or loan.		x	30	=
37. Vacation.		x	13	=
38. Changing to a new school.		x	20	=
39. Changing to a different line of work.		x	36	=
40. Beginning or ceasing formal schooling.		x	26	=
41. Marital reconciliation with mate.		x	45	=
42. Pregnancy.		x	40	=
Your total score				

Scoring:

- Multiply the mean value by the number of times an event happened, and enter the result in the Your Score column.

- Add up your scores to get your total score and enter it at the bottom of the schedule. (Remember, if an event happened more than four times within the past year, give it a 4 in the Number of Times column. A 4 is the highest number that can be used in the Number of Times column.)

According to Dr. Holmes and his associates, the higher your total score, the greater your risk of developing stress-related symptoms or illnesses. Of those with a score of over 300 for the past year, almost 80 percent will get sick in the near future; of those with a score of 200 to 299, about 50 percent will get sick in the near future; and of those with a score of 150 to 199, only about 30 percent will get sick in the near future. A score of less than 150 indicates that you have a low chance of becoming ill. So, the higher your score, the harder you should work to stay well.

Because individuals vary in their perception of a given life event as well as in their ability to adapt to change, we recommend that you use this standardized test only as a rough predictor of your increased risk.

Stress can be cumulative. Events from two years ago may still be affecting you now. If you think that past events may be a factor for you, repeat this test for the events of the preceding year and compare your scores.

PREVENTION

Here are some ways you can use the Schedule of Recent Experience to maintain your health and prevent illness. You can use it to:

1. Remind yourself of the amount of change that has happened to you by posting the Schedule of Recent Experience where you and your family can see it easily.

2. Think about the personal meaning of each change that's taken place for you and try to identify some of the feelings you experienced.

3. Think about ways that you can best adjust to each change.

4. Take your time when making decisions.

5. Try to anticipate life changes and plan for them well.

6. Pace yourself. Don't rush. It will get done.

7. Take time to appreciate your successes, and relax.

8. Be compassionate and patient with yourself. It is not uncommon for people to become overwhelmed by all the stresses in their lives. It takes a while to put into effect coping strategies to deal with stress.

9. Acknowledge what you can control and what you cannot control and, when possible, choose which changes you take on.

10. Try out the stress-management and relaxation techniques presented in this book and incorporate the ones that work best for you into your personalized stress-management program.

SYMPTOMS CHECKLIST

The major objective of this workbook is to help you achieve symptom relief using relaxation and stress reduction techniques. So that you can determine exactly which symptoms you want to work on, complete the following checklist.

After you've used this workbook to master the stress reduction techniques that work best for your symptoms, you can return to this checklist and use it to measure your symptom relief.

Instructions: Rate your stress-related symptoms below for the degree of discomfort that they cause you, using this 10-point scale:

Slight discomfort			Moderate discomfort				Extreme discomfort		
1	2	3	4	5	6	7	8	9	10
Symptom (Disregard those that you don't experience)			*Degree of discomfort (1-10) now*				*Degree of discomfort (1-10) after mastering relaxation and stress reduction techniques*		
Anxiety in specific situations Tests Deadlines Competing priorities Interviews Public Speaking Other			_____ _____ _____ _____ _____ _____				_____ _____ _____ _____ _____ _____		
Anxiety in personal relationships Spouse Parents Children Other			_____ _____ _____ _____				_____ _____ _____ _____		
Worry									
Depression									
Anxiety									
Anger									
Irritability									
Resentment									
Phobias									

Fears		
Muscular tension		
High blood pressure		
Headaches		
Neck pain		
Backaches		
Indigestion		
Muscle spasms		
Insomnia		
Sleeping difficulties		
Work stress		
Other		

Important: Physical symptoms may have purely physiological causes. You should have a medical doctor eliminate the possibility of any such physical problems before you proceed on the assumption that your symptoms are completely stress-related.

TACTICS FOR COPING WITH STRESS

As a member of modern society, you have available to you a variety of methods to cope with the negative effects of stress. Doctors can treat your stress-related symptoms and diseases. Over-the-counter remedies can reduce your pain, help you sleep, keep you awake, enable you to relax, and counter your acid indigestion and nervous bowels. You can consume food, alcohol, and recreational drugs to help block feelings of discomfort. You may have diversions such as TV, movies, the Internet, hobbies, and sports. You can withdraw from the world into your home and avoid all but the most necessary contact with the stressful world around you.

Our culture rewards people who deal with their stress by working harder and faster to produce more in a shorter time. There are people who thrive in our rapid-paced culture who are referred to as "type A" personalities. The type A personality is a term that was coined in the 1970s to describe people who have a strong sense of time urgency, can't relax, are insecure about their status, are highly competitive, and are easily angered when they don't get their own way. The classic study of type A personality was the twelve-year-longitudinal study of over 3,500 healthy middle-aged men reported by Friedman and Rosenman in 1974 and estimated that type A behavior doubled the risk of coronary heart disease. Although this popular concept has received a great deal of interest in health psychology, recent research (Williams 2001) has indicated that only the hostility component of type A personality is a significant health-risk factor.

In 2006 an article presented in the *American Journal of Cardiology* (Denollet, et al.) discussed how certain personal traits can hurt heart health and proposed a new personality construct, referred to as type D or "distressed" personality. Type D behavior is characterized by the tendency to experience negative emotions (anger and hostility) and to inhibit these emotions while avoiding social contact with others. Both negativity and social withdrawal are associated with greater *cortisol* (a hormone that is closely related to cortisone in its physiological effects), increased reactivity to stress and risk for coronary heart disease and other stress-related diseases. However, it is anyone's guess whether the type D label will have the staying power that the type A label has had.

In contrast to anxious, chronically stressed people, certain individuals are less vulnerable to stress, according to University of Chicago research psychologist Suzanne Kobasa, and colleagues (1985). These "stress-hardy" individuals have a lower frequency of illness and work absenteeism. They view stressors as challenges and chances for new opportunities and personal growth rather than as threats. They feel in control of their life circumstances, and they perceive that they have the resources to make choices and influence events around them. They also have a sense of commitment to their homes, families, and work that makes it easier for them to be involved with other people and in other activities. According to Herbert Benson and Eileen Stuart, authors of *The Wellness Book* (1993), the incidence of illness is lowest in individuals who have these stress-hardy characteristics and who also have a good social support system, exercise regularly, and maintain a healthy diet.

In his popular book *Emotional Intelligence* (1995), Daniel Goleman refers to emotionally healthy people as individuals who consistently demonstrate self-awareness, self-discipline, and empathy. Goleman asserts through his book that "emotional intelligence" contributes to a person's ability to cope with stress.

In her book *The Tending Instinct* (2002), psychologist Shelley E. Taylor discusses how we are biologically programmed to care for one another. In her research, Taylor discovered that studies involving the "fight-or-flight response" involved only male subjects. She set out to see whether men and women deal with stress differently, and if so, how. She found that in times of stress, people (especially women) who are driven to turn to their social support group to give and receive support—instead of running or fighting—are much less likely to experience a prolonged stress response. Her theory is known as "tend and befriend." Taylor says, "Social ties are the cheapest medicine we have" (p. 165).

TACTICS FOR COPING WITH STRESS INVENTORY

Before you embark on a program of change, it is important to consider how you currently manage your stress.

Instructions: Listed below are some common ways of coping with stressful events. Mark those that are characteristic of your behavior or that you use frequently.

_____   1. I ignore my own needs and just work harder and faster.

_____   2. I seek out friends for conversation and support.

_____   3. I eat more than usual.

_____   4. I engage in some type of physical exercise.

_____   5. I get irritable and take it out on those around me.

_____   6. I take a little time to relax, breathe, and unwind.

_____   7. I smoke a cigarette or drink a caffeinated beverage.

_____   8. I confront my source of stress and work to change it.

_____   9. I withdraw emotionally and just go through the motions of my day.

_____   10. I change my outlook on the problem and put it in a better perspective.

_____   11. I sleep more than I really need to.

_____   12. I take some time off and get away from my working life.

_____   13. I go out shopping and buy something to make myself feel good.

_____   14. I joke with my friends and use humor to take the edge off.

_____   15. I drink more alcohol than usual.

_____   16. I get involved in a hobby or interest that helps me unwind and enjoy myself.

_____   17. I take medicine to help me relax or sleep better.

_____   18. I maintain a healthy diet.

_____   19. I just ignore the problem and hope it will go away.

_____   20. I pray, meditate, or enhance my spiritual life.

_____ 21. I worry about the problem and am afraid to do something about it.

_____ 22. I try to focus on the things I can control and accept the things I can't.

Adapted from the *"Coping Styles Questionnaire."* © 1999 by Jim Boyers, Ph.D., Kaiser-Permanente Medical Center and Health Styles, Santa Clara, CA.

Evaluate your results: The even-numbered items tend to be more constructive tactics and the odd-numbered items tend to be less constructive tactics for coping with stress. Congratulate yourself for the even-numbered items you checked. Think about whether you need to make some changes in your thinking or behavior if you checked any of the odd-numbered items. Consider experimenting with some even-numbered items you haven't tried before. This workbook will assist you in making these changes.

KNOWING YOUR GOAL

The goal of stress management is not merely stress reduction. After all, wouldn't life be boring without stress? As mentioned earlier, there is a tendency to think of stressful events or stressors only as negative (such as the injury or death of a loved one), but stressors are often positive. For instance, getting a new home or a promotion at work brings with it the stress of change of status and new responsibilities. The physical exertion of a good workout, the excitement of doing something challenging for the first time, or the pleasure of watching a beautiful sunset on the last day of your vacation are all examples of positive stress.

Distress or negative stress occurs when you perceive that the challenge facing you is dangerous, difficult, painful, or unfair, and you are concerned that you may lack the resources to cope with it. You can actually increase your ability to deal with distress by integrating into your everyday life positive activities such as solving challenging problems, practicing regular exercise workouts and relaxation techniques, staying in touch with enjoyable social contacts, following sensible dietary practices, and engaging in optimistic and rational thinking, humor, and play.

Performance and efficiency actually improve with increased stress, until performance peaks as the stress level becomes too great. Stress management involves finding the right types and amounts of stress, given your individual personality, priorities, and life situation, so that you can maximize your performance and satisfaction. By using the tools presented in this workbook, you can learn how to cope more effectively with distress as well as how to add more positive stress or stimulating challenges, pleasure, and excitement to your life.

SYMPTOM-RELIEF EFFECTIVENESS

Now that you've identified the major sources of your stress, your stress-related symptoms, and your current tactics for dealing with stress, it is time to choose one or two symptoms that bother you the most and select the techniques that you will use to relieve them. Defining and achieving a specific goal will give you a sense of accomplishment and motivate you to continue using the tools and ideas that give you the positive change you are seeking. Because everyone reacts differently to stress, we can't tell you which techniques will work best for you. However, the chart on the following pages will give you a general idea of what to try first and where to go from there.

Chapter headings for each stress reduction method are across the top, and typical stress-related symptoms are listed down the side. As you can see, more than one stress reduction technique can be effective for treating most symptoms. The most effective techniques for a particular symptom are marked with a boldface X, while other helpful techniques for the same symptom are indicated by a smaller and lighter X.

The techniques fall into roughly two categories: relaxation techniques that focus on relaxing the body, and stress reduction techniques that condition the mind to handle stress effectively. Your mind, body, and emotions are interrelated. In seeking relief from stress, you will obtain the best results by using at least one technique from each of these two broad categories. For example, if your most painful stress symptom is general anxiety, you might practice progressive relaxation and breathing exercises to calm your body and work on the exercises from chapter 12 on refuting irrational ideas and chapter 13 on facing worry and anxiety to reduce your mental and emotional stress. If your results on the Tactics for Coping with Stress Inventory indicate that you do not engage in regular physical exercise and/or your diet is not good, you will also want to refer to chapters 19 on nutrition and 20 on physical exercise to learn how improving these tactics can reduce your general anxiety.

SYMPTOM-RELIEF EFFECTIVENESS CHART

Symptoms

Techniques	Breathing	Progressive Relaxation	Meditation	Visualization	Applied Relaxation	Self-Hypnosis	Auto-genics
Anxiety in specific situations (tests, deadlines, interviews, presentations)	X	X	x	x	X	x	
Anxiety in your relationships (spouse, children, boss)	X	x				x	
General anxiety and worry	X	X	X	x	X		x
Depression	X		X				
Hostility, anger, irritability, resentment	X	x	x		X		x
Phobias, fears	X	X		x	X		
Muscular tension	X	X		x	x	x	X
High blood pressure	x	X	X				X
Headaches, neck pain, backaches	x	X	X	X	X	X	x
Indigestion	x	X	x			X	X
Insomnia, sleeping difficulties	x	X			X	X	x
Work stress	X	X			X		
Chronic pain	X	x	X	X	x	X	X

Symptoms

Techniques	Brief Combination Techniques	Focusing	Refuting Irrational Ideas	Facing Worry and Anxiety	Coping Skills Training for Fears	Anger Inoculation
Anxiety in specific situations (tests, deadlines, interviews, presentations)	x	X	x	X	X	
Anxiety in your relationships (spouse, children, boss)	x	X	x	X	x	
General anxiety and worry	x	x	X	X	x	
Depression		x	X			
Hostility, anger, irritability, resentment		X	X			X
Phobias, fears		x	x	X	X	
Muscular tension	x					x
High blood pressure	x					x
Headaches, neck pain, backaches		x				
Indigestion	x					
Insomnia, sleeping difficulties		x				
Work stress	X	X	X			x
Chronic pain	x	X	x			

Symptoms

Techniques	Goal Setting and Time Management	Assertiveness Training	Work-Stress Management	Nutrition	Exercise
Anxiety in specific situations (tests, deadlines, interviews, presentations)	X	x			
Anxiety in your relationships (spouse, children, boss)		X			
General anxiety and worry	X	x		x	X
Depression	x	X		x	X
Hostility, anger, irritability, resentment	X	X		x	X
Phobias, fears	x	x		x	x
Muscular tension	x				X
High blood pressure	x	x		X	X
Headaches, neck pain, backaches		x		x	X
Indigestion	x	x		X	x
Insomnia, sleeping difficulties				x	X
Work stress	x	x	X		
Chronic pain	X	x		x	X

Read chapter 2 before you move on to other chapters. Body awareness is the key to everything else in this workbook, and without it you cannot use any of these techniques effectively.

FURTHER READING

Amundson, M. E., C. A. Hart, and T. A. Holmes. 1986. *Manual for the Schedule of Recent Experience (SRE)*. Seattle: University of Washington Press.

Benson, H. 1985. *Beyond the Relaxation Response*. New York: Penguin Publishers.

————. 2000. *The Relaxation Response*. New York: HarperCollins Publishers.

Benson, H., and E. Stuart. 1993. *The Wellness Book: The Comprehensive Guide to Maintaining Health and Treating Stress-Related Illness*. New York: Simon & Schuster.

Denollet, J., S. S. Peterson, C. J. Vrints, and V. M. Conraads. 2006. Usefulness of type D personality in predicting five-year cardiac events above and beyond current symptoms of stress in patients with coronary heart disease. *American Journal of Cardiology* 97(7):970-973.

Friedman, M., and R. Rosenman. 1974. *Type A Personality and Your Heart*. New York: Knopf

Goleman, D. 1995. *Emotional Intelligence*. New York: Bantam Books.

Kobasa, S., S. Maddi, M. Puccetti, and M. Zola. 1985. Effectiveness of hardiness, exercise and social support as resources against illness. *Journal of Psychosomatic Research* 29:525–533.

Lazarus, R. S., and S. Folkman. 1984. *Stress Appraisal and Coping*. New York: Springer Publishing.

Lorig, K., H. Holman, D. Sobel, D. Laurent, V. Gonzalez, and M. Menor. 2006. *Living a Healthy Life with Chronic Conditions*. Palo Alto, CA: Bull Publishing.

Martin, P. R. 1998. *The Healing Mind: The Vital Links between Brain and Behavior, Immunity and Disease*. New York: St. Martin's Press.

McBrooks, C., K. Koizumi, and J. O. Pinkston, eds. 1975. *The Life and Contributions of Walter Bradford Cannon 1871–1945*. Albany: State University of New York Press.

Ornstein, R., and D. Sobel. 1995. *Healthy Pleasures*. Cambridge, MA: Perseus Press.

———. 1999. *The Healing Brain*. New York: Major Books.

Rabin, B. 1999. *Stress, Immune Function and Health: The Connection*. New York: Wiley-Liss.

Sapolsky, R. M. 2004. *Why Zebras Don't Get Ulcers: A Guide to Stress, Stress-Related Diseases, and Coping*. New York: W. H. Freeman.

Selye, H. 1978. *The Stress of Life*. New York: McGraw-Hill.

Sobel, D. S., and R. Ornstein. 1997. *The Healthy Mind, Healthy Body Handbook*. New York: Time-Life Books.

Taylor, S. 2002. *The Tending Instinct*. New York: Times Books.

Williams, R. B. 2001. Hostility: effects on health and the potential for successful behavioral approaches to prevention in treatments. In *Handbook of Health Psychology*, edited by A. Baum, T. A. Revenson, and J. E. Singer. Mahwah, New Jersey: Erlbaum.

2

Body Awareness

In this chapter you will learn:

> ✳ How the mind and body interact
>
> ✳ How to recognize tension in your body
>
> ✳ Exercises to recognize and let go of tension in your body

BACKGROUND

The ability to recognize how your body reacts to the stressors in your life can be a powerful skill. Most people are more aware of the weather, the time of day, or their bank balance than they are of the tension in their own bodies or their personal stress response. Your body registers stress long before your conscious mind does. Muscle tension is your body's way of letting you know that you are stressed, and body awareness is the first step toward acknowledging and reducing that stress.

You inevitably tense your body when you experience stress. When the stress is removed, the tension will also go away. Also, chronic muscular tension occurs in people with particular beliefs or attitudes and tends to tighten specific muscle groups. For example, a woman who believes that it is bad to express anger is likely to have chronic neck tension and pain, while a man experiencing a lot of anxiety about the future may develop chronic stomach problems. This chronic muscular tension restricts digestion, limits self-expression, and decreases energy. Every contracted muscle blocks movement.

Differentiating between your external awareness and internal awareness in order to separate the world from your physical reaction to it is important. *External awareness* includes all stimulation to the five senses from the outside world. *Internal awareness* refers to any physical sensation, feeling, emotional discomfort, or comfort inside your body. Much of the tension in your body isn't felt because most of your awareness is directed toward the outside world. Below, you will learn about exercises designed to locate and explore your body tension.

The importance of body states, their effect on consciousness, and their relationship to stress have been emphasized for many centuries by Eastern philosophies such as Zen, hatha yoga, and Sufism. During the last century, the work of Wilhelm Reich, originally a student of Freud, kindled Western psychiatry's interest in the body's interaction with emotional conditions. Two other therapies that concentrate on the body and its relationship to emotional stress are Fritz Perls' Gestalt therapy and Alexander Lowen's bioenergetic therapy. Both of these therapies work closely with the mind-body relationship. Becoming aware of how your body responds to stress will give you some important information about your personal stress response that you can then use to develop a stress-management plan.

BODY INVENTORY

The following exercises promote body awareness and will help you identify areas of tension in your body.

Internal Versus External Awareness

1. First focus your attention on the outside world. Start sentences with "I am aware of." (For example, "I am aware of the cars going by outside the window, papers moving, the coffee perking, the breeze blowing, and the blue carpet.")

2. After you've become aware of everything that is going on around you, shift to focusing your attention on your body and your physical sensations—your internal world. (For example, "I am aware of feeling warm, my stomach gurgling, tension in my neck, my nose tickling, and a cramp in my foot.")

3. Shuttle back and forth between internal and external awareness. (For example, "I am aware of the chair pressing against my buttocks, the circle of yellow light from the lamp, my shoulders hunching up, the smell of bacon.")

4. Practiced during your free moments throughout the day, this exercise allows you to separate and appreciate the real difference between your inner and outer worlds.

Body Scanning

Close your eyes. Starting with your toes and moving up your body, ask yourself, "Where am I tense?" Whenever you discover a tense area, exaggerate it slightly so you can become even more aware of it. Be aware of the muscles in your body that are tense. Then, for example, say to yourself, "I am tensing my neck muscles … I am hurting myself … I am creating tension in my body." Note that all muscular tension is self-produced. At this point, be aware of any life situation that may be causing the tension in your body and think about what you could do to change that.

Letting Go of Your Body

Lie down on a rug or a firm bed and get comfortable. Pull your knees up until your feet rest flat on the floor (or bed) and close your eyes. Check yourself for comfort. (This may require shifting your body around.) Become aware of your breathing.... Feel the air move into your nose, mouth, and down your throat into your lungs. Focus on your body and let all of the parts come into your awareness spontaneously. What parts of your body come into awareness first? What parts are you less aware of? Become aware of which parts of your body you can feel easily and which parts of your body have little sensation. Do you notice any difference between the right and left side of your body? Now become aware of any physical discomfort you are feeling. Become aware of this discomfort until you can describe it in detail. Focus and be aware of what happens to this discomfort. It may change.... Scan your body for any residual tension or discomfort and let it go with each exhalation. Continue letting go for five to ten minutes, allowing your body to take over.

STRESS-AWARENESS DIARY

Some parts of the day are more stressful than others, and some stressful events are more likely to produce physical and emotional symptoms than others. Certain types of stressful events often produce characteristic symptoms. For this reason, keeping a record of stressful events, as well as symptoms that may have been a stress reaction, is useful. Make extra copies of the blank form on the next page for your own diary.

Keep a stress-awareness diary for two weeks. Make a note of the time that a stressful event occurs and the time you notice a physical or emotional symptom that could be related to the stress.

STRESS-AWARENESS DIARY

Date: _____   Day of the week: _____

Time	Stressful Event	Symptom
_____	_____	_____
_____	_____	_____
_____	_____	_____
_____	_____	_____
_____	_____	_____
_____	_____	_____
_____	_____	_____
_____	_____	_____
_____	_____	_____
_____	_____	_____
_____	_____	_____
_____	_____	_____
_____	_____	_____
_____	_____	_____
_____	_____	_____
_____	_____	_____
_____	_____	_____
_____	_____	_____

The following stress-awareness diary was recorded one Monday by a department store clerk:

Time	Stressful Event	Symptom
8 A.M.	Alarm doesn't go off, late for work, only had time for coffee	Slight headache, jittery
9:30 A.M.	Boss reprimands me for being late	
9:50 A.M.		Worry, depression, shallow breathing
11 A.M.	Customer is rude and insulting	
11:15 A.M.		Anger, tightness in stomach.
12:20 P.M.	Only have 10 minutes for lunch, eat some chips	
2:30 P.M.		Slight headache
3 P.M.	Presentation to senior manager	Nervous, sweating
5 P.M.	Heavy commute, late for dinner with family	
6 P.M.	Argument with son	Anger, pounding headache
6:35 P.M.	Wife defends son	Anger, tension in neck, back, and stomach
10 P.M.		Worrying, not able to sleep

As you can see, the diary identifies how particular stresses result in predictable symptoms. An interpersonal confrontation and just coffee for breakfast is followed by stomach tension. Rushing may cause *vasoconstriction* (tightening of the blood vessels), and eating virtually nothing all day is likely to cause low blood sugar for this individual, who, not surprisingly, experiences anger and various physical symptoms when he arrives home to face more confrontation. You can use your stress-awareness diary to discover and chart your stressful events and characteristic reactions.

As you use these body-awareness exercises, you will begin to recognize where your body stores muscular tension. When you allow yourself increased awareness, you can find ways to let go of the tension you discover. Along with the release of tension, you will experience increased energy and a sense of well-being.

To keep a convenient record of how you feel before and after your relaxation exercises, use the following Record of General Tension.

RECORD OF GENERAL TENSION

Rate yourself on this 10-point scale before and after you do your relaxation exercise.

1	2	3	4	5
totally relaxed no tension	very relaxed	moderately relaxed	fairly relaxed	slightly relaxed

6	7	8	9	10
slightly tense	fairly tense	moderately tense	very tense	extremely tense

Week of _____	Before session	After session	Comments
Monday			
Tuesday			
Wednesday			
Thursday			
Friday			
Saturday			
Sunday			

Your increased awareness of your body's response to stressful events is an integral part of learning how to manage the stress in your life, as opposed to letting it manage you. This chapter will help you begin that process.

FURTHER READING

Benson, H. 2000. *The Relaxation Response*. New York: Harper Paperbacks.

Benson, H., and E. Stuart. 1993. *The Wellness Book: The Comprehensive Guide to Maintaining Health and Treating Stress-Related Illness*. New York: Simon & Schuster.

Borysenko, J. 1993. *Minding the Body, Mending the Mind*. Reading, MA: Bantam Doubleday Dell Publications.

Goleman, D., and J. Gurin, eds. 1995. *Mind Body Medicine: How to Use Your Mind for Better Health*. Yonkers, NY: Consumer Reports Books.

Jaffe, D. 1982. *Healing from Within*. New York: Bantam Books.

Knaster, M. 1996. *Discovering the Body's Wisdom*. New York: Bantam Books.

Lorig, K., H. Holman, D. Sobel, D. Laurent, V. Gonzalez, and M. Menor. 2000. *Living a Healthy Life with Chronic Conditions*. Palo Alto, CA: Bull Publishing.

Lowen, A. 1994. *Bioenergetics*. New York: Viking-Penguin.

Perls, F., and F. S. Perls. 1973. *The Gestalt Approach and Eye Witness to Therapy*. New York: Science and Behavior Books.

Scheller, M. D. 1993. *Growing Older, Feeling Better*. Palo Alto, CA: Bull Publishing.

3

Breathing

In this chapter you will learn to:

✳ Use breathing to increase your awareness of your inner experience

✳ Use breathing to release tension and relax

✳ Use breathing to reduce or eliminate symptoms of stress

BACKGROUND

Breathing is the fundamental necessity of life that most people take for granted. With each breath of air, you obtain oxygen and release the waste product: carbon dioxide. Poor breathing habits diminish the flow of these gases to and from your body, making it harder for you to cope with stressful situations. Certain breathing patterns may actually contribute to anxiety, panic attacks, depression, muscle tension, headaches, and fatigue. As you learn to be aware of your breathing and practice slowing and normalizing your breaths, your mind will quiet and your body will relax. Breath awareness and good breathing habits will enhance your psychological and physical well-being, whether you practice them alone or in combination with other relaxation techniques.

Let's examine a breath. When you inhale, air is drawn in through your nose, where it is warmed to body temperature, humidified, and partially cleansed. Your diaphragm, a sheetlike muscle separating the lungs and the abdomen, facilitates your breathing by contracting and relaxing as you breathe in and out.

Your lungs are like a tree with many branches (*bronchial tubes*) that carry air to elastic air sacs (*alveoli*). The alveoli have the balloonlike ability to expand when air is taken into the lungs and contract when air is let out. Small blood vessels (*capillaries*) surrounding the alveoli receive oxygen and transport it to your heart.

Your heart pumps oxygenated blood to all parts of your body. An exchange takes place in which blood cells receive oxygen and release carbon dioxide, a waste product that is carried back to your heart and lungs, and then exhaled. This efficient method of transporting and exchanging oxygen and carbon dioxide is vital to sustain life.

When you breathe, typically, you use one of two patterns: (1) chest or thoracic breathing, or (2) abdominal or diaphragmatic breathing.

Chest or *thoracic breathing* is a common malady of modern life that is often linked with lifestyle, stress, anxiety, or other forms of emotional distress. It is shallow and often irregular and rapid. When air is inhaled, the chest expands and the shoulders rise to take in the air. Chronic shallow chest breathing or frequent breath holding can be associated with chronic stress, tension, poor posture, tight clothing, purposely holding in the stomach and pushing out the chest, sedentary lifestyle, painful feelings, or long periods of focused attention in which people forget to breathe regularly.

Too little oxygen and a carbon dioxide buildup in the body associated with breath holding can contribute to feelings of fatigue and depression. Rapid, shallow chest breathing often associated with the stress response and anxiety can result in symptoms such as light-headedness, heart palpitations, weakness, numbness, tingling, agitation, and shortness of breath. Too much carbon dioxide is exhaled, and (due to an imbalance in oxygen to carbon dioxide levels in the blood) too little oxygen reaches the brain and other parts of the body. In acute or extreme cases, rapid chest breathing is easily recognized as hyperventilation; but milder and slower chest breathing can go unnoticed for years.

Abdominal or *diaphragmatic breathing* is the natural breathing of newborn babies and sleeping adults. Inhaled air is drawn deep into the lungs as the abdomen expands, making room for the diaphragm to contract downward. Air is exhaled as the abdomen and the diaphragm relax. Diaphragmatic breathing is deeper and slower than shallow chest breathing, as well as more rhythmic and relaxing. The respiratory system is able to do its job of producing energy from oxygen and removing waste products.

By increasing your awareness of your breathing patterns and shifting to more abdominal breathing, you can balance the oxygen and carbon dioxide blood levels in your body, normalize your heart rate, and reduce the muscle tension and anxiety present with stress-related symptoms or thoughts. Diaphragmatic breathing is the easiest way to elicit the relaxation response.

SYMPTOM-RELIEF EFFECTIVENESS

Breathing exercises have been found to be effective in reducing generalized anxiety disorders, panic attacks and agoraphobia, depression, irritability, muscle tension, headaches, and fatigue. They are used in the treatment and prevention of breath holding, hyperventilation, shallow breathing, and cold hands and feet.

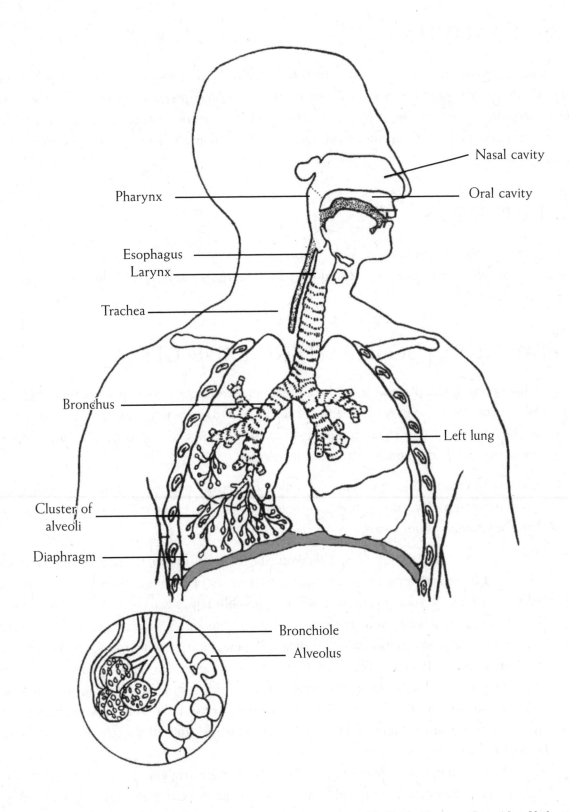

Nasal cavity

Oral cavity

Pharynx

Esophagus

Larynx

Trachea

Bronchus

Left lung

Cluster of alveoli

Diaphragm

Bronchiole

Alveolus

Adapted from *The Anatomy Coloring Book* by Wynn Kapit and Lawrence M. Elson, Harper & Row, New York, 1977.

TIME TO MASTER

A breathing exercise can be learned in a matter of minutes and some of its benefits experienced immediately. Regular practice of a breathing exercise can have profound effects in a matter of weeks if not days. After you've tried the exercises presented in this chapter, develop a breathing program incorporating those exercises you find most helpful and follow your program daily for the best results.

INSTRUCTIONS

This chapter is divided into four sections: (1) preparing to do breathing exercises, (2) breathing basics, (3) breathing for tension release and increased awareness, and (4) breathing for symptom control or release.

PREPARING TO DO BREATHING EXERCISES

1. Choose a time and place to learn these breathing exercises where you won't be disturbed. While you are learning to do them, try to do your daily practice in the same place and at the same time. However, a number of these exercises, once mastered, can be done anywhere you find yourself in a stressful situation.

2. It's best to breathe through your nose, unless otherwise instructed. If needed, clear your nasal passages before doing breathing exercises. If you can't clear them, it's okay to breathe through your mouth.

3. Think about what position is best for you. If your goal in practicing a breathing exercise is to be relaxed and maintain optimal awareness of your experience, do it from a seated position. If your goal is to relax and possibly fall asleep, practice it lying down. If you are seated while you do these exercises, remember to maintain good posture with your head comfortably balanced on your spine, your arms and legs uncrossed, and your feet firmly placed on the floor. Note that as a beginner, you will find it easier to learn how to breathe diaphragmatically lying down. Here are two lying down positions:

    If you have back problems, the "knees raised" pose is best. Bend your knees and move your feet about eight inches apart, with your toes turned slightly outward. Make sure that your spine is straight.

    When you use the "dead body" pose, your legs are straight and slightly apart, your toes pointed comfortably outward, your arms at your sides and not touching your body, your palms are up, and your eyes are closed.

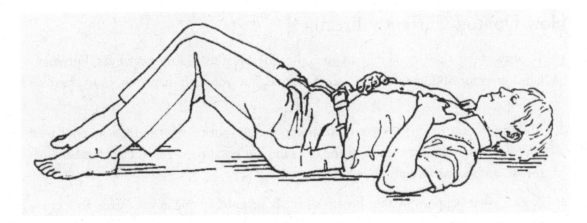

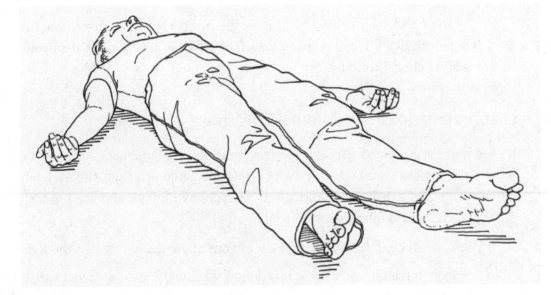

4. Whatever position you choose, take a moment to check in with yourself before beginning your breathing exercise. Scan throughout your whole body, releasing points of obvious tension and shift your position, if necessary, to be more comfortable.

BREATHING BASICS

It is useful to observe how you are currently breathing before you learn how to use breathing as a relaxation skill.

How Do You Currently Breathe?

1. To answer the question "How do you currently breathe?" close your eyes. Put your right hand on your abdomen at the waistline, and put your left hand on your chest, in the center.

2. Without trying to change your breathing, simply notice how it feels as cool fresh air enters your nose, passes through the hairs in your nasal passage, reaches the back of your throat, and descends into your lungs.

3. Notice what happens as that breath of fresh air enters your lungs. What happens when you exhale? Observe your breath for a while without making any effort to make it different. Take your time.

4. Which hand rises the most when you inhale—the hand on your chest or the hand on your abdomen?

    If your abdomen expands and rises the most when you inhale, you are breathing diaphragmatically. If your abdomen doesn't move or if it moves less than your chest, you are shallow chest breathing.

Diaphragmatic or Abdominal Breathing

1. Lie on your back and gently place one hand on your abdomen and one hand on your chest and follow your breathing. Notice how your abdomen rises with each inhalation and falls with each exhalation. Alternatively, put a book on your abdomen, place your hands at your sides, and follow your breathing.

2. If you experience difficulty breathing into your abdomen, try one of the following:

    a. Exhale forcefully to empty your lungs. This will create a vacuum that will pull a deep breath into your abdomen. If you find yourself drifting back to shallow chest breathing, you may need to repeat this.

    b. Press your hand down on your abdomen while you exhale and then let your abdomen push your hand back up as you inhale deeply.

    c. Imagine that your abdomen is a balloon and that as you inhale you are filling it with air.

    d. Lie on your stomach with your head resting on your folded hands. Inhale deeply into your abdomen so you can feel your abdomen pushing against the floor.

3. Is your chest moving in harmony with your abdomen or is it rigid? Although most of the action is in your abdomen when you breathe diaphragmatically, your chest does move a

little. As you inhale, first your abdomen, then your middle chest, and then your upper chest will rise in one smooth movement. You might want to imagine filling a glass with water from the bottom to the top as you inhale.

4. Once you know what it feels like to breathe diaphragmatically, you can use this option to deepen and slow your breath even more. Smile slightly, inhale through your nose, and exhale through your mouth, as though you are breathing out through a straw. Take long, slow, deep breaths that raise and lower your abdomen. Focus on the sound and feeling of your breathing as you become more and more relaxed.

5. When thoughts, feelings, and sensations catch your attention, just notice them and return to your breathing.

6. Practice diaphragmatic breathing for about five or ten minutes at a time, once or twice a day. Gradually extend the time you do this to twenty minutes.

7. At the end of each diaphragmatic-breathing session, take a little time to notice (and enjoy) how you feel.

8. Optional: You may want to scan your body for tension at the beginning and end of each breathing practice session. Compare the level of tension you feel at the end of the exercise with the tension level you felt when you began. Use the Record of General Tension in chapter 2 to monitor your progress.

SPECIAL CONSIDERATIONS

1. Once you become at ease with breathing diaphragmatically, check in with how you are breathing from time to time throughout your day. Are you breathing diaphragmatically? Shallowly? Are you holding your breath? Take a few diaphragmatic breaths. Concentrate on your abdomen moving up and down, the air moving in and out of your lungs, and the feeling of relaxation that deep breathing gives you. Then resume your normal activities.

2. If you have difficulty checking in with your breathing throughout the day, designate an external cue as a reminder to pay attention to your breath. An *external cue* is anything you know you will notice at least several times a day: the steering wheel of your car, your wristwatch, or a sign posted on your door that says "Breathe."

3. When you've learned to relax using diaphragmatic breathing, you can use it to lower your tension level whenever you anticipate you're going to be in a stressful situation, during that situation, and after that situation ends. Although it's not a panacea, most people report that diaphragmatic breathing helps them get through difficult situations more easily.

4. At first, diaphragmatic breathing may feel awkward, especially if you have been a shallow chest breather. As a beginner, it is useful to exaggerate the abdominal movement in this exercise in order to experience what it feels like. Once you have this movement down, you don't need to exaggerate it and you can place your hands at your sides. With practice, diaphragmatic breathing will feel more natural.

5. Diaphragmatic breathing is an integral part of most breathing exercises, as well as part of most of the other relaxation techniques you will be learning in this workbook, so be sure that you've mastered it before you move on.

BREATHING FOR TENSION RELEASE AND INCREASED AWARENESS

Letting Go of Tension

1. Inhale diaphragmatically as you say to yourself "breathe in."

2. Hold your breath a moment before you exhale.

3. Exhale slowly and deeply as you say to yourself "relax."

4. Pause and wait for your next natural breath.

5. As you inhale slowly and then hold your breath for a moment, notice the parts of your body that tense up.

6. As you exhale, feel the tension naturally leaving your body. With each exhalation, you will feel more and more relaxed, as you let go of more and more tension.

7. When thoughts, feelings, and sensations catch your attention, just notice them and return to your breathing.

8. Practice five to twenty minutes at a time.

9. Once you've mastered this exercise, practice using it several times a day in neutral situations, that is, nonstressful situations. Finally, start using it in stressful situations to reduce your tension. Simply take several diaphragmatic breaths, say the words "breathe in" and "relax," and let go of the tension on the exhalation. Focus on the sensations of relaxation.

10. Remember that you may need to exhale before you can breathe in deeply.

Mindful Breath Counting

In the preceding exercises, you may have noticed that your mind tends to wander to bodily sensations, noises, daydreams, plans, worries, judgments, and so forth. This is natural but it can hinder your ability to let go of the stresses in your life and thereby inhibit relaxation. Mindfully counting your breaths provides you with a way to observe your experience that will help you calm your mind, as well as relax your body.

Being *mindful* means being aware of your experiences in the here and now as an objective and friendly observer without getting caught up in those experiences. An objective observer is like a scientist who steps back and looks at what is happening in an experiment without judgment or expectation, open to learning something new. A friendly observer is compassionate without being swept away by what is going on. Of course, this is easier said than done. Fortunately, the more you practice this mindfulness mind-set, the easier it becomes. In addition, each time you lose track of your point of focus (in this case, your breath and the counting of your breaths) and bring it back to your attention, you are strengthening your ability to attend.

1. Practice this exercise sitting up to enhance mindfulness awareness. Later, if you like, you can use it in bed as a technique to help you fall asleep.

2. Use slow, deep diaphragmatic breathing.

3. Count each exhalation to yourself. When you reach the fourth exhalation, start over again at one. Here is how you do it: inhale … exhale ("one") … inhale … exhale ("two") … inhale … exhale ("three") … inhale … exhale ("four") … inhale … exhale ("one") … and so forth.

4. As other thoughts enter your consciousness or as your mind goes blank, simply observe those thoughts or the blankness without judgment or expectation, and then return to counting your breaths.

5. If you lose track of your count, simply start over again at "one."

6. Optional: If you like, you can label each of your thoughts, feelings, and sensations as they arise. Say to yourself "thought," "feeling," or "sensation," and then return to counting your breaths. You can make up your own labels, but keep it simple. The purpose of labeling is to increase your objectivity and emotional distance from potentially charged material.

7. Continue counting your exhalations in sets of four for ten minutes. Gradually increase to twenty minutes.

Here is an example of a few moments of a beginner's experience with Mindful Breath Counting:

Inhale … "remember to breathe into my belly…that's a thought" … exhale ("one") … inhale …exhale ("two") … inhale … exhale ("three") … "My shoulders are really tight … sensations … thought …" inhale … exhale ("four") … inhale … "Oh, it feels good to let go of that tension … sensation, feeling, thought …" exhale ("one") … inhale … exhale ("two") … "Did I lock the front door when I came home? Tension in my chest, holding my breath … Yes, relief … thoughts, sensations, feelings … I can't do this … thought, remember to breathe … now where was I? … more thoughts" … Inhale … exhale ("one") ….

1. To learn more about mindfulness, turn to chapter 5, Meditation.

2. When you practice any relaxation exercise and you find your mind has wandered, you can gently bring your attention back to your original point of focus.

3. Adopting an objective and compassionate awareness of your experience in the here and now when you practice relaxation exercises can help you develop and strengthen these qualities in your everyday life.

Once you have learned to return to your breath and your counting when you notice yourself being distracted, you may prefer to drop the counting and use your breath as the point of focus for your meditation.

Little Tension Releasers

During the day, there are many moments when you can benefit from a short time-out. For example, when you catch yourself sighing or yawning. This is generally a sign that you are not getting enough oxygen. Since a sigh or a yawn actually does release a bit of tension, you can practice sighing or yawning at will as a way to relax. Make a conscious effort to sit or stand up straight when you do this.

Sighing

1. Sigh deeply, letting out a sound of deep relief as the air rushes out of your lungs.

2. Don't think about inhaling—just let the air come in naturally.

3. Repeat whenever you feel the need for it.

Yawning

1. Open your mouth wide.

2. Stretch your arms over your head.

3. Yawn (loudly if you can).

4. Repeat as needed.

Diaphragmatic breathing

1. Step back mentally from what you are doing.

2. Notice how you feel.

3. Take three slow, relaxing, deep diaphragmatic breaths.

4. Notice how you feel.

5. Repeat as needed.

Note: Sometimes you don't have time to step back mentally and check in with yourself about how you're feeling. Nevertheless, you can still get a bit of tension release by breathing diaphragmatically a few times.

BREATHING FOR SYMPTOM CONTROL OR RELEASE

Abdominal Breathing and Imagination

The following exercise combines the relaxing benefits of diaphragmatic breathing with the curative value of positive autosuggestion.

1. Place your hands gently on your solar plexus (the point where your ribs start to separate above your abdomen). Get comfortable and begin to relax as you breathe diaphragmatically for a few minutes.

2. Imagine that energy is rushing into your lungs with each incoming breath of air and being immediately stored in your solar plexus. Imagine that this energy is flowing out to all parts of your body with each exhalation. Make a mental picture of this energizing process.

3. Continue doing this exercise for at least five to ten minutes a day on a daily basis.

Alternatives to step 2:

Keep one hand on your solar plexus and move the other hand to a point on your body that hurts. As you inhale, imagine energy coming in and being stored. As you exhale, imagine the energy flowing to the spot that hurts and stimulating that spot. As you continue to inhale more energy, imagine this energy driving out the pain with each exhalation. Keep a clear picture of this process in your mind as you alternately stimulate the spot that hurts and then drive out the pain.

Keep one hand on your solar plexus and move the other hand to a point on your body that has been injured or is infected. Imagine the energy coming in and being stored as you inhale. As you exhale, imagine that you are directing energy to the affected point and stimulating it, driving out the infection or healing it. Picture this process in your mind's eye.

Alternate Breathing

Most people will find this relaxation exercise useful, but those suffering from tension or sinus headaches often find it particularly beneficial. Begin by doing five cycles, and then slowly raise the number to between ten and twenty-five cycles.

1. Sit in a comfortable position with good posture.

2. Rest the index and second finger of your right hand on your forehead.

3. Close your right nostril with your thumb.

4. Inhale slowly and soundlessly through your left nostril.

5. Close your left nostril with your ring finger and simultaneously open your right nostril by removing your thumb.

6. Exhale slowly and soundlessly and as thoroughly as possible through your right nostril.

7. Inhale through your right nostril.

8. Close your right nostril with your thumb and open your left nostril.

9. Exhale through your left nostril.

10. Inhale through your left nostril, beginning the next cycle.

Breath Training

The following exercise, adapted from Masi (1993), has also been called "breathing retraining." Individuals with panic disorder or agoraphobia find it particularly helpful. When most people feel panic, they have a tendency to gasp, take in a breath, and hold onto it. The resulting sensation of fullness and inability to get enough air in turn produces quick, shallow breathing or hyperventilation. Hyperventilation can trigger a panic attack. Breath training provides a crucial counting or pacing procedure to help counteract this process. Here are the steps to follow:

1. Exhale first. At the first sign of nervousness or panic, at the first "what if" thought that you might pass out, have a heart attack, or be unable to breathe, *always* exhale. It is important to exhale first so that your lungs open up and you'll feel as though there's plenty of room to take a good deep breath.

2. Inhale and exhale through your nose. Exhaling through your nose will slow down your breathing and prevent hyperventilation. If you can't breathe through your nose, inhale through your mouth and exhale slowly through your mouth by slightly pursing your lips and pretending that you are blowing out through a straw.

3. When you are first learning this technique, lie on your back with one hand on your abdomen, and the other hand on your chest. Exhale first, and then breathe in through your nose, counting, "One ... two ... three." Pause a second, and then breathe out through your mouth, counting, "One ... two ... three ... four." Make sure that your exhalation is always longer than your inhalation. This will prevent you from taking short, gasping panic breaths.

4. After you feel comfortable doing step 3, you can slow your breathing even further. Breathe in and count, "One ... two ... three ... four"; pause and breathe out, counting, "One ... two ... three ... four ... five." Keep practicing these slow, deep breaths, pushing the hand on your abdomen up but allowing very little movement for the hand on your chest. When your mind wanders, refocus on your breathing.

Alternative positions:

Lie on your stomach with your hands folded under your head. Continue to count "one ... two ... three" as you breathe in and "one ... two ... three ... four" as you breathe out. As in step 4 above, breathe even more slowly by counting to four as you inhale and to five as you exhale.

Step 4 can also be done while you are standing, walking, and sitting. Pace your steps to match the same slow rate of your breathing.

When paced breathing feels comfortable and natural, you can replace counting with the words "in" as you inhale and "calm" as you exhale. Maintain the same pace, making each exhalation last slightly longer than each inhalation. Breathe in through your nose and breathe out through your mouth. Remember to always exhale first.

FINAL THOUGHTS

You will find it easier to relax your body, calm your mind, and cope with the stresses in your life when you practice a breathing relaxation exercise at least once or twice a day for twenty minutes. Make a plan right now to set aside time for this on a daily basis. In addition, remember to check in with your breathing from time to time throughout your day, especially when feeling stressed. If you catch yourself holding your breath or breathing shallowly and/or quickly, consciously take a few diaphragmatic breaths.

FURTHER READING

Benson, H., and E. Stuart. 1993. *The Wellness Book: The Comprehensive Guide to Maintaining Health and Treating Stress-Related Illness.* New York: Simon & Schuster.

Farhi, D. 1996. *The Breathing Book: Good Vitality Through Essential Breath Work.* New York: Owl Books.

Hendricks, G. 1995. *Conscious Breathing: Breathwork for Health, Stress Release and Personal Mastery.* New York: Bantam Books.

Lewis, D. 2004. *Free Your Breath, Free Your Life: Conscious Breathing Can Relieve Stress, Increase Vitality, and Help You Live More Fully.* Boston: Shambhala Publications.

Speeds, C. 2004. *Ways to Better Breathing.* London: Anness Publishing.

RECORDINGS

Hendricks, G. 2005. *The Art of Breathing and Centering: Discovering the Powerful Gifts of the Air You Breathe!* New York: Audio Renaissance.

Lewis, D. 2005. *Natural Breathing* (3 Audio CDs). Louisville, CO: Sounds True.

Masi, N. 1993. *Breath of Life.* Plantation, FL: Resource Warehouse.

McKay, M. 1987. *Progressive Relaxation and Breathing.* Oakland, CA: New Harbinger Publications.

4

Progressive Relaxation

In this chapter you will learn to:

* Distinguish between tense and relaxed muscles

* Progressively relax all of the muscles of your body

* Relax quickly in stressful situations

BACKGROUND

You cannot have the feeling of warm well-being in your body and at the same time experience psychological stress. Progressive relaxation of your muscles reduces pulse rate, blood pressure, and the startle reflex, as well as reducing perspiration and respiration rates. Deep muscle relaxation, when successfully mastered, can be used as an antianxiety pill.

Edmund Jacobson, a Chicago physician, published the book *Progressive Relaxation* in 1929. In it he described his deep muscle relaxation technique, which he asserted required no imagination, willpower, or suggestion. His technique is based on the premise that the body responds to anxiety-provoking thoughts and events with muscle tension. This physiological tension, in turn, increases the subjective experience of anxiety. Deep muscle relaxation reduces physiological tension and is incompatible with anxiety: The habit of responding with one blocks the habit of responding with the other.

Jacobson's original progressive relaxation procedures might take many months or even years to learn, but Joseph Wolpe (1958) developed a short form for these procedures that included verbal suggestions to relax. This abbreviated form can be mastered in a matter of days or weeks. Wolpe made this streamlined version a part of his systematic desensitization protocol for the treatment of phobias. He found that once they relaxed, clients were more capable of tolerating and responding adaptively to situations they were afraid of.

SYMPTOM-RELIEF EFFECTIVENESS

Excellent results have been found with progressive relaxation techniques for the treatment of muscular tension, anxiety, depression, fatigue, insomnia, neck and back pain, high blood pressure, mild phobias, and stuttering.

TIME TO MASTER

One to two weeks, employing two fifteen-minute sessions per day.

INSTRUCTIONS

Many people do not know which of their muscles are chronically tense. When you practice progressive relaxation, you focus on the sensations of tension in one particular muscle group at a time. Then, when you release that tension, you focus on the sensations of relaxation in that same muscle group. You move progressively through your whole body from one muscle group to the next, repeating this procedure. Using progressive relaxation techniques, you learn to identify particular muscle groups and to distinguish between the sensations of tension and deep relaxation.

Progressive relaxation can be practiced lying down or seated in a chair. Each muscle group is tensed from five to seven seconds and then released and relaxed for twenty to thirty seconds. These lengths of time are simply rules of thumb and don't have to be slavishly adhered to. This procedure is repeated at least once. If a particular muscle is difficult to relax, you can practice tensing and releasing it up to five times.

Once the procedure is familiar enough to be remembered, keep your eyes closed and focus your attention on just one muscle group at a time. Another option is to purchase a professional recording such as the one listed in the Recording section of this chapter.

The instructions for progressive relaxation are divided into two sections. The first part deals with the basic procedure, which you may wish to record and replay while practicing. This will familiarize you with the muscles in your body that are most commonly tense. If you do record these instructions, be sure to pause long enough for tensing and relaxing. The second section shortens the procedure by simultaneously tensing and relaxing many muscles at one time, so that deep muscle relaxation can be achieved in a very brief time period.

The Three Basic Levels of Tensing

There are three basic levels of tensing that you can use when you practice progressive relaxation. With experience, you can decide which level of tensing is most pleasant and effective for your needs.

1. *Active tensing* involves tensing a particular muscle group as tightly as you can without hurting yourself, studying the sensations of tension, then releasing the tension and studying the sensations of relaxation in that same area. While you are tensing one part of your body, the rest of your body is relatively relaxed. Remember to breathe diaphragmatically (it's easy to forget to breathe this way, especially during the tensing phase). Active tensing is the level of progressive relaxation described in italics below. By really exaggerating the tension, you are likely to feel where you carry chronic tension; the tense place may actually be sore. For people who have no injuries and who are not extremely tense, active tensing is recommended as the method of choice, at least for the first time you practice progressive relaxation. Some people prefer using this level every time they practice progressive relaxation, because tensing the muscles fatigues the muscle fibers and releasing the tension feels very relaxing and good. It's a little like setting down heavy bags you've been holding while standing in a long line.

2. *Threshold tensing* is the same as active tensing except that it involves tensing a particular muscle group slightly (just enough so that you notice the tension; it's barely noticeable to the human eye). Threshold tensing should be used for areas of your body that are injured or very tense to avoid pain or injury. Many people prefer to use threshold tensing once they've become familiar with the basic muscle groups through active tensing because threshold tensing takes less effort and feels less invasive. Some people use threshold tensing from the beginning because of health issues or extreme tension.

3. *Passive tensing* is the same as active tensing except that during the "tensing phase" you simply notice any tension that is present in a particular muscle group. You can use the same basic procedure described below in italics and substitute the words "Notice the tension in your _____" whenever the instructions call for tensing a muscle. If you feel no tension in a particular muscle, do threshold tensing or simply notice the sensations that are there. You may prefer to use passive tensing on a regular basis once you are familiar with active and threshold tensing. You will find that a round of progressive relaxation using passive tension, following a round of either active or threshold tensing, can deepen your state of relaxation.

VERBAL SUGGESTIONS

As you are releasing tension, you may also find it helpful to say to yourself one or more of the following expressions:

Let go of the tension.
Calm and rested.
Relax and smooth out the muscles.
Let the tension dissolve away.
Let go more and more.
Deeper and deeper.

Basic Procedure

Get into a comfortable position in a quiet room where you won't be disturbed. You may want to loosen your clothing and remove your shoes. Begin to relax as you take a few slow, deep breaths.... Now as you let the rest of your body relax, clench your fists and bend them back at the wrist ... tighter and tighter ... feel the tension in your fists and forearms.... Now relax.... Feel the looseness in your hands and forearms.... Notice the contrast with the tension.... (If you have time, repeat this, and all succeeding procedures, at least one more time.) *Now bend your elbows and tense your biceps.... Tense them as hard as you can and observe the feeling of tautness.... Let your hands drop down and relax.... Feel that difference.... Turn your attention to your head and wrinkle your forehead as tight as you can.... Feel the tension in your forehead and scalp. Now relax and smooth it out. Imagine your entire forehead and scalp becoming smooth and at rest.... Now frown and notice the strain spreading throughout your forehead.... Let go. Allow your brow to become smooth again.... Squeeze your eyes closed ... tighter.... Relax your eyes. Let them remain closed gently and comfortably.... Now, open your mouth wide and feel the tension in your jaw.... Relax your jaw.... When your jaw is relaxed, your lips will be slightly parted. Notice the contrast between tension and relaxation.... Now press your tongue against the roof of your mouth. Experience the strain in the back of your mouth.... Relax.... Press your lips now, purse them into an "O." ... Relax your lips.... Feel the relaxation in your forehead, scalp, eyes, jaw, tongue, and lips.... Let go more and more....*

Now roll your head slowly around on your neck, feeling the point of tension shifting as your head moves ... and then slowly roll your head the other way. Relax, allowing your head to return to a comfortable upright position.... Now shrug your shoulders, bring your shoulders up toward your ears ... hold it.... Drop your shoulders back down and feel the relaxation spreading through your neck, throat, and shoulders ... pure relaxation, deeper and deeper....

Now breathe in and fill your lungs completely. Hold your breath. Experience the tension.... Now exhale and let your chest become loose.... Continue relaxing, letting your breath come freely and gently.... Notice the tension draining out of your muscles with each exhalation.... Next, tighten your stomach and hold. Feel the tension.... Relax.... Now place your hand on your stomach. Breathe deeply into your stomach, pushing your hand up. Hold ... and relax. Feel the sensations of relaxation as the air rushes out.... Now arch your back, without straining. Keep the rest of your body as relaxed as possible. Focus on the tension in your lower back. . . . Now relax. . . . Let the tension dissolve away.

Tighten your buttocks and thighs. . . . Relax and feel the difference. . . . Now straighten and tense your legs and curl your toes downward. Experience the tension. . . . Relax. . . . Straighten and tense your legs and bend your toes toward your face. Relax.

Feel the comfortable warmth and heaviness of deep relaxation throughout your entire body as you continue to breathe slowly and deeply. . . . You can relax even more as you move up through your body, letting go of the last bit of tension in your body. Relax your feet . . . relax your ankles . . . relax your calves . . . relax your shins . . . relax your knees . . . relax your thighs . . . relax your buttocks. . . . Let the relaxation spread to your stomach . . . to your lower back . . . to your chest. . . . Let go more and more. Feel the relaxation deepening in your shoulders . . . in your arms . . . and in your hands. . . . Deeper and deeper. Notice the feeling of looseness and relaxation in your neck . . . your jaw . . . your face . . . and your scalp. . . . Continue to breathe slowly and deeply. Your entire body is comfortably loose and relaxed, calm and rested.

Shorthand Procedure

Once you have mastered the basic procedure, use the following procedure to relax your muscles quickly. In this procedure, whole muscle groups are simultaneously tensed and then relaxed. As before, repeat each procedure at least once, tensing each muscle group from five to seven seconds and then relaxing from fifteen to thirty seconds. Remember to notice the contrast between the sensations of tension and relaxation.

1. Curl both fists, tightening biceps and forearms (Charles Atlas pose). Relax.

2. Roll your head around on your neck clockwise in a complete circle, then reverse. Relax.

3. Wrinkle up the muscles of your face like a walnut: forehead wrinkled, eyes squinted, mouth opened, and shoulders hunched. Relax.

4. Arch your shoulders back as you take a deep breath into your chest. Hold. Relax. Take a deep breath, pushing out your stomach. Hold. Relax.

5. Straighten your legs and point your toes back toward your face, tightening your shins. Hold. Relax. Straighten your legs and curl your toes, simultaneously tightening your calves, thighs, and buttocks. Relax.

SPECIAL CONSIDERATIONS

1. If you make a recording of the basic procedure to facilitate your relaxation program, remember to space each procedure so that enough time is allocated to experience the tension and relaxation before going on to the next muscle or muscle group.

2. As with all relaxation techniques, regular practice of progressive relaxation will enhance the speed and depth of your relaxation.

3. Be extra cautious when tensing your neck and back, because excessive tightening can result in muscle or spinal damage. Also, overtightening your toes or feet can result in muscle cramping.

4. People new to this technique sometimes make the error of relaxing tension gradually. This slow-motion release of tension may look relaxed, but it actually requires sustained tension. When you release the tension in a particular muscle, let it go instantly; let your muscles become suddenly limp.

5. Although initially you will learn progressive relaxation in a quiet place, eventually you will be able to use at least a shortened version of it anytime during the day when you notice you are tense.

FURTHER READING

Bernstein, D. A., T. D. Borkovec, and H. Hazlett-Stevens. 2000. *New Directions in Progressive Relaxation Training: A Guidebook for Helping Professionals*. New York: Praeger Publishing.

Bernstein, D. A., and C. R. Carlson. 1993. Progressive relaxation: Abbreviated methods. In *Principles and Practice of Stress Management*, second edition. Edited by P. M. Lehrer and R. L. Woolfold. New York: Guilford Press.

Jacobson, E. 1974. *Progressive Relaxation*. Chicago: University of Chicago Press, Midway Reprint. Out of print.

McGuigan, F. J. 1993. Progressive relaxation: Origins, principles and clinical applications. In *Principles and Practice of Stress Management*, second edition. Edited by P. M. Lehrer and R. L. Woolfold. New York: Guilford Press.

Wolpe, J. 1958. *Psychotherapy by Reciprocal Inhibition*. Stanford, CA: Stanford University Press.

————. 1992. *The Practice of Behavior Therapy*. New York: Pergamon Press.

RECORDING

McKay, M. 1987. *Progressive Relaxation and Breathing*. Oakland, CA: New Harbinger Publications.

5

Meditation

In this chapter you will learn to:

✳ Use basic meditation techniques

BACKGROUND

Meditation is the intentional practice of uncritically focusing your attention on one thing at a time. Exactly what that thing might be is relatively unimportant and varies from one tradition to the next. Often the meditator repeats, either aloud or silently, a syllable, word, or group of words. This is known as *mantra meditation*. Focusing on a fixed object such as a candle's flame or a flower can also anchor the attention. Many meditators find that a convenient and relaxing point of focus is the rising and falling of their own breath. But you can use anything as an object of meditation ... the calendar on your desk, the tip of your nose, or even your Aunt Mary's maiden name.

It is important to understand that the heart of meditation lies not simply in focusing on one object to the exclusion of all other thought, but rather in the attempt to achieve this type of focus. The nature of the mind is such that it does not want to stay concentrated. A myriad of thoughts will appear and seemingly interfere with the meditation. A typical meditation might go something like this (the meditator in this case has chosen the task of counting to three repeatedly):

One ... two ... this isn't so hard ... one ... two ... three ... one ... I'm not having many thoughts at all ... oh, oh, I just had a thought ... that was another one ... two ... my nose itches ... one ... I wonder if it's okay to scratch it ... darn, there was another thought. I've got to try harder ... one ... two ... three ... one ... two ... I was judging myself pretty harshly. I'm not supposed to do that ... one ... two ... three ... one ... I'm hungry ... wonder what I'll cook tonight ... one ... two ... three ... I'm having way too many thoughts ... I'll never get this right ... one ... two ... now don't judge ... one ... two ... three ... one....

Each time this meditator realizes that his mind has drifted to other thoughts, he chooses instead to dwell on the original object of his attention. By repeating this one moment of awareness, a moment that consists of noticing the thought and then refocusing the attention, over time a number of surprising realizations can become apparent:

- It is impossible to worry, fear, or hate when your mind is thinking about something other than the object of these emotions.

- It isn't necessary to think about everything that pops into your head. You have the ability to choose which thoughts you will think about.

- The seemingly diverse contents of your mind really can fit into a few simple categories: grudging thoughts, fearful thoughts, angry thoughts, wanting thoughts, planning thoughts, memories, and so on.

- You act in certain ways because you have certain thoughts that over your lifetime have become habitual. Habitual patterns of thought and perception will begin to lose their influence over your life once you become aware of them.

- Emotions, aside from the thoughts and pictures in your mind, consist entirely of physical sensations in your body.

- Even the strongest emotion will become manageable if you concentrate on the sensations in your body and not the content of the thought that produced the emotion.

- Thoughts and emotions are not permanent. They pass into and out of your body and mind. They need not leave a trace.

- When you are awake to what is happening right now and open to "what is," the extreme highs and extreme lows of your emotional response to life will disappear. You will live life with equanimity.

In 1968, Dr. Herbert Benson and his colleagues at Harvard Medical School decided to put meditation to the test. Volunteer practitioners of Transcendental Meditation were tested to see if meditation really could counter the physiological effects of stress. Benson scientifically proved that during meditation, the following physiological effects were observed:

1. Heartbeat and breathing rates slow down.

2. Oxygen consumption falls by 20 percent.

3. Blood lactate levels drop. (This level rises with stress and fatigue.)

4. Skin resistance to electrical current, a sign of relaxation, increases fourfold.

5. EEG ratings of brain-wave patterns indicate increased alpha activity, another sign of relaxation.

Benson (1997) went on to prove that any meditation practice could duplicate these physiological changes as long as the following four factors were present:

1. A relatively quiet environment

2. A mental device that provides a constant stimulus

3. A comfortable position

4. A passive attitude

With regular meditation, a person feels more focused and calm in her life, more capable of making new choices in the moment, and less prone to engage in struggle and reactive responses.

SYMPTOM-RELIEF EFFECTIVENESS

Meditation has been used successfully in the treatment and prevention of high blood pressure, heart disease, migraine headaches, and autoimmune diseases such as diabetes and arthritis. It has proved helpful in curtailing obsessive thinking, anxiety, depression, and hostility.

TIME TO MASTER

The benefits of meditation increase with practice: Levels of relaxation deepen. Attention becomes steadier. You become more adept at living in the present moment. For these three reasons, it is important to meditate regularly.

INSTRUCTIONS

The following sections address some important aspects of meditation: the importance of correct posture, the need to center yourself, and the amount of time to spend on the practice.

Establishing Your Posture

1. From the following, select a position that is comfortable for you:

- In a chair with your knees comfortably apart, your legs uncrossed, and your hands resting in your lap.

- Tailor-fashion (cross-legged) on the floor. This position is most comfortable and stable when a cushion is placed under your buttocks so that both knees touch the floor.

- On your knees with your big toes touching and your heels pointed outward so that your buttocks rest on the soles of your feet. Again, if you place a cushion between your feet for your buttocks to rest on, you will be able to hold the position for a much longer period of time (Japanese-fashion).

- The yoga "full lotus" position. This position requires so much physical conditioning that it is not recommended for beginners.

2. Sit with your back straight (but not ramrod rigid) and let the weight of your head rest directly on your spinal column. This can be accomplished by pulling in your chin slightly. Allow the small of your back to arch.

3. Rock briefly from side to side, then from front to back, and establish the point at which your upper torso feels balanced on your hips.

4. Close your mouth and breathe through your nose. Place your tongue on the roof of your mouth.

Centering Yourself

Being centered means deliberately keeping an area of calmness within yourself by conscious thought no matter how intensely your emotions might be churning. For that reason, being centered is sometimes compared to being the eye in the center of a hurricane. The following are three steps to centering yourself:

ESTABLISHING YOUR POSTURE

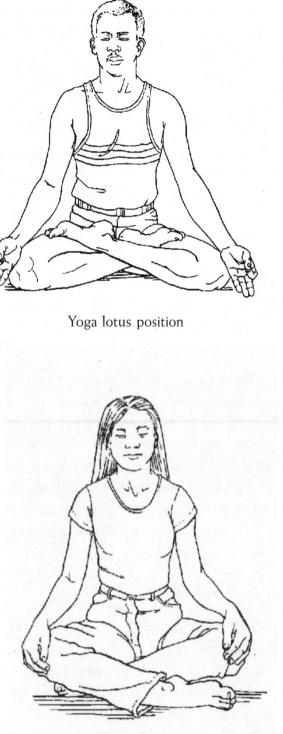

Yoga lotus position

Japanese-fashion

Tailor-fashion

GROUNDING

Close your eyes and focus on the place where your body touches the cushion or chair. What are the sensations there? Next, notice the places where your body touches itself. Are your hands crossed? Are your legs crossed? Pay attention to the sensation at these places of contact. Finally, focus on the way your body fills the space around you. Does it take up a lot of space or a small amount? Can you feel the boundary between your body and space? Notice the feelings there.

BREATHING

With your eyes closed, take several deep breaths and notice the quality of your breathing. Is it fast or slow? Deep or shallow? Notice where your breath rests in your body. Is it up high in your chest? Is it in the midsection around your stomach? Down low in your belly? Try moving your breath from one area to the other. Breathe into your upper chest, then into your stomach, then drop your breath into your lower belly. Feel your abdomen expand and contract as the air goes in and out. Notice how the upper chest and stomach areas seem almost still. This "dropped breath" is the most relaxing stance to meditate from. However, if you have difficulty taking deep belly breaths, don't worry. Your breath will drop of its own accord as you become more practiced in meditation.

ATTITUDE

Maintaining a passive attitude during meditation is perhaps the most important element in eliciting relaxation. It is important to realize that, especially as a beginner, you will have many thoughts and relatively few moments of clear concentration. This is natural and to be expected. Realize that your thoughts are not really interruptions but are an integral part of meditation. Without thoughts arising, you would not be able to develop the ability to let them go.

A passive attitude includes a lack of concern about whether you are doing things correctly, whether you are accomplishing any goals, or whether this meditation is right for you. Sit with the attitude of "I'm going to put in my time here, just sitting, and whatever happens is exactly what should happen."

A WORD ABOUT TIME

In general, any amount of time spent in meditation is more relaxing than not meditating at all. When you first begin to practice, maintain the meditation for only as long as is comfortable, even if this is just for five minutes a day. If you feel that you are forcing yourself to sit, you may develop an aversion to practicing meditation at all. As you progress in your practice and meditation becomes easier, you will find yourself wanting to extend your time. In terms of relaxation, twenty to thirty minutes once or twice a day is sufficient.

EXERCISES

The following exercises are divided into five groups:

- Group 1 explains the mechanics of three basic meditations. Try each one a few times, then settle on the one you like best. Practice it regularly, at least once a day.

- Group 2 consists of meditation exercises that will help you develop the skill of relaxing your muscle groups at will.

- Group 3 introduces you to mindfulness exercises. You don't have to go off by yourself and sit in silence in order to concentrate and build mindfulness. These exercises can be practiced anywhere and can be helpful in calming your body as it responds to stress throughout the day.

- Group 4 builds on the mindfulness techniques in group 3. In real life you may often find yourself in the presence of minor pain, annoyances, or disappointments, all of which cause you to tense up. By practicing feeling relaxed in response to small irritations while you meditate, you will become more adept at handling life's larger irritations when they occur.

- Group 5 teaches you how to let go of obsessive thoughts and feelings that make it difficult to relax because your mind wants to hold onto an idea or emotion that you experienced at an earlier time.

Group 1: Three Basic Meditations

Mantra Meditation

The mantra meditation is the most common form of meditation throughout the world. Before you begin, select a word or syllable that pleases you. Perhaps there's a word that has special meaning for you. Or you may use nonsense syllables, the sound of which you find pleasant. Benson recommends using the word "one." Many meditators prefer the mantra "om."

1. Find your comfortable posture and center yourself. Take several deep breaths.

2. Chant your mantra silently to yourself. Say the word or syllables over and over within your mind. When your thought strays, note that; then bring your attention back to your mantra. If you notice any sensations in your body, note the feeling; then return to the repetition of your own special word. You needn't force it. Let your mantra find its own rhythm as you repeat it over and over again.

3. If you have the opportunity, you may want to try chanting your mantra aloud. Let the sound of your voice fill you as you relax. Notice whether the sensations in your body are different from those you felt when you chanted silently. Which is more relaxing?

4. Remember that meditation is to be practiced with awareness. You may find that the repetition of a mantra, especially when repeated silently, can easily become mechanical. When this happens, you may have the sense that an inner voice is repeating your mantra while you are actually lost in thought or rapidly approaching sleep. Try to stay aware of each repetition of each syllable.

Sitting Meditation

The simplest way to begin meditation is by focusing on your breath.

1. Choose a comfortable sitting posture.

2. Bring your attention to the gentle rise and fall of your breath. Like ocean waves coming in to the shore and going out, your breath is always there. You can focus on your inhale and exhale, the sensations of your breath entering your nose or mouth, or the sensations of your breath filling your lungs and diaphragm.

3. Whenever your mind wanders, gently bring your attention back to focus on your breath. Let your breath be your anchor to this present moment.

4. When you find yourself becoming distracted by thoughts, simply notice and acknowledge them.

5. One way to work with thoughts is to "name" them as you notice them. If you notice you are worrying, silently say to yourself, "Worry, worry, there is worry." You can name *planning, reminiscing, longing, thinking,* or whatever it is in just the same way: Label it and move on. This will help you to stop identifying yourself with your thoughts and to learn how to let go to create more spaciousness and peace.

This meditation can take between twenty and thirty minutes to do. With practice, you will become able to rest your attention on your breath more effortlessly and to let go of your thoughts more easily.

Breath-Counting Meditation

An alternative form of sitting meditation is the use of counting with the rhythm of the breath. Following the gentle ins and outs of the breath creates a sense of peace and restfulness.

1. Find your posture and center yourself. Take several deep breaths. Either close your eyes or fix them on a spot on the floor about four feet in front of you. Your eyes may or may not be focused.

2. Take deep but not forced belly breaths. As you do, focus your attention on each part of the breath: the inhale, the turn (the point at which you stop inhaling and start exhaling), the exhale, the pause (between the exhale and inhale), the turn (the point at which you start to inhale), the inhale, and so on. Pay careful attention to the pause. What are the sensations in your body as you pause between breaths?

3. As you exhale, say "one." Continue counting each exhale: "two … three … four." Then begin again with "one." If you lose count, simply start over.

4. When you discover that your mind has slipped into thought, note this, then gently return to the counting of your breath.

5. If a particular sensation in your body catches your attention, focus on the sensation until it recedes. Then return your attention to the inhale and the exhale and the counting of your breath.

SPECIAL CONSIDERATIONS

1. It is not necessary to feel as though you are relaxing while you meditate for you to actually become relaxed. You may feel as though you are thinking thousands of thoughts and are very restless. However, when you open your eyes at the end of your meditation, you will realize you feel much more relaxed than you did before you began meditating.

2. As your mind quiets with meditation, old or hidden pain can arise from your subconscious. If you find that when you meditate you suddenly feel angry, depressed, or frightened, try to gently allow yourself to experience the feeling without resistance and let go of the temptation to make sense out of your feelings. If you feel the need, talk to a friend, counselor, or meditation teacher.

3. You may hear or read about ideal conditions for meditation: for example, that you should meditate only in a quiet place, only two hours after you've eaten, or only in a position that you can hold comfortably for twenty minutes, and so on. Yes, these are ideal conditions, but life is seldom ideal. If the place isn't absolutely quiet or if the only time you have to meditate is right after lunch, don't let these small obstacles keep you from meditating. If you find yourself being particularly bothered by noises or the rumblings of a full stomach, simply incorporate the annoying sensation in with the object of your meditation.

4. If you adopt a daily sitting practice, you must understand that you may find there are stretches of time during which you will not want to meditate. Don't expect that your desire to meditate will grow constantly with your practice. If you feel discouraged, be gentle with yourself and try to work creatively on ways to make your practice more comfortable. Know that these periods of discouragement will go away by themselves in time. Here are two things you can do to help maintain a schedule: Pick a regular time of the day to meditate and honor it as you would any other appointment. Find a group to meditate with—the value of finding such a group cannot be overstated.

Group 2: *Releasing Muscular Tension*

The Inner Exploration or Body Scan

This exercise will help you to open to each part of your body, notice any sensation that is present, and let go of tension in your body.

1. Begin by becoming aware of the rising and falling of your breath in your chest and belly. You can ride the waves of your breath and let it begin to anchor you to the present moment.

2. Bring your attention to the soles of your feet. Notice any sensation that is present there. Without judging or trying to make it different, simply be present with the sensation. After a few moments imagine that your breath is flowing into the soles of your feet. As you breathe in and out you might experience an opening or softening and a release of tension. Just simply observe.

3. Now bring your attention to the rest of your feet, up to your ankles. Become aware of any sensation in this part of your body. After a few moments imagine that your breath, instead of stopping at the diaphragm, flows all the way down to your feet. Breathe into and out of your feet, simply noticing the sensations.

4. Proceed up your body in this manner with all the parts of your body—lower legs, knees, thighs, pelvis, hips and buttocks, lower back, upper back, chest and belly, upper shoulders, neck, head, and face. Take your time to really feel each body part and notice whatever sensations are present, without forcing them or trying to make them be different, then breathe into the body part and let go of it as you move on to your next body part.

5. Go back to your neck and shoulders or any part of your body that has pain, tension, or discomfort. Simply be with the sensations in a nonjudgmental way. As you breathe,

imagine your breath opening up any tight muscles or painful areas and creating more spaciousness. As you breathe out, imagine the tension or pain flowing out of that part of your body.

6. When you reach the top of your head, scan your body one last time for any areas of tension or discomfort. Then imagine that you have a breath hole at the top of your head, much like the blowholes that whales or dolphins use to breathe. Breathe in from the top of your head, bringing your breath all the way down to the soles of your feet and then back up again through your whole body. Allow your breath to wash away any tension or uncomfortable sensations.

The entire body scan can take anywhere from a few minutes to thirty minutes. Ideally, try to allow for twenty to thirty minutes to complete a body scan each day.

Moving Band Meditation

1. Find your posture, center yourself, and take several deep breaths.

2. Imagine that a three-inch-wide band encircles the top of your head. Focus your attention on the part of your head surrounded by the imaginary band. Notice the sensations. Is there any tension in your forehead? If so, try to relax it. Are there any other sensations in this area? Focus on them for a moment.

3. Lower the imaginary band three inches—the width of the band. Again, focus your attention on the area encompassed by the band. Really try to feel around in there. What does the back of your eyeball feel like? The right wall of your nose? How are the muscles of your upper lip set? Any tension? Try to completely relax this area of your head. Breathe deeply and whisper to yourself, "Let it go, let it all go."

4. Continue to move the band down your body. Focus intently on any sensations. Wherever you notice tension, try to release it. As you do, take several deep belly breaths and relax. See if you can be aware of how the muscles feel as they relax.

5. When the band gets down to your torso, imagine that it goes around one arm, then across your upper body, around the other arm, then across your back. Scan a section of each arm and your torso at the same time as though they were one part. Notice the sensations where your arms are separate from your body. What do these boundaries feel like? Can you make the sensation of the boundaries less distinct so that your arms feel as though they are merging with your torso? Is there any tension? In your shoulders? Your back? If so, relax these areas.

6. Move the band down your torso and arms to your legs, noting tension and releasing it. Focus on the sensation where your legs touch each other (if they do), and where they touch the floor. Again, feel the sensations at the points of contact, then try to experience the sensation of your legs merging together.

This exercise can be practiced in two different ways. Try both ways and see which is more relaxing for you:

1. Move the band slowly down your body, carefully experiencing each sensation, noting all the points of tension, and letting them go.

2. Quickly lower the band down your body. Move it as soon as your attention has given the encompassed area a brief scan. If practiced this way, repeat the entire exercise several times in a row.

Group 3: Mindfulness and Present-Moment Awareness

Much of our stress comes from thinking about the past or worrying about the future. When you live in the present moment and your attention is focused on what you are doing right now, there is no room for anything else to enter—including regrets, anticipation of rejection or failure, or anything else that might be stressful.

In the meditative state, your attention is focused on the object of meditation, whether that's the inhale, the exhale, or the mantra that quiets the mind and allows you to be more in the present moment. When thoughts of past or future, desires or aversions, or anything else arise, note this and then turn your awareness gently back to the present. This concentration on the here and now allows your body and mind to enter a state of relaxation.

Mindfulness meditation is a form of meditation that offers both deep relaxation and insight. It cultivates a way of being in a harmonious relationship with what is, whether that's nagging or obsessive thoughts, uncomfortable feelings, external stressors, or physical discomfort. By fully opening to what is present in your internal experience and not resisting or pushing it away, you can cultivate a deep acceptance and ability to rest more fully in the present moment. In the beginning stages of mindfulness practice, present-moment awareness is usually cultivated by focusing on the breath. Beginning practices can also include focusing on sounds, feelings, or body sensations. The body scan or a mindful movement discipline such as yoga, tai chi, or qi gong can also help cultivate mindfulness.

Whatever your focus of attention, a gentle, nonjudgmental, and embracing attitude should be used to encounter what arises during your course of meditation. The stories you tell yourself about what you notice and the reactivity to *what is* creates your suffering or pain. Use a bare-bones (that is, a primary or low-level) attention to simply notice wherever your attention goes during meditation, let go of it without judgment, and return to the object of focus that you've chosen. If you find yourself creating a story about it, such as, *Oh my left knee is really hurting, it will never stop, it's going to get worse* ... simply notice the thought or story and return back to your breath without getting caught up in the content of your thoughts. Continue this process throughout the sitting period. Meditating in this way actually trains you to encounter stressors in your life, whether internal or external, in a similar fashion. When you encounter stressors, catch yourself before you go into a habitual reaction that leads to suffering—rather than getting stuck in reactivity, breathe, pause, and make new choices about how to respond. Make choices that bring you healthier thinking, relaxation, insight, health, connection with others, and more love.

Eating Meditation

You eat every day, but how often do you really pay attention to what you are eating while you are eating it? Do you usually eat with other people? In front of the TV? While reading a book? Can you usually finish a three-course meal in ten minutes or even less time?

The following is a conscious-eating meditation. Try it someplace where it is unlikely anyone will want to come over and eat with you. For the sake of this example, the food in question is a cheese sandwich.

1. Sit down in front of your food and take several deep breaths. Note the food's color, shape, and texture. Does it seem appealing to you? Can you barely restrain yourself from gobbling it up? Whatever you're feeling, notice it.

2. Be aware of your intention to begin eating. Move your hand slowly toward the sandwich. As you do this, make a quiet mental note of the action. You may say to yourself, "Reaching ... reaching ... reaching." By labeling your actions you are more likely to keep in mind your purpose—to stay aware. As you pick up the sandwich, notice that you are "lifting ... lifting ... lifting."

3. Watch your hand move the sandwich closer to your mouth. When it nears your mouth, take a moment to smell the food. What smells do you recognize? Can you smell the mayonnaise? How is your body reacting to the smell? Is your mouth watering? Notice the sensation of your body desiring food.

4. As you take your first bite, feel your teeth penetrate the bread. When the bite is complete, how is the food positioned in your mouth? How does your tongue position the food so that it's between your teeth? Begin chewing slowly. What are the sensations in your teeth? Your tongue? How does your tongue move when you chew? What tastes are you experiencing? The tomato? The cheese? What part of your tongue experiences the taste? Where is your arm? Did you put it back on the table? If so, did you notice the motion?

5. When you swallow, try to be aware of how the muscles in your esophagus contract and relax as they push the food to your stomach. Where is the food when you have finished swallowing? Can you feel the sensations in your stomach? Where is your stomach? What size is it? Is it empty, full, or somewhere in between?

6. As you continue to eat your sandwich, try to stay aware of as many sensations as you can. Silently label each movement if this helps. Try eating with the hand you don't normally use, because the awkwardness may serve as a reminder to pay attention. As with your basic meditation, when thoughts arise, notice them and then return your attention to your food.

Walking Meditation

Most people cover miles in the course of their daily routines. This makes walking a good opportunity to practice mindfulness. Focus on the act of walking much the same way as you focus on your breath in sitting meditation. You can do the walking meditation either indoors or outdoors.

1. Stand up and relax your abdominal muscles. Take several deep belly breaths. Feel your abdomen expand and contract with each breath. Begin walking. As you practice this exercise, try to continue breathing from this relaxed stance. Mentally repeat the word "in" with each inhalation and "out" with each exhalation as you walk.

2. Try to arrange it so that one of your feet touches the ground at the beginning of each *in* breath and each *out* breath, without forcing your breathing too much. Now, see how many steps seem natural to take during each inhalation and each exhalation.

3. As with all meditations, when thoughts or images interrupt your focus, make a mental note of this and then return to your walking and breathing.

4. Pay attention to the sensations of walking. Concentrate on your feet and lower legs. Notice which muscles contract and which relax as you lift your legs up and down. Which part of your foot touches the ground first? Pay attention to how your weight shifts from one foot to the other. What are the feelings in your knees as they bend and straighten? And, while you're at it, pay attention to the ground. What is its texture? Is it hard or soft? Notice any cracks or stones. How does the sensation of walking on grass differ from that of walking on a sidewalk? Catch your thoughts, let them go, and return to your awareness of the details of your present moment.

5. An alternative way to practice the walking meditation is to count your steps in time with your breathing as you walk. If you are taking three steps during each inhalation

and exhalation, mentally say to yourself, "In ... two ... three. Out ... two ... three. In ... two ... three ... " and so on. Your *in* breaths may be longer or shorter than your *out* breaths and therefore may accommodate either more or fewer steps. Or your step count may vary from breath to breath. Just pay attention and readjust your walking to the ins and outs of your breathing as needed.

Seeing Meditation

You can gaze meditatively at something during a meeting, on a bus, or in a waiting room. This is a wonderfully inconspicuous meditation practice that can be practiced anywhere.

1. Find an object within your line of vision that you might want to fix your eyes on. Take several belly breaths as you glue your eyes to the object. Let it capture your interest, as though it were the only object in the vicinity. Try not to judge what you are seeing, or have any thoughts about it at all. See if you can have the experience of "just seeing." When thoughts arise, note them and then return your focus to the object.

2. Try practicing this exercise with different types of objects. Here are a few suggestions:

   - Concrete objects—objects with a definite size and shape that are usually stationary.

   - Natural objects—such as clouds, sand, a pile of dry leaves, the ocean, and so on.

   - Vastness—any large, uniform surface such as a wall or a finely patterned rug.

   - Moving objects—a crowd of people, cars on a busy street, and so on. With objects of this nature, don't follow individual shapes with your eyes. Instead, fix your eyes on a point in space and let the movement pass in front of your field of vision.

Any simple activity can become a meditation when you try to continuously focus your attention on it. Another good mindfulness exercise is to choose an activity you do every day, preferably a short one, and then concentrate on every action and every sensation involved in that activity. Use the type of mental notation discussed earlier, under Eating Meditation, if that helps. You could practice concentrating when you shave, brush your teeth, wash dishes, fold clothes, or pull weeds. As thoughts occur, note them, and then go back to the task with renewed concentration. While engaged in this activity, it is often helpful to use your nondominant hand (though you might not want to do this while shaving). The resulting awkwardness will serve as a constant reminder that you want to concentrate on what you are doing.

Group 4: Mindfulness of Pain or Discomfort

As a rule, most people respond to pain, irritation, or any physical discomfort by trying to build a solid wall of tightness around it, attempting to block off the feeling or to avoid it entirely. However, the more you resist pain, the more it hurts. And the more it hurts, the more you will try to resist it. This vicious cycle produces one big knot of pain and resistance that is extremely difficult to untie.

An alternative way to deal with pain is to learn to soften around it. This means you first acknowledge the pain's presence, and then simply allow yourself to experience both physically and mentally whatever it is that hurts. Be your own good nurse, hold your own hand, tell yourself it's all right, and then sit with yourself compassionately as you experience sensations of discomfort.

When you open to an irritation, you consciously relax your tense, clenched muscles around the spot that hurts. You focus on the hurting itself, without all the tightness you tend to add to it.

Softening also means that you notice but disregard your thoughts about how awful the discomfort is, how you have to move, how you have to scratch, how you can't stand it, and so on. Softening is like working the hard lumps out of a mound of clay so that you can feel a tiny pearl in the center. It's like removing screens placed around a candle flame so that you can see it clearly. It's like thawing out the frozen core of a large piece of meat so that you can remove the bone. It's like cleaning layers of grime off the outside of a window so that you can see what's inside more clearly.

The following exercise introduces minor irritations into your basic meditation. By practicing with small irritations in a safe setting, you can begin to understand the process of softening.

Don't Move

1. Find your posture and center yourself. Take several deep breaths.

2. Make an agreement with yourself that for a preset period of time you will not move. Then begin your basic meditation.

3. As time passes, you may find yourself moving your head or shifting in your seat without realizing it. This is fine. Note the movement and return to your meditation. After a while you will be able to notice your intention to move a part of your body before you actually move it.

4. Once you are able to identify your intention to move, try to focus on what exactly your desire is. Do you want to squirm around in your chair? Stretch your back muscles?

Maybe you have an itch, or an ant is crawling across your foot. Try to precisely identify the uncomfortable sensation. Remember, don't move.

5. As you focus on the discomfort, try to soften around it. If muscle groups are tightening, try to relax them. Check these muscle groups often, because they will not want to stay relaxed. Where is your breath? Is it high in your chest? If so, try to drop it into your belly. Focus on the sensation of discomfort. What is the feeling here? Stay with it for a while.

6. When time is up, move your body slowly to the position you've been wanting to sit in. Focus on the sensations. Is the relief immediate? Is the relief gradual? In what way does your body feel better? Is there any tension? If so, release it.

Any irritating sound or sensation can be used as a focal point for meditation. Focusing on your body's minor aches or the sound of a lawn mower or a dog barking can teach you how your body responds to life's irritations. Once you realize this, you can begin to learn how to soften around such irritations.

Group 5: Letting Go of Thoughts

This highly structured exercise is found in many cultures in one form or another. In it, you passively observe the flow of your thoughts, feelings, and perceptions, one after another, without being concerned with their meaning or their relationship to one another. This will allow you to see what's on your mind and then let it go.

1. Find your posture and center yourself. Take several deep breaths.

2. Close your eyes and imagine yourself sitting at the bottom of a deep pool of water. When you have a thought, feeling, or perception, see it as a bubble and let it rise away from you and disappear. When it's gone, wait for the next one to appear and repeat the process. Don't think about the contents of the bubble. Just observe it. Sometimes the same bubble may come up many times, or several bubbles will seem related to each other, or the bubbles may be empty. That's okay. Don't allow yourself to be concerned with these thoughts. Just watch them pass in front of your mind's eye.

3. If you feel uncomfortable imagining being underwater, imagine that you are sitting on the bank of a river, watching a leaf drift slowly downstream. Imagine one thought, feeling, or perception as the leaf, and then let it drift out of sight. Return to gazing at the river, waiting for the next leaf to float by with a new thought. Or, if you prefer, you can imagine your thoughts rising in puffs of smoke from a campfire.

The practice of meditation can bring focus, insight, and a sense of renewal to your life. Give yourself the gift of meditation and all of its benefits.

FURTHER READING

Benson, H. 1997. *Timeless Healing: The Pow\er of Biology and Belief.* New York: Scribner.

Brantley, J. 2007. *Calming Your Anxious Mind: How Mindfulness and Compassion Can Free You from Anxiety, Fear, and Panic.* Oakland, CA: New Harbinger Publications.

Goldstein, J. 1987. *The Experience of Insight.* Boston: Shambhala Publications.

Goldstein, J., and J. Kornfield. 1991. *Seeking the Heart of Wisdom.* Boston: Shambhala Publications.

———. 1995. *The Path of Insight Meditation.* Boston: Shambhala Publications.

Hewitt, J. 1990. *The Complete Yoga Book.* New York: Shocken Books.

Kabat-Zinn, J. 1990. *Full Catastrophe Living: Using the Wisdom of Your Body and Mind to Face Stress, Pain, and Illness.* New York: Delacorte.

———. 1995. *Wherever You Go, There You Are: Mindfulness Meditation in Everyday Life.* New York: Hyperion.

———. 2005. *Coming to Our Senses: Healing Ourselves and the World Through Mindfulness.* New York: Hyperion.

Kornfield, J. 1993. *A Path with Heart: A Guide Through the Perils and Promises of Spiritual Life.* New York: Bantam Doubleday Dell.

LeShan, L. 1999. *How to Meditate.* New York: Little, Brown.

Thich Nhat Hahn. 1989. *The Miracle of Mindfulness.* Boston, MA: Beacon Press.

———. 1992. *Peace Is Every Step: The Path of Mindfulness in Everyday Life.* New York: Bantam Books.

———. 2005. *Being Peace.* Berkeley, CA: Parallax Press.

RECORDINGS

Goleman, D. 1989. *The Art of Meditation* (Audio CD). New York: Holzbrink.

Kabat-Zinn, J. 2005. *Guided Mindfulness Meditation* (Audio CD). Louisville, CO: Sounds True.

———. 2005. *Mindfulness for Beginners* (Audio CD). Louisville, CO: Sounds True.

Thich Nhat Hanh. 2005. *Touching Peace* (Audio CD). Berkeley, CA: Parallax Press.

6

Visualization

In this chapter you will learn to:

✳ Use your imagination to relax

✳ Manage stress-related conditions

✳ Create a safe and relaxing place in your mind

BACKGROUND

You can significantly reduce stress with an enormously powerful force: your imagination. The practice of positive thinking for the treatment of physical symptoms was popularized by Emil Coué, a French pharmacist, around the turn of the nineteenth century. He believed that the power of the imagination far exceeds that of the will. It's hard to will yourself into a relaxed state, but you can imagine relaxation spreading through your body, and you can visualize yourself in a safe and beautiful refuge. Coué asserted that all of your thoughts become reality—you are what you think you are. For example, if you think sad thoughts, you feel unhappy. If you think anxious thoughts, you become tense.

In order to overcome the feeling of unhappiness or tension, you can refocus your mind on positive, healing images. When you predict that you are going to be lonely and miserable, your prediction will probably come true, because your negative thoughts will be reflected in your asocial behavior. A woman who predicts that she will get a stomachache when her boss yells at her is likely to have her thoughts take a somatic form. Coué found that organic diseases such as fibrous tumors, tuberculosis, hemorrhages, and constipation are often worsened when you focus on them. His patients were recommended to say aloud, upon awakening, at least twenty times a day, the now-famous phrase "Every day in every way I am getting better and better."

Coué also encouraged his patients to get into a comfortable, relaxed position when retiring, and then to close their eyes and practice general relaxation of all their muscles. As they started to doze off in the "stage of semi-consciousness," he suggested that they introduce into their minds any desired idea, for example, "I am going to be relaxed tomorrow." Coué understood that this is a way of bridging your conscious and unconscious minds and allowing your unconscious to make a wish come true.

In the twentieth century, Carl Jung used a technique for healing that he referred to as "active imagination." He instructed his patients to meditate without any goal or program in mind. Images would come to consciousness that the patient was to observe and experience without interference. Later, if desired, the patient could actually communicate with the images by asking them questions or talking to them. Jung used active imagination to help the individual appreciate his or her rich inner life and learn to draw on its healing power in times of stress. Jungian and Gestalt therapists have since devised several stress reduction techniques using the intuitive, imaginative part of the mind.

Today, visualization is practiced and studied in cancer and pain centers throughout the country. Stephanie Matthews and O. Carl Simonton, who pioneered the use of visualization with cancer patients, wrote *Getting Well Again* in 1980. Two other visualization scientists, therapists, and writers are Jeanne Achterberg, who wrote *Imagery in Healing* in 1985, and Connecticut surgeon and Yale professor Bernie S. Siegel, who wrote *Love, Medicine, and Miracles* in 1986.

Shakti Gawain, author of *Creative Visualization* (2003) and *Living in the Light* (1998), states that visualization is a form of energy that creates life and life's happenings. Everything is energy and our mind creates our world, much as a movie projector projects a world upon a blank screen.

SYMPTOM-RELIEF EFFECTIVENESS

Visualization is effective in treating many stress-related and physical illnesses, including headaches, muscle spasms, chronic pain, and general or situation-specific anxiety. Visualization is used to prepare patients for surgery, to boost the effects of chemotherapy, to increase focus in sports competition, and to enhance well-being.

TIME TO MASTER

Symptom relief can be immediate or may take several weeks of practice.

INSTRUCTIONS

Types of Visualization

Everybody visualizes. Daydreams, memories, and inner talk are all types of visualization. You can harness your visualizations and consciously employ them to better yourself and your life.

Visualizations are mental sense impressions you create consciously to relax your body and relieve stress. There are three types of visualization for change:

1. **Receptive visualization.** With this type, you relax, empty your mind, sketch an image of a scene, ask a question, and wait for a response. For example, you might imagine you are on a beach and the sea breeze is caressing your skin. You can hear and smell the sea. Then you might ask "Why can't I relax?" And the response might surface into your consciousness; for example, "Because you can't say no to people," or "Because you can't detach yourself from your husband's depression."

2. **Programmed visualization.** Create an image, replete with sights, taste, sounds, and smells. Then, imagine a goal that you want to attain or a healing that you want to accelerate. For instance, Harriet used programmed visualization when she started running. For her first race, she visualized her race on that course daily. She would feel the pressure of running up a hill, the exhaustion after several miles, and the sprint to the finish line. When she finally ran that race, she set a state record for her age group that still holds.

3. **Guided visualization.** Again, visualize your scene in detail, but omit crucial elements. Then wait for your subconscious, or your inner guide, to supply the missing pieces in your puzzle. Jane imagines visiting a special place where she likes to relax. She constructs the smells, tastes, sounds, touch, and sights associated with the place, a forest clearing that she used to visit with the Girl Scouts. She sees herself roasting marshmallows over a campfire at twilight. (There are no mosquitoes.) She imagines her Girl Scout leader, someone she loves, and asks the leader how she can relax. Sometimes the Scout leader reminds her of songs she used to love and she tells Jane to sing them whenever she feels tense. Sometimes she reminds Jane of old jokes and old times that made Jane laugh, and she tells Jane that she needs to laugh more. Often the leader gives Jane a hug, to remind her that she is loved and that she needs to search for affirmations of that love.

Rules for Effective Visualization

1. Loosen your clothing, lie down in a quiet place, and softly close your eyes.

2. Scan your body, seeking tension in specific muscles. Relax those muscles as much as you can.

3. Form mental sense impressions. Involve all your senses: sight, hearing, smell, touch, and taste. For instance, imagine you are in the midst of a green forest with beautiful trees, vivid blue sky, and fluffy white clouds. Then add the sounds: wind in the trees, water running, birdcalls, and so on. Imagine you can hear pine needles crunching underfoot.

Include the feel of the ground under your shoes, the smell of pine, and the taste of a grass stem or mountain spring water.

4. Use affirmations. Repeat short, positive statements that affirm your ability to relax now. Use the present tense and avoid negatives, such as "I am not tense," in favor of positive versions, such as "I am letting go of tension." Here are some other examples of affirmations:

   Tension flows from my body.

   I can relax at will.

   I am in harmony with life.

   Peace is within me.

5. Practice creating your visualization three times a day. Visualization practice is easiest when done in the morning and at night while you lie in bed. After some practice, you will be able to visualize while waiting in the doctor's office, at the service station, before going into a parent-teacher conference—even during an IRS audit.

BASIC TENSION AND RELAXATION EXERCISES

1. Eye Relaxation (Palming)

Place your palms directly over your closed eyes. Block out all light without putting too much pressure on your eyelids. Try to see the color black. You may see other colors or images, but focus on the color black. Use a mental image to remember the color black (black fur, black object in the room).

Continue this way for two to three minutes, thinking and focusing on black. Lower your hands and slowly open your eyes, gradually getting accustomed to the light. Experience the sense of relaxation in the muscles that control the opening and closing of your eyes.

2. Metaphorical Images

Lie down, close your eyes, and relax. Visualize an image for tension and then replace it with an image for relaxation. The best images are those you make up yourself. But to get you started, images for tension might include the following:

- The color red
- The screech of chalk on a blackboard
- The tension of a cable

- The scream of a siren in the night

- The glare of a searchlight

- The smell of ammonia

- The confinement of a dark tunnel

- The pounding of a jackhammer

These tension images during visualization can soften, expand, and fade, creating relaxation and harmony:

- The color red can fade to pale blue.

- The chalk can crumble into powder.

- The cable can slacken.

- The siren might soften to a whisper of a flute.

- The searchlight might fade into a soft rosy glow.

- The smell of ammonia might soften into the smell of lemon or a rose.

- The dark tunnel might open into a light, airy beach.

- The jackhammer can become the hands of a masseuse kneading your muscles.

As you scan your body, apply a tension image to a tense muscle. Allow it to develop into your relaxation image. For example, if your neck is tense, you may visualize a tightened vise. Imagine the vise opening as you say an affirmation such as "Relax" or "I can relax at will."

End by reciting your affirmation. Speak to the specific tenseness as you apply your relaxation image. Observe what happens to your tension.

3. Creating Your Special Place

In creating your special place you will be making a refuge for relaxation and guidance. This place can be indoors or out. When structuring your place, follow these few guidelines:

- Allow a private entry into your place.

- Make it peaceful, comfortable, and safe.

- Fill your place with sensuous detail. Create a middle ground, foreground, and background.

- Allow room for an inner guide or other person to be there with you comfortably.

A special place might be at the end of a path that leads to a pond. Grass grows under your feet, the pond is about thirty yards away, and mountains are in the distance. You can feel the coolness of the air in this shady spot. The mockingbird is singing. The sun is bright on the pond. The honeysuckle's pungent odor attracts the bee buzzing over the flowers with their sweet nectar.

Or your special place might be a sparkling clean kitchen, with cinnamon buns baking in the oven. Through the kitchen window you can see fields of yellow wheat. A window chime flutters in the breeze. At the table there's a cup of tea for your guest.

Try recording this exercise and playing it, or have a friend read it aloud to you slowly:

To go to your safe place, lie down and be totally comfortable. Close your eyes. . . . Walk slowly to a quiet place in your mind. . . . Your place can be inside or outside. . . . It needs to be peaceful and safe. . . . Picture yourself unloading your anxieties, your worries. . . . Notice the view in the distance. . . . What do you smell? . . . What do you hear? . . . Notice what is before you. . . . Reach out and touch it. . . . How does it feel? . . . Smell it. . . . Hear it. . . . Make the temperature comfortable. . . . Be safe here. . . . Look around for a special spot, a private spot. . . . Find the path to this place. . . . Feel the ground with your feet. . . . Look above you. . . . What do you see? . . . Hear? . . . Smell? . . . Walk down this path until you can enter your own quiet, comfortable, safe place.

You have arrived at your special place. . . . What is under your feet? . . . How does it feel? . . . Take several steps. . . . What do you see above you? What do you hear? Do you hear something else? Reach and touch something. . . . What is its texture? Are there pens, paper, paints nearby, or is there sand to draw in, clay to work? Go to them, handle them, smell them. These are your special tools, or tools for your inner guide to reveal ideas or feelings to you. . . . Look as far as you can see. . . . What do you see? What do you hear? What aromas do you notice?

Sit or lie in your special place. . . . Notice its smells, sounds, sights. . . . This is your place and nothing can harm you here. . . . If danger is here, expel it. . . . Spend three to five minutes realizing you are relaxed, safe, and comfortable.

Memorize this place's smells, tastes, sights, sounds. . . . You can come back and relax here whenever you want. . . . Leave by the same path or entrance. . . . Notice the ground, touch things near you. . . . Look far away and appreciate the view. . . . Remind yourself that this special place you created can be entered whenever you wish. Say an affirmation such as "I can relax here" or "This is my special place. I can come here whenever I wish."

Now open your eyes and spend a few seconds appreciating your relaxation.

4. Finding Your Inner Guide

Your inner guide is an imaginary person or animal that clarifies and instructs. This being is your link to your own inner wisdom and to your subconscious. Your inner guide can tell you how to relax and can clarify what is causing your stress. With practice, you can meet your inner guide in your special place whenever you want.

Perhaps you already have an inner guide, a deceased parent or another spiritual presence. If so, invite this person into your special place and ask him or her to show you how to relax.

Try this exercise after reading it all the way through first, or record it, or have a friend read it aloud to you.

Relax and follow the path to your special place, as you have been doing. Invite an inner guide to your place. Wait. Watch your guide's path. Notice a speck in the distance. Wait. Watch your guide's approach. Listen to the footfalls. Can you smell the guide's fragrance? As your guide gains shape and clarity, if you feel unsafe, send it away. Wait for other guides until you find one you like, even though its appearance may surprise you or seem odd.

When your guide is comfortable, ask him or her questions. Wait for the answers. An answer may be a laugh, a saying, a feeling, a dream, a frown, or a purr. Ask your guide, "How can I relax? What is causing my tension?" When your guide answers, you will probably be surprised at the simplicity and clarity of its answers.

Before your guide leaves you, or immediately after, say your affirmation to yourself. Affirm your ability to relax with a simple "I can relax here" or "I can relax at will."

Do this exercise several times a day for at least seven days. By the seventh day, you will probably have found a guide and some answers.

One student who lost his mother, his house, and whose father is unable to care for him uses his mother as his inner guide. He goes to her to relax, to seek guidance when pressure from his life and his peers feels overwhelming. She doesn't say much, but her presence and her look of approval or disapproval is often enough to calm him.

Another person's guide can create relaxation simply because of the emptying of the mind that occurs in her presence. Words are rarely spoken, but her guide's actions and silence guide her.

Each person's inner guide is different and instructs in a unique manner.

5. Listening to Music

Listening to music is one of the most common forms of relaxation. However, each person gives his or her own meaning to music. It's important, therefore, that when you want to listen to music for the purpose of relaxation, you select music you find peaceful and soothing. If possible, make or buy a half-hour recording of uninterrupted relaxing music that you can play daily or whenever you decide to use music to relax. Note that the repetition of the same music that helped you relax in the past carries a positive association that is likely to be beneficial in the future.

To get the most out of your music session, find a half hour of uninterrupted time to be alone. Put on the music you have chosen, settle back in a comfortable position, and close your eyes. Mentally scan your body, noting areas of tension, pain, and relaxation. Be aware of your mood as you focus your attention on the music. Each time an unrelated thought enters your head, note it and then discard it, remembering your goal of focusing on the music and relaxing. Say an affirmation, such as "Relax" or "Music relaxes me." When the music ends, allow your mind to scan your body again and become aware of how it feels. Does your body feel different than before you started listening to music? Is there any difference in your mood?

SPECIAL CONSIDERATIONS

1. If you have trouble receiving impressions from all of your senses, work on your strongest sense first. The others will improve in time.

2. Practice often—three times a day. And be patient; it takes time.

3. If making your own recording doesn't work, you might want to buy one. There are some listed at the end of this chapter.

4. Remember to laugh. Laughter reduces emotional and physical tension by producing an internal massage. Laughing stimulates your circulatory, respiratory, vascular, and nervous systems. When the internal spasms of laughter subside, the release of pressure reduces muscle tension and creates a feeling of well-being. In his book *Anatomy of an Illness* (2005), Norman Cousins describes how he used laughter to overcome a rare and painful illness. Laughter takes your attention off yourself and your situation. It provides you with the distance necessary to gain perspective on a situation that you may be taking too seriously.

Visualization can help you to relax and can assist you in bringing focus and clarity to your life. When practiced on a regular basis, it will increase your sense of well-being.

FURTHER READING

Achterberg, J., B. Dossey, and L. Kolkmeier. 1994. *Rituals of Healing: Using Imagery for Health and Wellness*. New York: Bantam Books.

Cousins, N. 1990. *Head First: The Biology of Hope and the Healing Power of the Human Spirit*. New York: Penguin Books.

————. 2005. *Anatomy of an Illness.* New York: W. W. Norton & Company.

Epstein, G. 1989. *Healing Visualization: Creating Health Through Imagery.* New York: Bantam Books.

Gawain, S. 2002. *Creative Visualization: Use the Power of Your Imagination to Create What You Want in Life.* New York: New World Library.

————. 2003. *Creative Visualization.* London: Full Circle Publishing.

Klein, A. 1989. *The Healing Power of Humor.* Los Angeles: J. P. Tarcher.

————. 1998. *The Courage to Laugh.* Los Angeles: J. P. Tarcher.

Ornstein, R. 1996. *The Psychology of Consciousness.* San Francisco: W. H. Freeman.

Russman, M. 2000. *Healing Yourself.* New York: H J Kramer.

Siegel, B. 1990. *Love, Medicine, and Miracles.* New York: Harper & Row.

Simonton, O. C., S. Matthews-Simonton, and J. L. Creighton. 1992. *Getting Well Again.* New York: Bantam Books.

Wells, V. 1990. *The Joy of Visualization: 75 Creative Ways to Enhance Your Life.* Vancouver: Raincoast Books.

RECORDINGS

Gawain, S. 2002. *Creative Visualization Meditations* (Audio CD). New York: New World Library Audio.

Visualization for Stress Reduction. 1992. Oakland, CA: New Harbinger Publications.

Visualization for Healing Injuries. 1992. Oakland, CA: New Harbinger Publications.

New Harbinger Publications
5674 Shattuck Ave.
Oakland, CA 94609
www.newharbinger.com
(800) 748-6273

Recordings of Emmett Miller, MD
www.drmiller.com/index_main.html
(800) 528-2737

7

Applied Relaxation Training

In this chapter you will learn to:

❋ Relax quickly in stressful situations

BACKGROUND

Applied relaxation training brings together a number of proven relaxation techniques, including some already covered in this book. The combined effect is both rapid and powerful, helping you reverse the effects of high stress in less than a minute. Because the program is progressive, you will be adding new features to the exercise over the course of several weeks, while taking away other features once they have become habitual. Eventually, you will be able to achieve deep relaxation in twenty to thirty seconds, quickly calming both your body and your mind when you encounter a stressful situation.

The Swedish physician L.-G. Öst developed applied relaxation in the late 1980s. Öst worked with phobic patients who needed rapid and reliable methods to cut through the anxiety that struck when they encountered phobic situations. Finding that the technique could achieve high rates of success even with severely phobic patients, Öst realized that applied relaxation could be helpful in a variety of life situations, from daily quarrels and frustrations to difficulty falling asleep at night.

In general, the program first teaches you to relax by using a physical relaxation process. You then progress to a conditioned relaxation response and, finally, you learn to relax on command. You will also progress from practicing in a relaxed exercise setting to using the technique in real-life situations.

SYMPTOM-RELIEF EFFECTIVENESS

Although applied relaxation was first developed to treat patients with phobias, it has a wide range of applications in other areas, including panic disorder, generalized anxiety disorder, headaches (tension, migraine, and mixed), back and joint pain, epilepsy in both children and adults, and tinnitus. In clinical practice, applied relaxation training has also proven useful for sleep-onset insomnia, for cardiac neurosis (being needlessly preoccupied with the possibility of heart attack and typically requiring repeated reassurances from one's doctor), and for cancer patients with chemotherapy-induced nausea (Öst 1987). Öst found that almost everyone can learn applied relaxation and that 90 to 95 percent of the patients in his studies experienced benefits from the training.

TIME TO MASTER

You will notice some relaxation after just one or two sessions of applied relaxation training. Remember that this is a progressive program. Each new stage will help you relax more quickly and more deeply, until you can relax at will in less than a minute. Don't rush yourself. You'll want to master each step of the program before you move on to the next step. Allow yourself one to two weeks, with two practice sessions a day, to feel comfortable with each step. If this sounds like a lot of time, keep in mind that your practice sessions can become the most refreshing part of your day.

Clinical applications of applied relaxation have ranged from an unusually quick two-week course for inpatients suffering from tinnitus to a fourteen-week program for inpatients with panic disorders (Öst 1987). A middle range is more usual; generally, you can expect to spend from five to eight weeks progressing through the program.

INSTRUCTIONS

Applied relaxation training involves learning five separate stages. Each stage builds on the one before it, so be sure to follow all five stages in their listed order.

1. Progressive Muscle Relaxation

Progressive muscle relaxation will help you recognize the difference between tension and relaxation in each of your major muscle groups. Surprising as it may sound, these distinctions are easy to overlook. Once you can really feel the difference between a tense muscle and a deeply relaxed one, you will be able to identify your chronic trouble spots and consciously rid them of their locked-in tension. You will also be able to bring your muscles to a deeper state of relaxation after you relax them than you could have if you hadn't tensed them first. Follow the instructions described under Basic Procedure in chapter 4. Give yourself one to two weeks to master the technique, with two fifteen-minute practice sessions per day. Your goal should be to relax your entire body in one fifteen-to-twenty-minute session.

2. Release-Only Relaxation

Now that you've felt the difference between tensing and relaxing each muscle group, you're ready to move on to the next stage of applied relaxation training. As you might guess from its name, release-only relaxation cuts out the first step in progressive muscle relaxation: the tensing step. This means that you can cut the time down by half (or more) that you need to achieve deep relaxation in each muscle group.

With practice, you'll find that mental focus alone is enough to drain your muscles of their tension, with no need for you to tense them first. Developing this skill depends on your ability to recognize the difference between clenched muscles and deeply relaxed ones. Be sure that you're comfortable with progressive muscle relaxation before you begin the following release-only instructions.

A. Sit in a comfortable chair with your arms at your sides and move around a bit until you're comfortable.

B. Begin to focus on your breathing. Breathe in deeply and feel the pure air fill your stomach, your lower chest, and your upper chest. Hold your breath for a moment as you sit up straighter ... and then breathe out slowly through your mouth, feeling all your tension and worries blow out in a stream of air. After you've exhaled completely, relax your stomach and your chest. Continue to take full, calm, even breaths, noticing that you become more relaxed with each exhalation.

C. Now relax your forehead, smoothing out all the lines. Keep breathing deeply . . . and now relax your eyebrows. Just let all the tension melt away, all the way down to your jaw. Let it all go. Now let your lips separate and relax your tongue. Breathe in and breathe out and relax your throat. Notice how peaceful and loose your entire face feels now.

D. Roll your head gently and feel your neck relax. Release your shoulders. Just let them drop all the way down. Your neck is loose, and your shoulders are heavy and low. Now let the relaxation travel down through your arms to your fingertips. Your arms are heavy and loose. Your lips are still separated because your jaw is relaxed too.

E. Breathe in deeply and feel your stomach expand and then your chest. Hold your breath for a moment and then breathe out slowly in a smooth stream through your mouth.

F. Let the feeling of relaxation spread to your stomach. Feel all the muscles in your abdomen release their tension as it assumes its natural shape. Relax your waist and relax your back. Continue to breathe deeply. Notice how loose and heavy the upper half of your body feels.

G. Now relax the lower half of your body. Feel your buttocks sink into the chair. Relax your thighs. Relax your knees. Feel the relaxation travel through your calves to your ankles, to the bottoms of your feet, all the way down to the tips of your toes. Your feet feel warm and heavy on the floor in front of you. With each breath, feel the relaxation deepen.

H. Now scan your body for tension as you continue to breathe. Your legs are relaxed. Your back is relaxed. Your shoulders and arms are relaxed. Your face is relaxed. There's only a feeling of peace and warmth and relaxation.

I. If any muscle felt hard to relax, turn your attention to it now. Is it your back? Your shoulders? Your thighs? Your jaw? Tune in to the muscle and now tense it. Hold it tighter and release. Feel it join the rest of your body in a deep, deep relaxation.

The directions for release-only relaxation may seem simpler than those for progressive muscle relaxation, but the tasks involved are actually a bit more complex. Be certain that you drain all of the tension out of each muscle you focus on. Don't let the tension creep back in as you turn your attention to different muscles. When you stand up after a session of release-only relaxation, you should feel at least as relaxed as you did after a session of progressive muscle relaxation.

Of course, you don't want to stress yourself by forcing and pushing yourself through a set of strict directions. Allow your body to relax, rather than forcing it. If you have trouble with a particular step, take a deep breath and try it again—or skip it. Let negative, critical thoughts blow away with each breath and hold onto the feeling of success and deepening peace.

Allow yourself one to two weeks with two practice sessions a day to master release-only relaxation. When you can relax your entire body in one five-to-seven-minute session, you're ready to move on to step 3.

3. Cue-Controlled Relaxation

Cue-controlled relaxation reduces the time you need to relax even further—down to two or three minutes in most cases. In this stage, you will focus on your breathing and condition yourself to relax exactly when you tell yourself to relax. The instructions will help you build an association between a cue—for example, the command "relax"—and true muscle relaxation. Be sure that you are comfortable with release-only relaxation before you begin to work with cue-controlled relaxation.

A. Make yourself comfortable in your chair, with your arms on your lap and your feet flat on the ground. Take a deep breath and hold it for a moment. Concentrate on blowing the worries of the day far, far away as you release the air from your mouth in a smooth stream. Empty your lungs as you feel your stomach and your chest relax.

B. Now begin to relax yourself, from your forehead all the way down to your toes, using the release-only technique. See if you can relax yourself completely in thirty seconds. If you need more time, that's fine.

C. You feel peaceful and at ease now. Your stomach and chest are moving in and out with slow, even breaths. With each breath, the feeling of relaxation deepens.

D. Continue to breathe deeply and regularly, saying "breathe in" to yourself as you inhale and "relax" as you exhale.

Breathe in … relax …

Breathe in … relax …

Breathe in … relax …

Breathe in … relax …

Breathe in … relax …

Feel each breath bring peace and calm in and float worry and tension out.

E. Continue to breathe this way for several minutes now, saying these words to yourself— "breathe in" and "relax"—while you breathe. Focus all your attention on the words in your head and on the process of breathing. Feel your muscles relax more and more deeply with each breath. Let the word "relax" crowd every other thought from your mind. Close your eyes if you can, to deepen your focus.

F. Now listen to the words again as you continue to breathe in … and relax.

Breathe in … relax …

Breathe in … relax …

Breathe in … relax …

Breathe in … relax …

Breathe in … relax …

G. Continue to breathe, saying these words in your head, for a few more minutes. Now, feel each breath bring peace and calm in and float worry and tension out.

H. If you have time, repeat the entire process of cue-controlled relaxation after a recovery period of between ten and fifteen minutes.

Practice cue-controlled relaxation twice a day, as you did with the earlier practices.

After each session, you may want to make a note of the amount of time you needed to relax and how deeply relaxed you became. Most people find that the actual time required to relax at this stage is shorter than they imagine. Aim to relax completely using cue-controlled relaxation within two to three minutes before moving on to rapid relaxation.

4. Rapid Relaxation

Rapid relaxation can bring the time you need to relax down to thirty seconds. Being able to relax that quickly can mean real relief during stressful situations. It's a good idea to practice rapid relaxation many times a day as you move through different activities and states of mind.

In rapid relaxation, you will pick a special relaxation cue. Choose something that you see regularly throughout the day, such as your watch or a certain clock or the picture you pass as you walk down the hall to the bathroom. If you can, mark that special cue with a piece of colored tape while you're practicing this technique.

When you're ready to begin, look at your special cue. Breathe in and relax. Breathe in and relax. Continue to look at your cue and think "relax." Breathe in and relax. You are breathing deeply and evenly, and you continue to think "relax" each time you exhale. Let the relaxation spread throughout your body. Scan your body for tension and relax as much as possible in every muscle that isn't needed for whatever activity you are currently doing.

Every time you look at your cue throughout the day, go through these three simple steps:

A. Take two or three deep, even breaths, exhaling slowly through your mouth.

B. Think "relax" each time you exhale, as you continue to breathe deeply.

C. Scan your body for any tension. Focus on those muscles that need to relax and empty them of tension.

Try to use your relaxation cue fifteen times a day to relax quickly in natural, nonstressful situations. This will instill the habit of checking yourself for tension and moving back to a state of deep relaxation throughout the day. After your first few days of practice, you may want to change the color of the tape on your relaxation cue—or even change the cue altogether. This will keep the idea of relaxation fresh in your mind. Finally, see if you can use rapid relaxation to calm yourself during one or two particularly stressful moments of the day. (The next stage, applied relaxation, will help you refine this ability but it's a good idea to open yourself up early to the idea of relaxation during a crisis.)

When you feel comfortable with rapid relaxation and are able to achieve a state of deep relaxation in twenty to thirty seconds many times during the day, you are ready to move on to the final stage of applied relaxation training.

5. Applied Relaxation

The final stage of applied relaxation training involves relaxing quickly in the face of anxiety-provoking situations. You will use the same techniques that you practiced in rapid relaxation, beginning your deep breathing the moment you notice a stress reaction setting in.

If you're unsure of your body's particular stress warning signs—such as rapid breathing, sweating, or an increased heart rate—turn to the exercises for body awareness in chapter 2. The earlier you can identify the physiological signs that accompany stress, the more effectively you can cut in on a stress reaction before it builds.

As soon as you note a sign of stress—if you catch your breath, feel your heart leap, or feel a flush of heat—begin your three steps:

A. Take two to three deep, even breaths.

B. Think these calming words to yourself as you continue to breathe deeply:

Breathe in … relax …
Breathe in … relax …
Breathe in … relax …

If you prefer, you need only hear yourself think "relax" each time you exhale.

C. Scan your body for tension and concentrate on relaxing the muscles that you don't need to continue your activity. For example, if you are sitting at a computer, you can consciously relax the lower part of your body, your abdomen, and much of your head. The muscles in your eyes, back, neck, shoulders, chest, arms, and hands may need to remain somewhat tense in order for you to look at the monitor and type on the keyboard.

To begin coming close to the feeling of your stress reaction, start by practicing these instructions after you have run up a flight of stairs or completed some jumping jacks. When you feel confident, visualize a stressful situation such as a fight with your spouse or an unpleasant encounter with your boss. (Chapter 6 provides ideas and exercises to help you build your visualization skills.) Practice using these three steps when you encounter a stressful situation in real life. Take a brief moment to collect yourself and remember the three steps and then put them into effect immediately. No one but you needs to know what you're doing, and you and those around you will all benefit from the calmness with which you approach the crisis at hand.

Be patient with yourself. Applied relaxation is a skill, and as with any other skills you will refine your ability with practice. Note that the chances are good that you won't feel complete relief the first time you try to cut through a deeply stressful situation with applied relaxation. Observe the improvements that you do make. Most people are able to stop anxiety from increasing with relatively little practice. From that point, it's just a few short steps to actually decreasing the anxiety and replacing panic with a feeling of calmness and control.

SPECIAL CONSIDERATIONS

If you have progressed methodically from one step of applied relaxation to the next, by now, you should have the control you need to bring your body to a state of deep and full relaxation.

As with any other skill, you'll want to practice applied relaxation regularly to keep yourself in top form. Make it a habit to scan your body for tension at least once a day. Focus on ridding your body of that tension using the rapid-relaxation technique. Whatever activity you may be engaged in, you can bring yourself to a calm and deep relaxation.

If there are times when your anxiety doesn't seem to respond or you worry that you've forgotten the skill you once had, remember that setbacks do happen. No treatment can guarantee permanent freedom from anxiety attacks or stress. View setbacks as an opportunity to practice applied relaxation. At other times, enjoy the feeling of deep relaxation that you have achieved. Remind yourself that you can bring yourself there whenever you need to.

You may find it useful to make an audio recording to guide yourself through the exercises described in this chapter. A recording will help you focus on relaxing your body and free you to close your eyes. To make a recording, use the instructions for each step as your script. Speak in a slow, even voice and be sure not to rush through the process.

Another way to learn applied relaxation is to practice it following the instructions on the audiotape *Applied Relaxation Training*. (See Recording below.)

FURTHER READING

Öst, L.-G. 1987. Applied relaxation: Description of a coping technique and review of controlled studies. *Behavior Research Therapy* 25:397–409.

———. 1988. Applied relaxation vs. progressive relaxation in the treatment of panic disorder. *Behavior Research Therapy* 26:13–22.

RECORDING

Fanning, P., M. McKay, and N. Sonenberg. 1991. *Applied Relaxation Training* (Audiotape). Oakland, CA: New Harbinger Publications.

8

Self-Hypnosis

In this chapter you will learn to:

* Use self-suggestions for deep relaxation and positive change

* Fight stress and stress-related illnesses

* Alleviate specific problems such as insomnia

BACKGROUND

Hypnosis is a term derived from the Greek word for sleep. In some ways, hypnosis is similar to sleep: there is a narrowing of consciousness accompanied by inertia and passivity. Hypnosis is very relaxing. But unlike sleep you never completely lose awareness during hypnosis. While hypnotized, you are able to respond to things going on around you. Although hypnosis is usually done with eyes closed to facilitate concentration and imagination, it also can be done with the eyes open.

Hypnosis allows you to experience your thoughts and images as real. While you are hypnotized you willingly suspend disbelief for the moment, just as you do when you become absorbed in a compelling fantasy or play. For instance, when you watch a violent chase scene in a movie, your mind and body respond in many ways as though you were actually participating in the chase: your muscles tense, your stomach churns, your heart rate increases, and you feel excited or scared. The brain-wave patterns traced on an electroencephalogram (EEG) during hypnosis resemble the patterns that typically occur during the actual activities that the hypnotized person is imagining (participating in a chase, relaxing at the beach, playing a musical instrument, and so on).

You may think that you have never been hypnotized but, in fact, you are no stranger to hypnosis. Often, when you concentrate on something of great interest to you, you enter hypnosis without any formal induction. Daydreaming, for example, is a hypnotic state. Long-distance driving is highly conducive to hypnosis (and commonly results in amnesia for various parts of the trip). You may have entered a form of light hypnosis many times while trying to remember a shopping list, a past sequence of events, or while watching TV and feeling a strong emotion such as fear.

In this chapter you will learn to use self-hypnosis to experience positive thoughts and images of your own choosing for the purpose of relaxing and reducing stress. You can learn self-hypnosis quickly and safely. There are no reported cases of harm resulting from self-hypnosis. Because hypnosis is your experience of your own thoughts and images, it can take place only when your participation is active and voluntary. (This is true even when you are undergoing hypnotic induction by someone else.) You can extend, modify, or shorten any of the hypnosis exercises in this chapter to meet your specific needs.

SYMPTOM-RELIEF EFFECTIVENESS

Self-hypnosis has been clinically effective with symptoms of insomnia, minor chronic pain, headache, nervous tics and tremors, chronic muscular tension, and minor anxiety. It is a well-established treatment for chronic fatigue. You may also consider using self-hypnosis for any subjective experience that could be improved with positive words and images (for example, the rapid heartbeat, cold sweaty palms, and knotted stomach associated with anticipatory anxiety).

CONTRAINDICATIONS

Poor candidates for hypnosis include people who are disoriented due to organic brain syndrome or psychosis, people who are severely mentally retarded, and people who are paranoid or hypervigilant.

TIME TO MASTER

Significant relaxation effects can be achieved within two days. To become proficient in the skill of self-hypnosis, practice the basic hypnotic induction once a day for a week. Then adapt the basic induction to your personal goals by adding specific hypnotic suggestions. Plan on practicing this modified induction until you no longer need to practice because you will have mastered the skill.

INSTRUCTIONS

The Power of Suggestion

The first step in self-hypnosis is to appreciate the power of suggestion. Here are two simple exercises that can demonstrate the power of suggestion:

POSTURAL SWAY

1. Stand up with your eyes closed and imagine holding a suitcase in your right hand.

2. Imagine bigger and bigger suitcases weighing down your right side, pulling you over.

3. After two or three minutes, open your eyes and notice any changes in your posture.

4. Close your eyes again and imagine that the north wind is blowing you, pushing you back on your heels. Feel the gusts. Notice if your weight is shifting in response to your imagination.

POSTURAL SUGGESTION

1. Stretch both of your arms in front of you at shoulder level. With eyes closed, imagine a weight being tied onto your right arm as it strains to stay up.

2. Imagine a second weight, and then a third. Feel the strain in your arm as it gets heavier and heavier, heavier and heavier.

3. Now imagine that a huge balloon filled with helium has been tied to your left arm and is tugging it up into the air … higher and higher … higher and higher.

4. Open your eyes and notice where your arms are relative to each other.

Most people who try these two exercises notice that their bodies move at least a little in response to these self-suggestions. If you don't notice any movement, practice the exercises a few more times. If you still don't notice even the slightest amount of movement, hypnosis may not be for you.

Personalized Self-Induction

The second step in self-hypnosis is to learn how to write a self-induction script. The following suggestions will provide you with a basic outline for self-induction that you can adapt and change to suit your particular style and purposes.

Position. If possible, sit in a reclining chair or comfortable high-backed chair with support for your arms, hands, neck, and head. Choose a comfortable position with your feet flat on the floor and your legs and arms uncrossed. Loosen your clothing. You may prefer to remove contact lenses or glasses.

Time. Set aside at least thirty minutes to do this exercise without being interrupted.

Key word or phrase. Choose something that is the opposite of your problem and hence the essence of the goal for which you are using hypnosis. For instance, if your problem is anxiety prior to giving a public presentation, your goal and key phrase might be "Calm and clear" or "Relax now." You can repeat this statement slowly at the moment your eyes close and when you are imagining that you are in your special place (see below), so that the key word becomes associated with deep relaxation. A meaningful key phrase may occur to you spontaneously when you experience being in your special place during hypnosis. With enough practice, this key word or phrase will be sufficient to induce hypnosis quickly.

Breathing. After closing your eyes, take several deep breaths. Breathe deeply all the way down into your abdomen and feel the spreading sense of relaxation as you exhale.

Muscle relaxation. You will be relaxing your legs, arms, face, neck, shoulders, chest, and abdomen in that order. As you relax your legs and arms, the key phrase is "heavier and heavier, more and more deeply relaxed." As you relax your forehead and cheeks, the key phrase is "smooth and relaxed, letting go of tension." As you relax your jaw, the key phrase is "loose and relaxed." Your neck, too, becomes "loose and relaxed." Your shoulders are "relaxed and drooping." You relax your chest, abdomen, and back by first taking a deep breath. As you exhale, use the key phrase "calm and relaxed."

Staircase or path to a special place. You will count each step going down to that peaceful place, and with each step you will become more and more relaxed. Count backward slowly from ten to zero. Each number you count is a step going down. Imagine that saying each number and taking each step helps you to feel more deeply relaxed. You can count backward from ten to zero once, twice, or even three times. Each complete count will deepen your relaxation.

Your special place. Your special place can be any place you feel secure and at peace; for instance, a meadow or beach or your bedroom. When you arrive at your special place, you'll look around and notice the shapes and colors. You'll listen to the sounds, and smell the fragrances of your special place. You will also notice the temperature and how your body feels there.

Practice imagining being in your special place before attempting your first self-induction. Make sure that the image is detailed and evocative. If you are at the beach, make sure you can hear the waves crashing and hear the hiss of foam as the waves recede. See and hear the seagulls overhead. Notice the salty sea breeze, the warmth of the sun on your body, and the feel of the sand beneath you. Try to involve all your senses in building the scene: sight, sound, taste, smell, and touch.

Deepening hypnosis. Use the following four key suggestions over and over, in various combinations, until you feel a deep sense of calm and letting go.

1. *Drifting deeper and deeper, deeper and deeper*

2. *Feeling more and more drowsy, peaceful, and calm*

3. *Drifting and drowsy, drowsy and drifting*

4. *Drifting down, down, down into total relaxation*

Posthypnotic suggestion. Once you've spent time relaxing in your special place, you may wish to give yourself posthypnotic suggestions. Read the sections Hypnotic Suggestions and Practice Writing Hypnotic Suggestions, later in this chapter, for rules and techniques that will help you craft your posthypnotic suggestions.

Coming out of hypnosis. When it's time to end your trance, you can count back up from one to ten. In between numbers, tell yourself that you are becoming "more and more alert, refreshed, and wide awake." As you reach number nine, tell yourself that your eyes are opening. As you say the number ten, tell yourself that you are totally alert and wide awake.

Here is a summary of the key rules for a successful self-induction:

1. Allow at least twenty minutes to enter and deepen the hypnotic state.

2. Don't worry about success or how you are doing. Hypnosis will become easier with practice.

3. Always allow time to relax your muscles and take deep breaths.

4. Use compelling instructions ("I am feeling more and more heaviness in my arms").

5. Use adjectives such as "drowsy," "peaceful," "comfortable" during self-induction.

6. Repeat everything until the suggestion begins to take hold.

7. Use creative imagery. For example, to induce heaviness, imagine your legs as lead pipes. For lightness, imagine helium-filled balloons pulling up your arm or imagine floating on a cloud.

Basic Self-Induction Script

The third step to self-hypnosis is to record the basic script below and play it back for your initial inductions. When you read the induction aloud, speak in a monotone. Keep the tempo slow and monotonous. Pronounce one word after another with an even beat. Pause between each sentence. Speaking slowly, with little inflection, will help your mind drift and increase your relaxation and suggestibility. After some experience with this induction, you will be ready to write your own personalized self-induction.

Sit in a comfortable position with your arms and legs uncrossed. Let your eyes focus gently on a point in front of you ... take a deep, relaxing breath all the way down into your abdomen.... Take another slow, deep, relaxing breath ... and another.... Even though your eyes are getting tired, keep them open a little longer and take another deep breath ... and another.... Your eyes become heavier and heavier ... let them close, as you say to yourself [Insert your key word or phrase here].

Now you can begin to relax the muscles in your body. Let your legs begin to relax ... let your legs begin to feel heavy ... heavier and heavier as they relax. Your legs are heavier and heavier as they let go of the last bit of muscular tension.... Your legs are becoming more and more heavy and relaxed, heavy and relaxed.... Your arms, too, are becoming more and more heavy ... heavier and heavier as they let go of the last bit of muscular tension. You can feel gravity pulling them down.... You feel your arms growing heavier and heavier, more and more deeply relaxed. Your arms are letting go ... letting go ... letting go of tension as they become heavier and heavier ... more and more deeply relaxed. Your arms and legs feel heavy, heavy, and relaxed.... Your arms and legs feel totally relaxed as they let go of the last bit of muscular tension ... more and more heavy and relaxed....

And your face, too, begins to relax. Your forehead is becoming smooth and relaxed. Your forehead is letting go of tension as it becomes more and more smooth and relaxed.... And your cheeks too are becoming relaxed, smooth and relaxed. Your cheeks are relaxed and letting go of tension ... your forehead and cheeks are totally relaxed ... smooth and relaxed.... And your jaw can now begin to relax ... feeling more and more loose and relaxed. As your jaw becomes more and more deeply relaxed, feel the muscles letting go ... and your lips beginning to part ... and your jaw becoming more and more loose and relaxed.

Now your neck and shoulders can begin to relax. Your neck is loose and relaxed ... your shoulders are relaxed and drooping.... Feel your neck and shoulders becoming more and more deeply relaxed ... so loose and relaxed.... Now, take another deep breath, and as you exhale let the relaxation spread into your chest and stomach and back.... Take another deep breath and, as you exhale, feel yourself becoming calm and relaxed ... calm and relaxed. Take another deep breath ... and as you exhale, feel your chest and stomach and back become calm and relaxed ... calm and relaxed. Feel yourself drifting deeper and deeper ... deeper and deeper ... becoming more and more drowsy, peaceful, and calm. Drifting and drowsy ... drowsy and drifting ... drifting down, down, down into total relaxation ... drifting deeper and deeper ... deeper and deeper.

Now it's time to go to your special place ... a place of safety and peace. You can go down the stairway to your special place or down a path, and with each step you can count backward from ten to zero ... and with each step become more and more deeply relaxed. In ten steps you will be there ... feeling peaceful and safe as you move toward your special place. Now you grow more and more relaxed with each step. Ten ... nine ... eight ... seven ... six ... five ... four ... three ... two ... one ... zero.

[If you want to repeat this countdown two or even three times to deepen hypnosis, that's perfectly fine.]

Now see the shapes and colors of your special place … hear the sounds … feel the sensations of your special place … smell the smells of your special place. See it … feel it … hear it … smell it. … You can feel safe and calm in your special place, safe and calm. …

Feel yourself drifting deeper and deeper, deeper and deeper … more and more drowsy, peaceful, and calm. You feel drowsy and drifting, drifting and drowsy … drifting down, down, down into total relaxation. You are so relaxed, peaceful, and calm.

[Pause and spend time relaxing in your special place.]

Now you know that you can …

[Leave a blank space on the tape here for any posthypnotic suggestion that you wish to use. Give yourself time to repeat the suggestion at least three times.]

Now, when you are ready, it is time to come back up … to come all the way back, feeling alert, refreshed, and wide awake. Starting to come up now: one … two … three … four … more and more alert and aware … five … six … seven … more and more alert and awake … eight … nine … beginning to open your eyes … and ten … completely alert, refreshed, and wide awake. Alert, refreshed, and wide awake.

Abbreviated Inductions

An optional fourth step to self-hypnosis is to learn to do *abbreviated inductions*. These are shorthand techniques that can produce hypnosis in thirty seconds to two minutes. Here are some examples.

Pendulum drop. To make a pendulum, tie an object like a paper clip, pen, or ring to the end of a heavy thread ten inches long. Hold the thread in your dominant hand and let the pendulum dangle above the floor. Ask your subconscious for permission to go into hypnosis for two minutes. If the answer is yes, your eyes will want to close. As your eyes close, picture a candle flame. Take several deep breaths and allow yourself to slip into a deeper and deeper relaxation. Tell yourself that when you have entered hypnosis, your hand will relax and drop the pendulum. Count down slowly from ten to zero.

Yes repetition. Think the thought "yes" over and over, as you focus on an imagined candle flame. Go down the stairs or down a path to your special place while you continue to think "yes."

Eye fixation. Fix your eyes on a point slightly above your normal line of vision. Let your peripheral vision narrow and your eyes lose focus. Allow your eyes to close, accompanied by a feeling of drowsiness. To increase the drowsiness, roll your eyes up to the top of your head two or three times.

Key word or phrase. Breathe deeply and slowly, and repeat the key word or phrase that you used in your self-induction script. As you say the word or phrase, close your eyes and enter hypnosis.

These abbreviated methods are useful after you have become relatively proficient at self-hypnosis. Always remember to end an induction by suggesting that you will awaken refreshed and feeling fine.

Five-finger exercise. The next exercise has been used very effectively for relaxation. Memorize the following steps. After you have gone through them, you can use the feeling of calmness that follows to enter hypnosis.

1. Touch your thumb to your index finger. As you do that, go back to a time when your body felt healthy fatigue, such as just after swimming, playing tennis, jogging, or some other exhilarating physical activity.

2. Touch your thumb to your middle finger. As you do that, go back to a time when you had a loving experience. You may choose to remember a moment of sexual fulfillment, a warm embrace, or an intimate conversation.

3. Touch your thumb to your ring finger. As you do that, recall the nicest compliment you have ever received. Try to really accept it now. By accepting it, you are showing your high regard for the person who said it. You are really paying him or her a compliment in return.

4. Touch your thumb to your little finger. As you do that, go back to the most beautiful place you have ever been. Dwell there for a while.

The five-finger exercise takes less than ten minutes, but it pays off with increased vitality, inner peace, and self-esteem. It can be done any time you feel tension.

Hypnotic Suggestions

A fifth useful step to self-hypnosis is to learn how to give yourself positive suggestions for change. For best results, say these suggestions to yourself when you are in a relaxed and receptive frame of mind, such as when you are in your special place during the basic self-induction. Or you may find that you prefer to intersperse suggestions throughout an induction.

Remember that autosuggestions are thoughts and images that influence your subjective experience. Here's a list of rules to keep in mind when you are creating suggestions for yourself:

Autosuggestions are most effective when they are:

1. *Direct.* Tell yourself, "I will be calm, confident, and in control."

2. *Positive.* Avoid wording suggestions in a negative way, such as, "I won't feel tired tonight."

3. *Permissive.* Try saying "I *can* feel relaxed and refreshed tonight" instead of "I *will* feel relaxed and refreshed." However, some people do respond better to commands. You can experiment with both to find out which approach works best for you.

4. *About the immediate future, not the present.* "Soon the drowsiness is going to come upon me."

5. *Repeated at least three times.*

6. *Represented with a visual image.* If you are trying to overcome a feeling of exhaustion, imagine yourself bouncing along with springs on your feet and see yourself as looking athletic and happy.

7. *Reinforced with an emotion or sensation.* If you want to give up smoking cigarettes, imagine how bad the first one tasted or think of the unpleasant burning in your lungs. If you are attempting to improve your confidence for a first date, imagine the feeling of closeness and belonging that you are hoping to find.

8. *Not associated with the word "try."* That's because "try" implies doubt and the possibility of failure.

9. *Exaggerated at first when working toward the control of unpleasant emotions or painful physical symptoms.* Start out by suggesting that the negative emotion or symptom is growing more intense. You might say, "My anger is getting bigger. I can feel the blood pushing at my veins. I'm getting hot. My muscles are tensing." Bring the feeling up to a peak and then tell yourself that the emotion or symptom is diminishing. "My anger is subsiding. My heart is slowing and beating normally. My flush is receding. My muscles are loosening and beginning to relax." When an unpleasant emotion or symptom reaches its peak, it can only get better. Suggestion can speed that process of recovery. When you can turn your emotions and symptoms on and off during hypnosis, you will have gained enormous control over your life.

10. *Written out in advance.* After you've written it out, distill it into a catchword or phrase you can easily remember when you are in the hypnotic state.

Practice writing hypnotic suggestions. Once hypnotized and relaxed, your subconscious mind is more open to believing whatever you tell it. Many of the symptoms that bother you, as well as your habitual tension responses to stress, were learned through suggestion. They can be unlearned through suggestion. For example, if you watched your father get angry every time he was forced to wait, and if on the first occasion when you delayed him he became angry at you, you may have learned by suggestion to respond exactly the same way. You can use hypnosis to learn new methods of coping with delay. Suggestions such as "Waiting is a chance to relax" and "I can let go of rushing" may undo the old habit.

In order to get the flavor of how suggestions can be written, write down hypnotic suggestions that you could use for the following problems:

1. Fear of coming into a dark house at night

2. Chronic fatigue

3. Obsessive and fearful thoughts about death

4. Fear of illness

5. Minor chronic head or back pain

6. Chronic anger and/or guilt

7. Self-criticism and worry about making mistakes

8. Low self-esteem

9. Lack of motivation

10. Feelings of insecurity and self-consciousness in the presence of other people

11. Anxiety about an upcoming evaluation or test

12. Improving performance

13. Pain or muscle tension

14. Disease and injury

Now that you have written your own suggestions, examine these possible scripts for each of the fourteen problems.

1. Fear of coming into a dark house at night
   I can come in tonight feeling relaxed and glad to be home, safe and secure.

2. Chronic fatigue
   I can awaken refreshed and rested. I can enjoy the evening ahead. I can pace myself today so that I will accomplish my priorities. Whenever I feel my energy flagging, I can do the five-finger exercise or another relaxation technique and then return to my daily activities relaxed and revitalized.

3. Obsessive and fearful thoughts about death

   I am full of life now. I will enjoy today. Very soon I can let go of these thoughts. [Visualize a blackboard and see the date written there.]

4. Fear of illness

   My body is feeling healthy and strong more and more. Each time I relax, my body becomes stronger. [Visualize yourself as healthy, strong, and relaxed while doing a favorite activity.]

5. Minor chronic head or back pain

   Soon my head will be cool and relaxed. [Imagine cool images.] *Gradually I will feel the muscles in my neck and back loosen.* [Imagine smooth, flowing, loosening images.] *In an hour, they will be completely relaxed. Whenever these symptoms come back, I will simply turn my ring a quarter turn to the right and the pain will relax away.*

6. Chronic anger and/or guilt

   I can turn off anger and guilt because I am the one who turns it on. [Practice turning up and turning down the unwanted emotion.] *I will relax my body and breathe deeply.*

7. Self-criticism and worry about making mistakes

   When I catch myself being self-critical or worried, I can take a deep breath and let go. I can breathe out negative tension and breathe in positive energy. [Practice five-finger exercise.]

8. Low self-esteem

   Each day I will feel more capable and self-assured. I can do it. I am doing the best I can with my prevailing level of awareness. I can feel myself becoming happier and more successful every day. I can be kind to myself. I am liking myself more and more. I am an intelligent, creative, and talented person.

9. Lack of motivation

   I can feel confident that I will achieve my goals. I have the power within myself to change. I can see myself solving my problems and getting beyond them. The decisions I make are the right ones for now. I can put aside distractions and focus my attention on one goal. As I get into my project, I will get more and more interested in it. As I work toward my goal, step by step, new energy and enthusiasm will emerge. When I finish this, I will feel great! When I achieve my goal, I will reward myself. I deserve success.

10. Feelings of insecurity and self-consciousness in the presence of other people

    The next time I see Ben, I can feel secure in myself. I can respond to Ben in a firm and assertive manner. I can feel relaxed and at ease because I am perfectly all right. I can relax and enjoy the thought that there are people in my life who see me as a good friend, valuable coworker, and loving family member. Whenever I lace my fingers together, I will feel confidence flowing throughout my entire body.

11. Anxiety about an upcoming evaluation or test

    I can concentrate on my studies, remembering everything I need to know for the test. When I feel nervous, I will take a deep breath and relax. My mind is becoming more and more calm and sharp. When I successfully complete this test, I will reward myself with _____. I can imagine myself getting an A.

12. Improving performance

    I can be calm and in control in response to stressful situations. [Imagine yourself maintaining your cool and concentration in the face of specific pressures and fears.] *I can imagine myself playing a perfect game from start to finish.* [Reflect on every perfect move and strategy.] *I will achieve my goal.* [Be specific about your objectives and visualize them in detail.]

13. Pain or muscle tension

    I can see my back pain as a sword of dry ice burning and stabbing me. Now I see the sun shining, warming my back. The ice sword is gradually melting away into a puddle in the warmth of the sun and my pain is beginning to subside. My tension is starting to flow; as it flows, its color changes into a warm orange fluid moving slowly through my body toward my right shoulder, down my right arm, and into my clenched fist. When I am ready, I can let go of it. I can just scoop my pain up and throw it away. [Imagine a symbol that best represents your pain or tension. Have it interact with another symbol that eliminates the first symbol or transforms it into something more tolerable or makes it disappear.]

14. Disease and injury

    I can imagine a healing white light at the top of my head. I can see and feel it surrounding my entire body. I can feel it begin to move within my body, cleansing and healing as it slowly spreads throughout my entire body. I can imagine myself healthy, strong, and energetic while doing what I want to do.

Self-Hypnotic Induction for a Specific Problem

Another optional step is to consider how self-hypnosis might fit into an overall plan to solve a specific problem in your life. The specific problem addressed here is sleep disturbance. This section is adapted from Josie Hadley and Carol Staudacher's *Hypnosis for Change* (1996).

Before you are ready to begin self-hypnosis for a specific problem, there are a few issues you need to address. They are as follows:

Define your problem and your goal. Do you have difficulty falling asleep or staying asleep, or do you wake up too early? Is your sleep restless? Do you have great difficulty waking up in the morning? Once you have clearly labeled your problem, you can easily define your goal in the form of a positive autosuggestion. For example, "I can fall asleep quickly and easily." "I will wake up refreshed and alert at the appropriate time." Or "Soon I will be able to sleep deeply and continuously throughout the night."

Identify and eliminate any possible external factors that may be contributing to your problem. Ask yourself what might be interfering with getting a good night's sleep. Is your bedroom a comfortable place that invites sleep, or is it filled with clutter, noise, and light? Do you spend half the night coping with a restless bed partner and staring at a glowing clock face that keeps reminding you of how much sleep you are losing? Are you consuming too many stimulants during the day? You need to address these problems before you use self-hypnosis for better sleep, since you cannot expect self-hypnosis to solve these problems for you.

Notice what you are telling yourself that may be contributing to your problem. For example, people who have difficulty with sleep often focus on time. They say things to themselves like "If I don't get to sleep by midnight, I know I won't be able to sleep at all." If you tend to worry, your mind can go wild when you turn off the light. "I really blew it today. Wait until my boss finds out!" "I know I didn't study enough for the test tomorrow." Do you use the quiet hours of the night to solve problems? "Until this question is answered, we can't go on!" "I'll tell her I didn't mean what I said, and then she'll say … "

If part of your problem has to do with what you are telling yourself, you can use the chapters Refuting Irrational Ideas, Facing Worry and Anxiety, and Anger Inoculation to help you identify and change the way you think. If you are being kept awake by your thoughts, here are some suggestions to calm your mind before you fall asleep.

- If you are a clock watcher, turn the clock to the wall, direct your thoughts away from time, and tell yourself "As I rest, my mind will become calm and my body will relax."

- If you tend to dwell on the negative or on things that you cannot control, think about the positive things you did during the day.

- If you are a nighttime problem solver, write your to-do list *before* you go to bed and then make an agreement with yourself to put aside your problems until tomorrow when you are at your sharpest and to save the night for restorative sleep.

When you create your own sleep induction, be sure to write in positive suggestions that incorporate these ideas to reinforce your new desired behavior.

Record an induction tailored to your particular problem. Begin by recording the basic induction up through the section about your special place, and then add your special suggestions. For sleep disturbance, you might add the following script to the basic induction.

Now just linger in your special place. There's no place to go, nothing to do. Just rest, just let yourself drift and float, drift and float into a sound and restful sleep. And as you drift deeper and deeper, imagine the positive things that you can think and do to allow yourself a sound and restful sleep. Your new positive thoughts are true. You have released negative thoughts and feelings. You have released stress and tension from your mind and body. Each new positive statement becomes stronger and stronger as you continue to drift deeper and deeper into relaxation. Just let yourself drift deeper and deeper into sleep. Just let those positive statements float in your mind as you drift into a sound and restful sleep.

Now become aware of how comfortable you feel, so relaxed, your head and shoulders are in just the right position, your back is supported, and you are becoming less aware of all the normal sounds of your surroundings. As you drift deeper and deeper you may experience a negative thought or worry that is trying to surface in your mind and disrupt your slumber and your rest. Simply take that thought and sweep it up as you would sweep up crumbs from the floor and place that thought or worry into the box. The box has a nice tight lid. Put the lid on the box and place the box on the top shelf of your closet. You can go back to that box at another time, a time that is more appropriate, a time that will not interfere with your sleep. As other unwanted thoughts appear, sweep them up and place them in the box, put the lid on the box, and place it on the top shelf of your closet to let them go. Let them go and continue to drift deeper and deeper into sleep.

Shift your thoughts back to your positive thoughts and positive statements. Just let these thoughts flow through your mind, thoughts such as, "I am a worthwhile person." [Pause.] "I have accomplished many good things." [Pause.] "I have reached positive goals." [Pause.] Just let your positive ideas flow through your mind. Let them flow and drift, becoming stronger and stronger as you drift deeper and deeper into sleep.

You may begin to see them slowly fade, slowly fade, as you become even more relaxed, sleepier, more drowsy, more relaxed. Just imagine yourself in your peaceful and special place, smiling, feeling so good, so comfortable, so relaxed. [Pause.] From your special place you can easily drift into a sound and restful sleep, a sound and restful sleep, undisturbed in a sound and restful sleep. You sleep through the night in a sound and restful sleep. If you should awaken, you simply imagine your special place once again and drift easily back into a sound and restful sleep, a sound and restful sleep. Your breathing becomes so relaxed, your thoughts wind down, wind down, wind down, and relax. You drift and float into a sound and restful sleep, undisturbed throughout the night. You will awaken at your designated time feeling rested and refreshed.

Now there's nothing to do, nothing to think about, nothing to do but enjoy your special place, your special place that is so peaceful for you, so relaxing. Just imagine how it feels to relax in your special place. You may become aware of how clean and fresh your special place smells, or you may become aware of the different sounds of your special place, of the birds singing in the background or the water cascading over river rocks in a stream. Or you may become aware of how warm the sun feels as you lounge in a hammock or how cool the breeze feels from the ocean air. Or you may experience something else that is unique and wonderful in your special place. Just experience it, drift and float, all thought just fading, drifting into a sound and restful sleep. Just drift into a comfortable, cozy, restful sleep, your body feeling heavy and relaxed as you sink into your bed, so relaxed, just drifting into sleep ... sleep ... sleep ... sleep ... sleep ... sleep. ...

SPECIAL CONSIDERATIONS

Do not practice a hypnotic induction in a car or in any other situation where your safety requires you to be fully alert and able to respond quickly. After an induction, always make sure that you are completely awake and alert before reentering such situations.

Some people, especially those who are sleep-deprived, fall asleep during self-hypnosis. If sleep is not your goal and you have this problem, you may want to shorten the induction so that you are awake to hear the suggestions specifically geared to your goals. Keep in mind that many people who think they are asleep during hypnosis are still able to hear and benefit from positive suggestions. If you are prone to falling asleep, practice it sitting up and use a timer to wake yourself up rather than worry about being late for your next activity.

You may find that as the symptom you are concerned about fades, you lose your motivation to continue practicing self-hypnosis. This is a typical experience and nothing to worry about. If your symptom returns at a later time, you can use self-hypnosis again.

You can use your key phrase when you experience your symptom or anytime you feel tense or uncomfortable in a stressful situation. Although you are unlikely to feel as relaxed as you do after a full self-hypnotic induction, you will still experience some measure of relief. In this way, your key phrase can also serve as a reminder that you do have a choice about how you respond to stress.

Whether you are using self-hypnosis to relax or to accomplish some other goal, you are likely to be pleasantly surprised by the power of positive suggestion.

FURTHER READING

Alman, B. M., and P. Lambrou. 1991. *Self-Hypnosis: The Complete Manual for Health and Self-Change.* New York: Brunner-Mazel.

Hadley, J., and C. Staudacher. 1996. *Hypnosis for Change: A Manual of Proven Techniques.* 3rd ed. Oakland, CA: New Harbinger Publications.

Haley, J. 1993. *Uncommon Therapy: The Psychiatric Techniques of Milton Erickson.* New York: Norton.

Hunter, C. R. 1998. *Master the Power of Self-Hypnosis.* New York: Sterling Publications.

Rosen, S. 1998. *My Voice Will Go with You.* New York: W. W. Norton.

MacKanzie, R. 2005. *Self-Change Hypnosis.* Victoria, BC, Canada: Trafford Publishing.

Soskis, D. A. 1986. *Self-Hypnosis: An Introductory Guide for Clinicians.* New York: W. W. Norton.

9

Autogenics

In this chapter you will learn to:

* Respond quickly to verbal commands to relax

* Return your body to a balanced, normal state

* Calm your mind

* Resolve specific physical problems

BACKGROUND

Autogenic training (AT) has its origins in research on hypnosis conducted by the famous brain physiologist Oskar Vogt at the Berlin Institute during the last decade of the nineteenth century. Vogt taught some of his experienced hypnotic subjects to put themselves into a trance that had the effect of reducing their fatigue, tension, and painful symptoms like headaches. It also seemed to help the subjects deal more effectively with their everyday lives. They usually reported that when their fatigue and tension lifted, they felt warm and heavy.

Johannes H. Schultz, a Berlin psychiatrist, became interested in Vogt's work. He found that his subjects could create a state very much like a hypnotic trance just by thinking of heaviness and warmth in their extremities. Essentially, all they had to do was relax, be undisturbed, sit in a comfortable position, and concentrate passively on verbal formulas that suggested they feel warmth and heaviness in their limbs. Schultz combined some of Vogt's autosuggestions with some yoga techniques and in 1932 published his new system in the book *Autogenic Training*.

In its present form, AT not only provides you with the recuperative effects of traditional hypnosis, it also frees you from dependence on a hypnotist. With skillful use of AT, you can learn to induce the feelings of warmth and heaviness associated with relaxation whenever you choose.

Schultz's verbal formulas fall into four main categories of exercises:

1. Verbal formulas to normalize the body

2. Verbal formulas to calm the mind

3. Autogenic modification exercises designed to address specific problems

4. Meditative exercises to develop mental concentration and creativity

This introductory chapter will teach you to use verbal suggestions to relax your body, calm your mind, and help you resolve specific problems.

The verbal formulas to normalize the body fall under six standard themes. The formulas are aimed at reversing the fight-or-flight response state, or high-alarm state, that occurs when anyone experiences physical or emotional stress.

1. The first standard theme is *heaviness*, which promotes relaxation of the voluntary muscles used to move your arms and legs. There are seven verbal formulas that suggest the theme of heaviness (see Set 1 under Autogenic Verbal Formulas).

2. The second standard theme is *warmth*, which brings about peripheral vasodilatation. As you say the verbal formula "My right hand is warm," the smooth muscles that control the diameter of the blood vessels in your hand relax so that more warming blood flows into your hand. This helps reverse the pooling of blood in the trunk and head characteristic of the fight-or-flight reaction to stress.

3. The third standard theme focuses on *normalizing cardiac activity*. The verbal formula is simply "My heartbeat is calm and regular."

4. The fourth standard theme *regulates the respiratory system*. The verbal formula says "It breathes me."

5. The fifth standard theme *relaxes and warms the abdominal region*. The formula to say is "My solar plexus is warm."

6. The last standard theme *reduces the flow of blood to the head* while you say "My forehead is cool."

The verbal formulas to calm the mind are used in conjunction with these six themes and serve to intensify the effect of the themes.

SYMPTOM-RELIEF EFFECTIVENESS

Autogenic training has been found to be effective in the treatment of muscle tension and various disorders of the respiratory tract (hyperventilation and bronchial asthma), the gastrointestinal tract (constipation, diarrhea, gastritis, ulcers, and spasms), the circulatory system (racing heart, irregular heartbeat, high blood pressure, cold extremities, and headaches), and the endocrine system (thyroid problems). AT is also useful in reducing general anxiety, irritability, and fatigue. It can be employed to modify your reaction to pain, increase your resistance to stress, and reduce or eliminate sleeping disorders.

CONTRAINDICATIONS

AT is not recommended for children under the age of five, people who lack motivation, or those with severe mental or emotional disorders. Prior to beginning AT, it is essential that you have a physical exam and discussion with your medical doctor about what physiological effects AT will likely have on you. Those with serious diseases such as diabetes, hypoglycemic conditions, or heart conditions should be under the supervision of a medical doctor while in AT. Some people experience an increase in blood pressure and a few have a sharp drop in blood pressure when they do these exercises. If you have high or low blood pressure, you should check with your medical doctor to be sure that AT is regularizing it. If you feel very anxious or restless during or after AT exercises or experience recurring disquieting side effects, you should continue AT only under the supervision of a professional AT instructor.

Autogenic instructor training is offered in some universities and is practiced by educators, mental health therapists, and complementary medicine practitioners.

TIME TO MASTER

In the past, AT specialists recommended moving at a slow but sure and steady pace, taking many months to master all six themes. We've found this timetable unrealistic for people who want and typically get some positive results in the very first session of AT. Others require a week or two of regular practice to experience relaxation. Plan on practicing your autogenic formulas at least twice a day for twenty minutes. If you find this is too long for you, shorten the length of the session and add more sessions each day.

By the end of one month of regular practice, you should be able to relax quickly using all six themes. At that time you may choose to use all six themes in one twenty-minute relaxation exercise, or perhaps only a few themes that rapidly bring about deep relaxation for you. For instance, the formulas "My arms and legs are warm and heavy," "My heartbeat is calm and regular," and "It breathes me" may be sufficient to induce immediate relaxation. You should experiment to find what works best for you.

INSTRUCTIONS

How to Facilitate Your Relaxation When Doing AT

- Keep external stimuli to a minimum.

- Choose a quiet room where you won't be disturbed.

- Keep the room temperature at a moderately warm, comfortable level.

- Turn the lights down low.

- Wear loose clothing.

- Choose one of the following three basic AT postures:

  1. Sit in an armchair in which your head, back, and extremities are supported and you are as comfortable as possible.

  2. Sit on a stool, slightly stooped over, with your arms resting on your thighs, your neck relaxed, and your hands draped between your knees.

  3. Lie down on your back with your head supported and your legs about eight inches apart, your toes pointed slightly outward, and your arms resting comfortably at your sides but not touching your body.

- Scan your body to be sure that the position you chose is tension-free. In particular, look for overextension of your limbs such as unsupported arms, head, or legs, tightening of the limbs at the joints, or a crooked spine. If any of these overextensions exist, continue moving and supporting your body until you are well-supported and comfortable, with no overextensions.

- Close your eyes or pick a point in front of you to softly focus on.

- Take a few slow, deep, and relaxing breaths before you begin to repeat your autogenic formulas.

How to Practice the Six Basic Autogenic Themes to Normalize Your Body

There are two ways to learn the six basic autogenic themes. The first option is to make a recording of the verbal formulas and listen to it twice a day. Or, you can memorize and practice one set of verbal formulas at a time until you include all of the themes in your practice. Slowly repeat each formula over and over to yourself, keeping up a steady silent verbal stream.

As a general rule of thumb, repeat each formula four times, saying it slowly (taking about five seconds) and then pausing for about three seconds. Using the first three verbal formulas of the first set as an example, you would say to yourself, "My right arm is heavy.... My right arm is heavy.... My right arm is heavy.... My right arm is heavy." This should take you about half a minute. Then you would say to yourself, "My left arm is heavy.... My left arm is heavy.... My left arm is heavy.... My left arm is heavy...." Then, "Both of my arms are heavy.... Both of my arms are heavy.... Both of my arms are heavy.... Both of my arms are heavy...." The entire set should take you less than four minutes. If you are focusing on memorizing one set at a time, you can repeat the set up to twenty minutes in one practice session or create many minipractice sessions of one or a few sets throughout the day. If you are recording the verbal formulas, be sure to leave about half a minute between each formula for silent repetition.

As you silently repeat a verbal formula, "passively concentrate" on the part of the body it refers to. In other words, just notice what happens without harboring any expectations or judgments. Passive concentration does not mean spacing out or going to sleep. You remain alert to your experience without analyzing it. This casual attitude is contrasted with active concentration, which occurs when you fix your attention on certain aspects of your experience and have an interest and goal-directed investment in it. *Active concentration* is essential for such tasks as preparing a new recipe or fixing a car. *Passive concentration* is required for relaxation.

At first, you will not be able to maintain perfect passive concentration. Your mind will wander. That's natural. When you find this happening, just return to the formula as soon as possible. In addition, you may experience some initial symptoms known as "autogenic discharges," which are normal but distracting. For example, you may sense a change in your weight or temperature, tingling, "electrical currents," involuntary movements, stiffness, some pain, anxiety, a desire to cry, irritability, headaches, nausea, or illusions. At times, you may experience fascinating insights or feelings of bliss. Whether you have pleasant or unpleasant experiences, just note them and return to your AT formulas. Remember that these experiences are transitory, they are not the purpose of AT, and they will pass as you continue to practice.

When you are ready to stop an AT session, say to yourself, "When I open my eyes, I will feel refreshed and alert." Then open your eyes and breathe a few deep breaths as you stretch and flex your arms. Be sure that you are not still in a trancelike state when you return to your regular activities.

Read the helpful hints and cautionary notes in the Special Considerations section at the end of this chapter before you begin to practice AT.

AUTOGENIC VERBAL FORMULAS FOR NORMALIZING THE BODY

Set 1

My right arm is heavy.
My left arm is heavy.
Both of my arms are heavy.
My right leg is heavy.
My left leg is heavy.
Both of my legs are heavy.
My arms and legs are heavy.

Set 2

My right arm is warm.
My left arm is warm.
Both of my arms are warm.
My right leg is warm.
Both of my legs are warm.
My arms and legs are warm.

Set 3

My right arm is heavy and warm.
Both of my arms are heavy and warm.
Both of my legs are heavy and warm.
My arms and legs are heavy and warm.
It breathes me.
My heartbeat is calm and regular.

Set 4

My right arm is heavy and warm.
My arms and legs are heavy and warm.
It breathes me.
My heartbeat is calm and regular.
My solar plexus is warm.

Set 5

My right arm is heavy and warm.
My arms and legs are heavy and warm.
It breathes me.
My heartbeat is calm and regular.
My solar plexus is warm.
My arms and legs are warm.
My forehead is cool.

Autogenic Formulas for Calming the Mind

The following formulas focus on mental rather than physical functions. They are intended to reinforce the effects of the autogenic verbal formulas for the six standard themes previously mentioned. Here is a list of examples:

I am calm and relaxed.

I feel quite quiet.

My whole body feels quiet, heavy, comfortable, and relaxed.

My mind is quiet.

I withdraw my thoughts from the surroundings and I feel serene and still.

My thoughts are turned inward and I am at ease.

Deep within my mind, I can visualize and experience myself as relaxed and comfortable and still.

I feel an inward quietness.

You may add one or more of these phrases for calming the mind at the end of each set of autogenic verbal formulas. But for the best results, intersperse them throughout each set. For example, the first set could be rewritten as follows:

My right arm is heavy.

I am calm and relaxed.

My left arm is heavy.

I am calm and relaxed.

Both of my arms are heavy.

I am calm and relaxed.

My right leg is heavy.

I am calm and relaxed.

My left leg is heavy.

I am calm and relaxed.

Both of my legs are heavy.

I am calm and relaxed.

Autogenic Modification Exercises

You can practice autogenic modification by making up what Schultz called "organ specific formulae" to deal with specific problems after you have mastered the six basic autogenic themes. For example, you can develop an *indirect formula* such as "My feet are warm" or "My shoulders are warm" each time you feel an embarrassing blush coming on. This allows you to passively attend to something other than the problem of blushing. At the same time, you move some of the blood from your head that would contribute to the blushing toward your feet. You might also use a *direct formula* such as "My forehead is cool."

When you experience persistent muscle pain or tension in a specific part of your body, use the autogenic verbal formulas to become generally relaxed. Then passively concentrate on the persistently tense or painful area and project the sensation of comfortably warm relaxation into that area. Repeat to yourself, "My [tense or painful area] is warm and comfortably relaxed."

If you have a headache, concentrate on the area that tends to tighten up most at the beginning of a headache. For instance, if it is your shoulders or neck or back of the head, passively concentrate on that area and project the sensation of warm relaxation into it, repeating to yourself, "My [tense area] is warm and comfortably relaxed." Occasionally, intersperse the formula with "My forehead feels comfortably cool." Never make the suggestion "My forehead feels warm" because that would stimulate vasodilatation in the area that could result in pain.

When you are troubled by a cough, you may want to use the verbal formula "My throat is cool, my chest is warm." To cope with asthma, use the same formula and add "It breathes me, it breathes me calm and regular."

When you are in a very relaxed state toward the end of an AT session, you are highly suggestible. This is a good time to use what Schultz called "intentional formulae." In other words, you tell yourself to do things that have been causing you difficulties. For example, if you want to stop smoking, say something over and over again such as, "Smoking is a dirty habit, and I can do without it." If you want to eat less, say "I have control over what I eat. I can eat less and be more attractive." These special intentional formulas should be believable, persuasive, and brief.

SPECIAL CONSIDERATIONS

1. When practicing the six basic autogenic themes, start with your dominant arm: if you write with your left hand, begin with your left arm. Repeat "My left arm is heavy" four times and then go on to the next phrase, "My right arm is heavy," and repeat it four times, and so on.

2. If you have trouble experiencing the physical sensations suggested by the verbal formulas, try imagery. Contemplate being in a nice warm shower or bath, or having your hand

submerged in a comfortably warm pan of water. Feel yourself sitting in the warm sun, or holding a nice warm mug of your favorite hot drink in your hand. Think about blood flowing gently through the fingertips of your hands and through your toes. Imagine lying under a comfortably heavy warm blanket or lying under the warm heavy sand at the beach. Recall a cool breeze or washcloth on your forehead.

3. Note that perhaps 10 percent of all people experimenting with AT never experience the basic sensations of heaviness or warmth. This doesn't matter. The formulas describing warmth and heaviness are used only to bring about a functional change in the body, which you may or may not feel. Just focus on doing the formulas correctly, and within two weeks of regular practice you should experience feelings of relaxation.

4. Some people experience a paradoxical response when they first practice the autogenic verbal formulas. For example, they feel light as they repeat the verbal formulas for heaviness, or they feel cool as they say the formulas for warmth. This is an indication that the body is responding to the formulas and will in time relax.

5. If you feel stuck or are experiencing unpleasant side effects while practicing one of the themes, move on to the next one and come back to the formula that is difficult for you at the end of your training period.

6. If you have trouble becoming aware of your heartbeat, lie on your back with your right hand resting over your heart. If you experience any discomfort or distress while becoming aware of your heartbeat, move on to another theme and come back to this one at the end of your training session, or skip it.

7. Skip the verbal formula "My solar plexus is warm" if you have ulcers, diabetes, or any condition involving bleeding from abdominal organs. If you notice dizziness or light-headedness when you practice the verbal formula "My forehead is cool," practice it lying down.

FURTHER READING

Goleman, D., and J. Gurin, eds. 1995. *Mind Body Medicine: How to Use Your Mind for Better Health.* Yonkers, NY: Consumer Reports Books.

Kermani, K. 1996. *Autogenic Training: The Effective Holistic Way to Better Health.* London: Souvenir Press.

Linden, W. 1990. *Autogenics: A Clinical Guide.* New York: Guilford Press.

Pelletier, K. R. 1977. *Mind as Healer, Mind as Slayer.* New York: Delta.

Peurifory, R. Z. 2005. *Anxiety, Phobias, and Panic: Taking Charge and Conquering Fear.* New York: Warner Books.

Sadigh, M. 2001. *Autogenic Training: A Mind-Body Approach to the Treatment of Fibromyalgia and Chronic Pain Syndrome.* Binghamton, NY: Haworth Press.

RECORDING

McManus, C. 2003. *Progressive Relaxation and Autogenic Training* (Audio CD). Produced by Carolyn McManus. Can be purchased on Amazon.com.

10

Brief Combination Techniques

In this chapter you will learn to:

* Tailor relaxation techniques to fit your specific needs

* Combine techniques for a more powerful effect

BACKGROUND

The relaxation exercises presented in this chapter are based on the work of many different thera-pists. They are creative blends of some of the techniques you've already learned. Learning several brief combination techniques can greatly benefit you for three reasons.

1. When you put two or more relaxation approaches together, the combination can have a *synergistic* effect. This means that the sum relaxation effect of the combined techniques is far greater than what you would achieve if you did each relaxation procedure individually. As you experiment with the material presented in this chapter, you'll learn which tech-niques are best at activating each other and combining for the most powerful effect.

2. The second reason that combining techniques is often more powerful than one technique by itself is that the sequence of the combination is structured to draw you deeper into the relaxation experience. Each technique builds progressively on the one before. For example, the relaxation you experience from visualizing a pleasant beach scene is more profound if you precede the visualization with some deep breathing. And if you follow the deep breathing and the beach scene with autogenic themes of heaviness and warmth, you have a sequence of techniques that builds one upon the other to activate a deeper relaxation response.

3. The third advantage to using the combination techniques presented here is their brevity. You can easily do any of these combined sequences during a ten-minute coffee break. Any time you have a few minutes to spare, they can help you center yourself and regain a sense of calmness.

The combination techniques presented here are merely suggestions. Although each one has been tested and proven useful, feel free to be inventive. Try your own unique combinations. Experiment with a different sequence. Because you are a unique person with unique needs and patterns of responses, it's important for you to add, delete, and modify until you have a brief combined relaxation sequence that really works for you.

SYMPTOM-RELIEF EFFECTIVENESS

The brief combination techniques presented here have been proven effective in the treatment of fight-or-flight symptoms and stress-induced physiological disorders. They are particularly helpful when your stress is work-related and requires brief but frequent booster sessions during the day to help you cope with mounting tensions.

TIME TO MASTER

If you have mastered the component techniques presented in earlier chapters, these combination approaches can be immediately and effectively applied. Otherwise, allow one to two weeks to use these combined approaches successfully.

INSTRUCTIONS

1. Stretch and Relax

A. While sitting in a chair, take a big stretch. Tighten your arms and pull them back so that you stretch your chest and shoulders. Stretch and tighten your legs at the same time by first pulling your toes up toward your knees and then pushing them out straight again.

B. Place one hand on your abdomen, just above your natural waist (where a belt would be most comfortable). Inhale slowly and deeply through your nose into your abdomen. Allow your hand to be pushed out by your exhale as much as feels comfortable. Take four more deep breaths using the same procedure.

C. Take hold of a pencil and suspend it by its point over a desk or table or the floor. Tell yourself that when you are deeply relaxed, the pencil will drop. The sound of the dropping pencil will be your signal to enter a healing five-minute trance. (If you prefer, you may omit the pencil and proceed with step C from here.) Close your eyes and say to yourself the key word or phrase that you've found most helpful in self-hypnosis. Tell yourself you will become more and more relaxed with each number as you count back-ward from ten to zero. After the countdown, repeat to yourself these four phrases, over and over, in any order: "I am drifting deeper and deeper, deeper and deeper.... I am more and more drowsy, peaceful, and calm.... I am drifting and drowsy, drowsy and drifting.... I am drifting down, down, down into total relaxation." If, by this time, your pencil has not already dropped, let go of it deliberately and remind yourself that you will now enjoy five minutes of peaceful self-hypnosis.

D. While in trance, visit your special place and enjoy the uniquely relaxing qualities of that environment. Really experience the sights, sounds, and sensations of your own special place. When it feels that you've been there long enough, count up from one to ten. Suggest to yourself that you are becoming more and more alert, refreshed, and wide awake as you count.

2. Abdominal Breathing and Imagination

This exercise combines the relaxing benefits of complete natural breathing with the curative value of positive autosuggestion.

A. Lie down on the floor on a rug or blanket in a "dead body" pose.

B. Place your hands gently on your solar plexus (the point where your ribs start to separate above your abdomen) and practice complete natural deep breathing for a few minutes.

C. Imagine energy is rushing into your lungs with each incoming breath of air and being immediately stored in your solar plexus. Imagine that this energy is flowing out to all parts of your body with each exhalation. Form a mental picture of this energizing process.

D. Continue doing this exercise on a daily basis for at least five to ten minutes a day.

3. Autogenic Breathing

A. Begin by taking slow, deep abdominal breaths as described in step 1B above. Become aware of your growing feeling of relaxation as each deep breath expands your diaphragm.

B. Visualize a beach. See the waves rolling up the sand, the seagulls wheeling overhead, a few puffs of fleecy clouds. Hear the roar of waves, and then the quiet. Hear the alter-nating roar, quiet, roar, quiet. Over the ocean sound you can hear the seagulls calling. Now feel the warm sand. Imagine it covering your body, warm and heavy. Really feel the weight of the sand on your arms and legs. Feel surrounded by warmth and comfort.

C. While visualizing the sand, continue to breathe as deeply as feels comfortable. Notice the rhythm of your breath. As you breathe in, say the word "warm" to yourself. Try to feel the warmth of the sand around your body. As you breathe out, say the word "heavy." Experience the weight of the sand on your limbs. Continue your deep breathing, thinking "warm" as you inhale and "heavy" as you exhale. Continue for at least five minutes. (Note: If after a time you feel more comfortable shifting to shallower breathing, allow yourself to do so.)

4. I Am Grateful

This exercise is particularly helpful as the day is wearing on and your sense of stress and frustration is rising. It is also an excellent sequence for relaxing and putting yourself in a pleasant frame of mind before you drift off to sleep.

A. Use the short form for progressive muscle relaxation outlined in chapter 4: (1) Curl fists, tighten biceps. (2) Wrinkle forehead and face like a walnut. (3) Arch back, take a deep breath. (4) Pull feet back, curl toes while tightening calves, thighs, buttocks.

B. Reflect on the events of your day so far, and select three things for which you feel grateful. These don't have to be major events. For example, you may be grateful for the warm shower you took this morning, a coworker helping you with a difficult project, your child giving you a hug and telling you she loves you, a lovely sunrise, and so on. Take a moment to relive and enjoy these experiences.

C. Continue to think back over your day. Recall three things you did that you feel good about. Remember, these don't have to be major feats. For example, you may feel good about saying no to something you really didn't want to do, taking time for yourself to exercise or relax, or being supportive to someone you like. Take a minute to reexperience those positive moments.

5. Deep Affirmation

A. Put your hand over your abdomen and begin taking slow, deep abdominal breaths, as described in step 1B above.

B. Close your eyes and continue to breathe deeply as you scan your body for tension. Start with your toes and move up your body. Notice any tension in your calves, thighs, and buttocks. Explore areas of tension in your back, abdomen, or chest muscles. Notice your shoulders and neck, your jaw, cheeks, and forehead. Check for tension in your biceps, forearms, and hands. Whenever you discover a tense area, exaggerate the tension slightly so that you can become more aware of it. Notice exactly which muscles in your body are tense and then say to yourself, "I am tensing my [insert the name of the muscle you're working with]. I am hurting myself . . . I am creating tension in my body . . . I will let go of that tension starting now."

C. Use the self-hypnosis exercise outlined in step 1C.

D. Select an affirmation to use while in trance. The following list of suggested affirmations is reprinted with permission from *Visualization for Change* (1994) by Patrick Fanning.

I can relax at will.

Tension is draining from my muscles.

I'm filled with peace, calm, and serenity.

I can turn my tension down like the volume on a radio.

Relaxation floods my body like healing, golden light.

I am in touch with my peaceful center.

I can look inward and find peace.

Relaxation is always within my grasp.

E. When you have relaxed long enough, count back up from one to ten. Suggest to yourself while you count that you are feeling more and more refreshed, alert, and wide awake.

6. The Tension Cutter

A. Take four deep abdominal breaths as described in step 1B.

B. Close your eyes. Visualize your tension by giving it a color and a shape. Now change the shape and color of your tension. Make it bigger or smaller, lighter or darker. Now see it moving farther and farther away from you. Watch it as it becomes smaller and smaller until it finally disappears from your awareness.

C. Now imagine your body filled with lights. See red lights for tension spots and blue lights for relaxed areas. Imagine the lights changing from red to blue in all the tension spots of your body. Be aware of any physical sensation you experience while you change to the blue light of relaxation. See all the lights in your body as blue and see the color blue becoming darker and darker. Feel yourself relaxing more deeply with each darker shade of blue you experience.

D. Now it's time for a minivacation. Here are two itineraries: pick one to enjoy or use them as a model for creating your own minivacation.

Vacation 1. Picture yourself in a forest. The light is clear and bright in places and dappled in others. As you take a long pleasant walk, you feel safe and comfortable. The air around you is cool and refreshing. You enjoy the bright spots of sunshine on the ground where sunlight filters down through the leaves. You are walking barefooted. The fallen leaves and moss feel soft and cool to your feet. You hear birdsongs and the soft rustle of wind through the trees. These sounds make you feel happy and comfortable. As you walk, your muscles feel looser and looser, heavier, and more relaxed. The forest carpet of leaves and moss feels so comfortable that you want to lie down on it and close your eyes to rest. Now you see a small stream. It is making a soft, bubbly noise. Next to the stream is a patch of tall, soft grass, lit and warmed by sunlight. It's a lovely place to rest and you sink down to your knees and roll gently over onto the soft, warm grass. You hear the bubbling stream, the birds' song, and the gentle wind. You are so deeply relaxed that every part of your body from your toes to the top of your head is loose and heavy.

Vacation 2. Picture yourself alone in a beach house with a view of the sea. The first rays of the morning sun light up the wall of your bedroom as you sink deeper into the warm, soft bed. You take a deep breath and notice how relaxed your muscles are. Outside you hear the sounds of seagulls and the rhythmic crashing of the waves. The waves roll in and out, in and out. Each wave makes you more and more deeply relaxed. In and out, in and out. You feel drowsy, heavy, and calm. You can feel the cool salt air coming through the open window and you roll over to see the sand and the waves and the blue sky. You take deep breaths of the air and your relaxation deepens with each breath. You feel safe and yet very free, unhurried, aware that the day ahead is full of possibilities.

7. Taking Control

A. Get comfortable, close your eyes, and begin noticing your breathing. Try to notice each breath and nothing else. As you exhale, say to yourself the word "one." Keep saying "one" with each exhalation.

B. When you feel sufficiently relaxed, turn your attention from your breathing to a situation you find stressful or difficult. See yourself handling that stressful situation confidently and successfully. See yourself saying and doing the appropriate thing to succeed. See yourself smiling, standing or sitting erectly. Now visualize yourself hesitating or making a small error, uncertain for a moment. But then you recover, you go on, confidently finishing the task, looking satisfied. You remind yourself, "I can handle this. I'm in control."

8. Accepting Yourself

A. Use the body scanning procedure from chapter 2 to become aware of how you are feeling in your body right now and what stressors might be contributing to how you feel.

B. Use abdominal breathing as described in step 1B to let go of the tension in your body and relax.

C. When you feel relaxed, make these suggestions to yourself: "I let go of 'shoulds.' … I accept myself with all my faults and weaknesses. … I breathe, I feel, I do the best I can." Rewrite this mantra in any manner that feels more authentic or true for you. Anything will work, as long as it carries the basic message that you accept yourself.

We also recommend that you review and consider incorporating the following combination techniques from these other chapters into your daily routine:

1. Mindful Breath Counting from chapter 3

2. Cue-Controlled Relaxation from chapter 7

3. Creating Your Special Place from chapter 6

FURTHER READING

Fanning, P. 1994. *Visualization for Change*. Oakland, CA: New Harbinger Publications.

RECORDINGS

The Relaxation and Stress Reduction Workbook Audio Program Series CD is sold separately by New Harbinger Publications. This is a source of audio exercises that you can use on a daily basis. The series consists of: Applied Relaxation Training, Body Awareness and Imagination, Progressive Relaxation and Breathing, and Stress Inoculation.

Fanning, P., and M. McKay. 1997. *The Daily Relaxer Series*. Oakland, CA: New Harbinger Publications.

Miller, E. 2003. *Letting Go of Stress* (Audio CD). Nevada City, CA: Emmett Miller. www .drmiller.com.

11

Focusing

In this chapter you will learn to:

* Listen to your body and your feelings

* Be more self-aware and self-accepting

* Use the wisdom of your body to guide positive change in your life

BACKGROUND

Although all of your senses are continually taking in information, your body's reactions to incoming stimuli often go unnoticed by your conscious mind. For example, when you were practicing the various relaxation exercises presented in the preceding chapters, you probably observed that when you take time out from a stressful day to relax and turn inward, you become more aware of how you feel physically and emotionally in the here and now. With this awareness, you can appreciate it when you feel good, and take action to feel better when you don't. By being more in tune with your body, you can respond sooner to subtle signs of tension and you can make wiser choices so that your body doesn't end up screaming at you in the form of symptoms like a headache or an anxiety attack before you can take care of yourself.

Focusing is another method you can use to listen to your body. The Focusing process can help you move from a stress-filled life to a life that better meets your needs. You'll be able to understand more completely how you feel about the situations and relationships in your life, know what you want in those situations and relationships, and how to make the needed changes. You'll be able to understand and begin the healing process for any of your emotional reactions that are out of proportion to the present day because they come from past hurts. You'll become kinder and gentler to yourself, more accepting of all your feelings, and more peaceful with and accepting of other people, too.

Do you remember times when you were nervous and you felt butterflies fluttering in your stomach or a heaviness weighing down your heart when you were sad? These are body sensations that contain meaning. In Focusing they are referred to as *felt senses*. Most likely you try to move beyond such feelings as quickly as possible because they're usually uncomfortable. But when you push past your felt senses by ignoring them, you miss out on opportunities to learn from them and to become more self-aware.

Focusing is a process that allows you to explore your felt senses and what they tell you about your emotions, how you feel about what's going on in your life, and what you can do to feel better. Focusing was discovered and developed by philosopher/psychologist Eugene Gendlin (1981) in the 1960s at the University of Chicago. It is based on his research into the question of why psychotherapy helps some clients and not others.

Gendlin noted that those clients who benefited most from therapy were the people who experienced "felt senses" (he invented the term). In other words, clients who were successful in therapy were those who tried to find the right words to express what they were feeling in their bodies about their problems in the moment. By contrast, unsuccessful clients stayed "in their heads," explaining and analyzing, rather than sensing something in their bodies about their problems that was, at first, hard to articulate.

Gendlin concluded that the ability to feel and explore your felt senses in the here and now is a key component of positive change. He linked this ability to what he called the *life-forward process* that all living organisms have naturally, but which we can lose touch with when we become separated from our inner wisdom. He developed methods to teach this awareness skill to his clients in therapy and later to people in all walks of life. He called it "Focusing."

SYMPTOM-RELIEF EFFECTIVENESS

Focusing can help you to become clearer about how you are feeling and what you want from life. It also can help you with making decisions, releasing addictions, unblocking your creativity, and dealing effectively with issues such as frustration, procrastination, self-criticism, low self-esteem, too much emotionality, and emotional numbness. Furthermore, Focusing has proved to be a viable stress-management technique (Weld 1992).

TIME TO MASTER

Plan on doing a month of daily half-hour Focusing sessions to learn the basics of how to use this skill. By then, you will know how useful it can be in your daily life. If obstacles arise that you are unable to overcome on your own or if you want more training, you can learn more about Focusing resources at the end of this chapter.

INSTRUCTIONS

The Power of Inner Presence

Presence is the ability to keep company with yourself and become a compassionate listener to your own emotions and felt senses. It is a key ability in the Focusing process. In the first two exercises, you are asked to remember times when you experienced Presence, using examples from your life. In the third exercise, you will practice offering Presence to your own feelings.

Exercise 1. The Shy Animal at the Edge of the Woods

- Imagine that you are taking a walk on a beautiful day, and you have all the time in the world to enjoy the day.

- When you pass by the edge of a small woodsy area, you catch sight of a shy animal peeking at you from between the trees. It's not a dangerous animal, just shy—perhaps a deer or a rabbit. Whatever shy animal comes to your imagination, that's fine.

- You stand still, hoping the animal will not run away, hoping this magical moment will continue one minute longer.

- What are the qualities or attitudes you would embody so the animal won't get scared and run away?

To answer that question, most people use words or phrases like: stillness, patience, warmth, empathy, love, acceptance, not being judgmental, allowing it to be as it is. It's amazing that we all know how to embody these qualities. These are the very qualities of Presence that are so important in Focusing.

Exercise 2. When Someone Listened to You

- Take a moment to recall a time when you told another person something meaningful to you, and you felt really heard by that person. Maybe this was someone in your family, a good friend, or a counselor.

- What did he or she do that gave you the impression you were being really heard? What qualities did you feel coming from that person? (Chances are they're the same kind of qualities you found in the previous exercise.)

- How did really being heard make you feel?

Did your listener give you his or her full attention? Did he or she give you the space, the sense of safety, and the encouragement you needed to express yourself? Did he or she acknowledge what you had to say? Do you remember how good it felt to be really heard? Maybe you clarified something. Perhaps you had a new insight. Maybe you came to a better understanding of yourself or some issue. It's possible that just saying what you had to say out loud to another person—and being heard—gave you a sense of relief or completion.

Here are some qualities of good listeners: They are usually friendly, interested, patient, curious, open, respectful, accepting, trustworthy, trusting, warm, empathic, and compassionate. Did your good listener have some of these qualities? How did he or she express them? Is this someone you would want to open yourself to again in the future?

Exercise 3. Presence with Yourself

- Take the next few minutes to observe how you feel in your body right now. Notice especially the areas of your throat, chest, and stomach (although any area of your body is welcome to come to awareness). Say to yourself "How am I, in here, right now?"

- When you become aware of something, let it be there.

- Gently acknowledge your feelings and sensations by saying to each one "Yes, I know you're there."

In this exercise, were you able to feel your feelings and sensations without wanting to make them different? Were you able to avoid being critical, analytical, or dismissive? How many of the qualities of the good listener did you just demonstrate?

Rather than trying to use your intellect to change how you feel, when you practice Focusing you allow your feelings to be as they are. When you keep your feelings company through Presence, they change naturally. No force or effort is needed. Cultivating the qualities of a good listener in Presence with your inner self will lead to a safe and trusting inner relationship in which your inner self feels heard, trusted, and accepted. Above all else, this is what Focusing is about.

You'll probably need to try this to believe it! So, let's try.

Practicing Focusing

There are many variations on the stages of Focusing; in fact, you can look up a number of them on the Internet. The approach presented in this chapter is based on *The Power of Focusing: A Practical Guide to Emotional Self-Healing* (Cornell 1996).

Here is an outline of the stages as you will practice them:

1. Choose an issue to work on.

2. Bring your attention into your body.

3. Give a gentle invitation to your felt senses and feelings.

4. Wait for a felt sense about your issue to form: Take the time to feel how your issue feels in your body.

5. Get to know your felt sense and begin to describe it in words and images.

6. Move back and forth between feeling your felt sense and describing it; find a description that fits the felt sense in the here and now.

7. Settle down to keep the felt sense company through Presence.

8. Be open and curious toward the felt sense, sense how it feels emotionally from its own point of view.

9. If the felt sense would like to tell you more, offer it gentle prompts to help it reveal itself.

10. Receive all that has come.

11. End the session with a gentle thank-you to your body.

Basic Focusing Instructions

PREPARING TO PRACTICE FOCUSING

1. Set aside thirty minutes a day in a quiet place where you will not be disturbed. If you have only ten minutes to focus, that's okay too. Be clear about when you plan to stop Focusing. You may want to use a timer, so your Focusing time has a limit. Be aware that, sometimes, your body will let you know that you are finished earlier than you had planned to be.

2. Keep a notebook by your side that you can use to record things that come up while you are Focusing that you want to remember. If you find it helpful, you can also write a few words during the Focusing session to stay alert and attentive.

3. Sit in a comfortable position that will allow you to stay alert. You can shift your position whenever you like. Be sure you are warm enough (or cool enough), and that your clothes are loose-fitting and comfortable.

4. Initially, practice Focusing where you won't be disturbed; later on, you can practice it in your everyday life.

5. You can choose a life issue to work on or you can be open to what your body brings up. It's a good idea to take a moment before you begin the session to decide which it will be. (Later in this chapter you'll find some tips for how to ask about specific issues.)

BRINGING YOUR ATTENTION INTO YOUR BODY

To bring your attention into your body, first take a few deep, relaxing breaths and either close your eyes or gaze downward without looking at anything in particular. Gently bring your awareness to your arms and your hands … your legs and your feet … and to the sensations of resting on the chair you're sitting on. Allow yourself to rest completely on the support that's there.

Now, sense into the middle area of your body: your throat … your chest … your stomach … your abdomen. If you have difficulty feeling a part of your body, move it around, wiggle it, or tense and release it. As you do this, pay attention to how it feels.

To be aware of all of your sensations, you need to be fully alert. If you start to drift off, open your eyes, stretch, and move around. Then bring your awareness back to your body. With more practice, you will be able to bring your awareness into your body more easily.

GIVING A GENTLE INVITATION TO A FELT SENSE

1. When your attention is resting gently in the areas of your throat, chest, stomach, and abdomen, you are now going to invite a felt sense to form.

2. If you have a specific issue you want to address, ask "What comes into my body about _____?" For example, "What comes into my body about the problem I am having with Steve?"

3. If you don't want to focus on a specific issue, let your body know that you are open to listening to whatever comes. Send out an open invitation by asking "What wants my awareness now?" Then wait, with your attention in that inner area of your body.

WAITING FOR THE FELT SENSE TO FORM

Rather than thinking about the problem, which will only give you more of what you already know, wait for a felt sense to form, which is how the whole issue or situation feels right now. At first, this body sense may be unclear. There will certainly be more to it than you could easily describe. If you aren't sure, you're probably on the right track! Welcome all sensations, emotions, memories, thoughts, and images that come up for you. Give yourself time. For example, "When

I think about this whole thing with Steve, I feel something in my chest … it's heavy … like a weight or something."

GETTING TO KNOW YOUR FELT SENSE: DESCRIBING IT

When you come in contact with a felt sense, greet it as you would a person. For instance, you might say "Hello," or "Yes, I know you're there." When you acknowledge it just as it is, notice how it responds to your greeting. Does it ease up, or get stronger, or does it do something else? For example, "When I greet this heaviness in my chest, it starts to feel a little lighter."

Let go for the moment your thoughts about the issue, your assumptions, and any previous realizations. Allow what you feel to be here freshly, as if you had never felt it before. (Perhaps you haven't!)

Now, from your fresh sensing of this felt sense, just as it is, in the here and now, allow a description to come of *what it feels like*. This could be in words, images, gestures, or even sounds. This is where it really pays to be a good listener.

RESONATING BETWEEN THE FELT SENSE AND ITS DESCRIPTION

1. Each time some kind of a description of the felt sense comes to you, check back with the felt sense to confirm whether it fits or not. For example, you feel "something" in your stomach. Patiently stay with it. Soon you may sense that this "something" has a quality of "tired." You can then take the word "tired" and check with the felt sense in your stomach: "Is the word 'tired' right?" If it doesn't fit, let it go. Then you might say to your felt sense, "'Tired' isn't right. *What does it feel like?*" It comes to you that it feels more like "drained." Checking back again with your felt sense, you might ask, "Is 'drained' right?" Perhaps the feeling you get from the felt sense is that "drained" is partly right, so you ask the felt sense, "So, 'drained' is part of it, and there's something more…?" Keep checking back with your felt sense with each new description until you find one that fits it with a satisfying sense of rightness. For example: "Drained, sucked dry."

2. When your description catches the essence of your felt sense, when the image, sound, gesture, word, or phrase fits perfectly, you will know because you'll feel an inner sense of rightness, a kind of satisfying inner "Yes, that's it."

3. If the felt sense changes, follow it with your awareness. Again search for a description of how the felt sense feels in the here and now. Once you have a match between the description and the felt sense, take the time to feel what this is like.

KEEP THE FELT SENSE COMPANY THROUGH PRESENCE

Saying "hello" and finding a satisfying description are similar to the first stages of getting to know someone. After saying "hello" and finding a description, you settle down for the rest of the conversation by imagining that you are sitting down next to this "something" inside you to get to know it better. It's best if you can find a relaxed quality of not being in a hurry; you are just keeping the felt sense company. You have all the time in the world.

BE OPEN AND CURIOUS TOWARD THE FELT SENSE; SENSE HOW IT FEELS EMOTIONALLY FROM ITS OWN POINT OF VIEW

Keep sensing the felt sense with a listening quality of Presence. Bring it your interested curiosity. Begin to sense its emotion. This is its own emotion, not how you feel about it. For example, to you it might be uncomfortable. But it itself might be scared. For instance, if you feel heavy in your chest, you might ask your felt sense, "What is the emotional quality of this heaviness?" You can even suggest some possibilities: *"Is it a sad heaviness?" "Is it a tired heaviness?"* Another way to say this is, you are sensing how *it* feels from *its* point of view. You can even ask your felt sense, "How do you feel from your point of view?"

OFFER YOUR FELT SENSE GENTLE PROMPTS TO HELP IT REVEAL ITSELF

1. If you sense that your felt sense would like to tell you more, you can offer gentle prompts in the form of unobtrusive questions, or invitations. Each time you ask a question, wait for an answer from your body. Observe how this whole thing feels in your body right now.

2. Skip the "why" questions. "Why" questions invite intellectual explanations that take you out of your body and into your rational mind. Instead of asking "Why," consider asking "What." Keep in mind that you haven't heard the message of your felt sense until you've learned something new.

3. Here are some "what" questions that will help your felt sense open up to you. Try to sense which question *it* would like to be asked.

What's the worst (or the best) of this whole thing?

What is it about this whole thing that brings this feeling?

What image captures this felt quality?

What do you [the felt sense] want me to know?

What is it not wanting to happen?

What is it wanting to happen?"

What would it feel like if it was all okay?

What is in the way of everything being all okay?

What is the question that needs to be asked?

4. After asking a question, wait patiently for a response from your body. If you like, you can suggest a possible answer to your question and listen to how your felt sense responds. For example, in response to "What is it not wanting to happen?" you might ask if it is not wanting you to be hurt or criticized. Then, sense how it responds.

5. Not all felt senses are unpleasant or uncomfortable. When you are Focusing on a positive felt sense, you may want to ask it if it has something that it wants to show you or give you. It is also useful to inquire what it needs to be in your life more of the time.

RECEIVING ALL THAT HAS COME TO YOU

At some point in the Focusing procedure, you will likely experience a new insight as well as a shift in your body that tells you that something has changed. Perhaps your body feels more open or you get a sense of relief or release. It may be quite pronounced or very subtle. It generally feels good. The insight may simply be that you feel more clear or definite, or it may be like an important missing piece to a puzzle or an "Aha experience," or an indication of what you need to do next. It is always something more than what you "knew" intellectually.

Whatever the enjoyable experience is for you, allow it to fill your body as much as it wants to. Let it settle in. Even though most shifts and insights will be small ones, take the time to feel them in your body, accept them, and appreciate them.

ENDING YOUR FOCUSING SESSION

1. A useful rule of thumb for ending is to give yourself one minute at the end for every ten minutes of Focusing. When it is close to stopping time, ask your felt sense if it feels okay to end the session in a couple of minutes or if there is something else it wants you to know. Occasionally, important information is revealed at this moment. Or you may get the feeling that you've done enough for now.

2. Change often takes place in small steps over time in Focusing. An issue may not be resolved in one session or even several. Remember, each session is an opportunity to

cultivate your relationship with your inner self and serves as a foundation for the next session.

3. Thank your body and your felt senses for being with you during this session. Even if the session revealed nothing new, let your inner self know that you appreciate spending time with it.

4. Let your body know that you will be back to continue the conversation that you have opened up, particularly if an issue is unresolved.

5. At the end of the session, go over what came up and perhaps take notes about your experiences in your journal so as not to forget them. It's often useful to write at least a phrase or an image in your journal to help you recall where you left off so that you can continue from there in your next session if you want to (and if your *felt sense* wants to). If you gained an important insight or felt that the shift in your body was particularly noteworthy, you may want to write about how your body feels and then tell the story of the entire session leading up to the shift, especially what came just before the insight or shift.

6. You also may want to create something, for example, to draw or sculpt what came to you. Or you may want to tell a trusted friend about your experience.

7. You may feel finished with this particular issue at this point, or this may be the first of many layers of meaning that will gradually peel away as you continue the Focusing.

CLEARING A SPACE

Another way to start your Focusing session, when you have a lot going on, is to use a step called "Clearing a Space." In "Clearing a Space," you take an inventory of your issues and then find the "all-okay" body sense that your body knows how to feel. Here is how you "clear a space":

- Once your awareness is in the middle part of your body, ask "How am I inside right now?" Pause for a while to sense the answer to that question from your body.

- Then ask "What's between me and feeling fine right now?" Don't answer with your mind; give your body time to form an answer. Be open to whatever comes up: "Problem with Steve.... Dirty house.... Bills.... Lonely.... Sad about Leo dying.... Noisy neighbors.... Promotion at work...."

- Greet each concern as it comes up without going into it, then say hello to it and set it somewhere outside of yourself. Perhaps you can imagine putting it a comfortable distance away from you on a table or on a shelf in the room. You can come back and focus on each one of these concerns in turn, if you like, at a later time. Return to your body and repeat this process by asking the question *"What's between me and feeling fine right now?"* until nothing else comes up.

- Finally, ask *"Which of these issues am I most drawn to work on today?"* Rather than deciding intellectually, listen to your body. You could also ask, "Which of these issues needs my attention the most right now?"

Sometimes, it may feel as though your list of issues is so long you'll never get to everything! Don't worry. Working on just one issue can change the way they all feel. Everything is connected to everything else.

When You Have Difficulty Finding Your Felt Sense

If you have difficulty getting a felt sense, remember that a felt sense can be anything you feel in your body—good, bad, or indifferent. Set aside your doubt for a little while and let yourself be open to all sensations, even the subtle ones. Notice, for instance, if there is a difference between how your stomach feels and how your chest feels. You can notice a difference even when it's difficult to describe what the difference is. Take your time to sense the difference and notice if a word, phrase, or image occurs to you that describes one or both areas of your body or the difference between the areas.

For example, you might find that your stomach is more relaxed than your chest, then you might notice feeling a band of tension around your chest. If you feel something, acknowledge it by saying, "Yes, I know you're there." As you continue to sit with this something, you can try on different words or various combinations of words such as "My stomach feels tight," "It feels cold ... and resigned." Or "It's sort of warm ... and hopeful." Even if you don't find the right description, you are at least paying attention to your inner self, and thereby building a relationship with your inner self that is essential for Focusing to work.

Focusing is not the same as getting in touch with your feelings. If you feel unhappy, take your time to sense where in your body you sense the unhappiness. Just doing this can bring a sense of relief: "Oh, it's in my heart. I thought it was all over my body!"

Focusing is about being *with* your feelings, not being *in* your feelings. When you sit with your feelings and have a conversation with them, you can appreciate them as parts of you that have something important to tell you. When you are *in* your feelings, they surround you, and you are at risk of being overwhelmed by them.

As you search for the right description of a felt sense, you may lose track of how you feel inside. Gently bring your awareness back inside to your felt sense. Does it still feel the same or has it changed? If it is the same, repeat the last description that seemed close or got some response. If it is different, how is it different? You can write down your descriptions in your journal as they come up so you can refer to what you wrote if you get lost.

Even if your felt sense feels the same, it is wise to check periodically to see if the description you originally came up with still fits. This is particularly true when you come back to a felt sense you worked on in a preceding Focusing session. If it has changed, look for a new description that fits it now.

When you get an image, pay attention to whether it is in your body or if you seem to be seeing it before your eyes. Here are some examples of body-felt images: "a block of dry ice in my stomach," "a sword piercing my heart," and "an expanse of green hills in my chest."

Here are some visual images that can seem to appear in front of your eyes rather than in your body: "I see a squall on the ocean," "I see a child clutching her teddy bear," and "I see a bronze sculpture of my husband." Treat body-felt images as felt senses. Show your visual image to your felt sense and ask it how it feels about the image. Each time the image changes, ask your body how it feels about it. In this way, you will stay with your body.

When you find something that makes it difficult for you to be a friendly and accepting listener to a felt sense, move your attention to the part of you that is having the reaction. This is referred to as "the feeling about the feeling." You may be annoyed about feeling frightened, impatient about feeling stuck, or anxious about feeling adventurous. This "feeling about the feeling" becomes the new felt sense. Rather than trying to ignore it, say hello to it and take time to get to know it. It will either relax once its meaning is acknowledged, in which case you can return to the first felt sense, or it will become the focus of your session.

SUGGESTIONS FOR FOCUSING ON SPECIAL PROBLEMS

In this section you will find suggestions to help you when you are Focusing on particular problems. Combine these with the instructions already described in this chapter to explore the issues that are relevant for you.

Strong feelings. When these threaten to overwhelm you, this indicates that something important wants to be heard. Imagine yourself sitting beside your strong feelings, willing to listen to what they have to tell you. Be sure to say "hello" to them. The sense of Presence is most important here. *You are not your feelings.* If you are saying "I'm sad," try saying instead, "I'm sensing that something in me is sad." Sometimes it helps to put a gentle hand on the place where you have the strong feeling, as if your hand is communicating, "Yes, I'm with you."

Habits. When you want to change a habit, bring awareness into your body and ask to get a felt sense of the part of you that wants to continue the habit. This might be the part of you that wants to eat junk food, smoke cigarettes, watch TV, or play games on the computer until all hours of the night. Just listen to this part of yourself. It hasn't been heard because you probably tend either to condemn it ("smoking is going to kill me") or make excuses for it ("I work so hard, smoking is one of my few pleasures"). Explore with this part of you what purpose it is pursuing from its point of view. Also, you may want to ask if there is another part of you that has been hiding beneath this habit.

Making decisions. When you need to make a decision about which of two or more options to choose, first do some research and weigh the pros and cons logically. Then, take one option at a time and explore how it feels in your body, by asking something like "What does moving to a larger apartment feel like in my body?" Once you have a felt sense, you will be able to do the Focusing with it, as already described. You can repeat this with the other option or options you are considering.

Physical Symptoms. When you want to learn the inner meaning of a physical symptom, first bring your awareness to the middle part of your body, and then to the location of the symptom. Say hello to the feeling there, spend some time sensing the felt quality of it, and confirm with your body the right description of it. You can then do the rest of the Focusing process with it. Sensing *its* emotion will be especially interesting.

Feeling stuck. When you want to take some action but you don't because you're feeling stuck, bring your attention to the middle part of your body and experience the felt sense of that part of you that doesn't want to take the action. Listen with compassion, for this is another part of yourself that has not had a voice. You may be astonished by what comes up.

Interpersonal problems. When you are having an interpersonal problem, bring your attention to the middle part of your body and ask your body to give you the feeling associated with this problem. Once you've found an accurate description for it, get to know it with the rest of the Focusing process.

Inner critic. When your inner critic gets in your way, you can turn toward it with a gentle hello. You can assume that it's worried about something. That's because inner critical voices are actually trying to protect us, just like worried parents. When this part of you realizes you are listening to it, it won't need to speak so critically anymore.

SPECIAL CONSIDERATIONS

1. Asking a felt sense what it wants allows you to understand it better. You don't have to do what a felt sense wants to do if you'd prefer not to. Simply acknowledging what it wants is often sufficient. However, if you avoid taking positive action in your life and your Focusing repeatedly indicates that taking that positive action is the right thing to do, you are likely to get stuck in Focusing, as well as in your life. The action that you take may

be a small one, not necessarily the big action that something in you wants, because that is what is possible at this time.

2. If your felt sense is not cooperating, go back and be sure that you are really in Presence. It is crucial to establish a trusting relationship with your body before it will feel safe enough to open up to you. If you are not in Presence, but are identified with another part of yourself that is trying to make something change, you'll need to say hello to this part of you, too, before trust and safety begin to return.

3. Although this chapter has presented Focusing as a process that you can do on your own, it is often practiced with a partner. One person listens and supports the other person as he or she uses Focusing to address his or her own issues out loud. Each person spends an equal amount of time as the listener and as the Focuser. An excellent way to learn to do Focusing with a partner or learn more about Focusing on your own is to attend a workshop or phone seminar. (See the resources listed at the end of this chapter.)

A REAL-LIFE EXAMPLE OF THE POWER OF FOCUSING

Lois was a retired grandmother who was unaccustomed to listening to her feelings and unaware of her body as a resource for this deep internal form of communication. But after hearing how much her daughter had gotten from learning Focusing, and with her own seventieth birthday coming soon, she was motivated to try Focusing herself. At first, she was afraid to stop her activities and carve out a space to focus on herself. Then one day, she locked herself in her bedroom and sat down with a notebook and pen beside her. She set her kitchen timer for thirty minutes, closed her eyes, took a few deep breaths, and turned her attention within to the inside of her body. She found this hard to do because she kept thinking of other people and things she needed to get done.

Finally, her mind settled down sufficiently so that she was able to become aware of how she felt in her body. Gently she felt her arms and her hands ... her legs and her feet ... her body's contact with the chair. She allowed her breathing to deepen, and she sensed the feeling of spaciousness that came into the middle of her body. Then she scanned through her entire body to sense how it was feeling. Her chest was tense.... So was her throat.... Her shoulders were aching.... Her stomach felt upset.... Inwardly, she said hello to each of these places and sensations. Then she waited.

Her throat became very tight and she began to cry as she thought, "Life is short and then you die...." She thought of some of the things that she had wanted to do with her life that she had not done, and her tears came more intensely. Then she remembered that in Focusing she was the listener to her inner feelings, in Presence. She put a gentle hand on her throat, and said *"Yes, I know you're there"* to her tears.

Lois said to herself, *"So many things that I wanted to do with my life that I haven't done.... How does that whole thing feel now in my body?"* She could feel a burning tightness in her throat, and acknowledged it by saying *"Hello, I know you are there."* Immediately, she felt her throat relax a little bit.

She began to sense for a description of what she felt in her throat. Each time she came up with a word or image, she checked with the felt sense in her throat to see if it was a good fit: *"Tense and burning ... is that right?"* She listened.... *"That's part of it ... tense, burning and ... sad?"* She waited.... *"A little sad ... something more ... more mad than sad."* This felt almost right. She said, *"Tense, burning, sad, and angry."* Lois felt something release in her throat as she realized that she was more angry than saddened about missing out on doing some of the things she wanted to do. Her throat felt more relaxed and energized, as did the rest of her body. She stayed with this insight and the feelings, and allowed them to sink in.

It felt right to go further and ask the felt sense in her throat this question: *"What is the worst aspect of this whole missing out on my life thing?"* After a while she got an image of herself silent during dinner on a cruise liner with her husband and a couple of their friends. Her husband and friends were bickering. She took this image to the felt sense in her throat and, after a while, she got the sense of being trapped. She checked with her felt sense to see if this was right ... it was almost right. She sat with her felt sense until the phrase "held hostage" came to mind, at which point she felt a perfect fit between the words and her felt sense. Along with this insight, she noticed that her throat was no longer tight and burning; instead it felt warm, open, and relaxed.

Lois took some time to allow the shift in her body and the new insight to sink in. Her kitchen timer was about to ring, so she asked her felt sense if there was anything else it wanted her to know, and nothing came up. She thanked her felt sense and her body for being with her during the session, and promised to return the following day to focus further on this issue. She wrote down the words "held hostage" and "more mad than sad" in her journal.

The next day in her Focusing session, it was a little easier to bring her attention into her body. From there she focused on the felt sense in her throat; it felt mostly relaxed but a little tense again. She remembered the words from the day before, and asked "This is about feeling held hostage, right?" She sensed that there was something more. She stayed with the tenseness, and repeated, "I feel held hostage, and ... what more?" After a while, she got a distinct sense of feeling guilty. So she checked with her felt sense in her throat: "I feel held hostage and I feel guilty?" That didn't feel quite right, so she discarded "guilty" and waited.

Then it occurred to her that she felt it was her fault that she was held hostage. When she checked this with her felt sense, she got the impression that this was closer to being right. Listening intently to her felt sense, she heard the words "I just go along with what others want," so she asked her felt sense, *"I just go along with what others want and end up feeling held hostage, right?"* This felt like a perfect fit; she felt tingly all over. She took her time to allow this insight and feeling to soak in.

She could have ended there, because this was a major breakthrough for her, but she wanted to know if there was anything she could do about her lifelong habit of going along with what others wanted. So she asked her felt sense, "What is it wanting to happen?" She waited for a response. Then, she remembered that in real life, the bickering couple that had come up for her in her image the day before had invited her and her husband to go on another cruise with them. She tried to return to her throat, but she couldn't dismiss this thought. Her throat felt tight and burning and she had a very strong urge to push this thought away and to scream "No!"

Finally, it occurred to her that saying no to the bickering couple was what her felt sense was wanting to happen, at which point she immediately felt a sense of relief and freedom that she had never experienced before. She sat with these feelings and this insight for quite a while; then, feeling fulfilled, she thanked her felt sense and her body for being with her in the session and promised to return to Focusing the next day. She wrote down her experience and insight and resolved to tell her husband that she wanted to turn down the couple's invitation.

As Lois continued Focusing, she became able to reclaim her feeling self, take new risks, and set new limits. When she thought about how simple it was, she laughed. She discovered that there was no major fallout when she expressed what she wanted or said no to what she didn't want. For example, her daughter was completely understanding when she stopped being an "ever-ready babysitter" for her grandchildren. She spent a number of Focusing sessions exploring what she wanted. She began to make suggestions to her friends about which restaurants she wanted to go to for their weekly luncheon. She redecorated an unused bedroom as her den to use for Focusing and her projects. She planned trips with her husband to places she wanted to go.

FINAL THOUGHTS

As you can see from Lois's story and hopefully your own experience, Focusing allows you to get a handle on what is true and important for you in the here and now. When you're feeling stressed out, it can help you get in touch with what stands between you and feeling better and can lead the way to show you what you can do about feeling stressed. Through Focusing, your issues can become better understood, resolved, or released; and if something more is needed, it will become clear. When you take on the role of good listener to your inner self, it is likely you will feel better after Focusing even if a session doesn't yield any insights simply because you are giving yourself the gifts of interested attention, respect, and acceptance.

FURTHER READING

Cornell, A. W. 1996. *The Power of Focusing: A Practical Guide to Emotional Self-Healing.* Oakland, CA: New Harbinger Publications.

———. W. 2005. *The Radical Acceptance of Everything.* Berkeley, CA: Calluna Press.

Gendlin, E. 1981. *Focusing.* New York: Bantam Books.

Weld, S. E. 1992. Stress management outcome: Prediction of differential outcome by personality characteristics. PhD diss, University of Ottawa, Canada.

WEBSITES

Ann Weiser Cornell, Focusing Resources: www.focusingresources.com

The Focusing Institute: www.focusing.org.

Inner Relationship Focusing: www.innerrelationship.com

12

Refuting Irrational Ideas

In this chapter you will learn to:

* Recognize how your thoughts influence your feelings, physical sensations, and behavior

* Assess your distressing thoughts

* Counteract your needless distressing thoughts

BACKGROUND

Almost every minute of your conscious life you are engaging in self-talk, your internal thought language. These are the sentences with which you describe and interpret the world. If your self-talk is accurate and in touch with reality, you function well. If it is irrational and untrue, you experience stress and emotional disturbance. Here is an example of irrational self-talk: "I can't bear to be alone." No physically healthy person has ever died merely from being alone. Being alone may be uncomfortable, undesirable, and frustrating, but you can live with it and live through it.

Another example of irrational self-talk might be, "I should never be cruel to my child. If I am, I'll know I'm a rotten person." The phrase "should never" allows no possibility of flaw or failure. When the inevitable quarrel occurs, you indict yourself as entirely rotten—all on the basis of a single incident.

Irrational ideas may be based on outright misperceptions ("When the airplane's wing shakes, I know it's going to fall off") or the perfectionist's "shoulds," "oughts," and "musts" ("I ought to keep quiet rather than risk upsetting anyone"). Inaccurate self-talk such as "I need love" is emotionally dangerous compared to the more realistic "I want love very much, but I don't absolutely need it, and can survive and feel reasonably happy without it." "How terrible to be rejected" is fear-producing in comparison to "I find it unpleasant, awkward in the moment, and feel regretful when I am rejected." Imperatives such as "I've got to be more helpful around the house" can be converted to more rational statements, such as "There would probably be more peace and compatibility in my home if I did a greater share of the work."

Albert Ellis developed a system to attack irrational ideas or beliefs and replace them with realistic statements about the world. He called his system "rational emotive therapy" and wrote about it, with coauthor Harper, in *A Guide to Rational Living* (1997) first published in 1961. Ellis's basic thesis is that emotions are only partially related to actual events. Between the event and the emotion is realistic or unrealistic self-talk. The self-talk produces the emotions. Your own thoughts, directed and controlled by you, are what create anxiety, anger, and depression. Ellis later renamed his system "rational emotive behavior therapy," stressing that people's actions as well as their emotions are influenced by their ideas. The image below shows how it works.

FEEDBACK LOOP

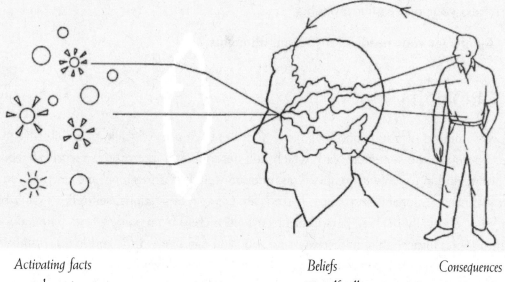

*Activating facts
and events*

*Beliefs
negative self-talk
(irrational ideas)*

*Consequences
emotions, sensations,
behaviors*

Example

Ellis's model is as simple as A, B, C:

ACTIVATING FACTS AND EVENTS

A mechanic replaces a fuel pump he honestly believes was malfunctioning, but the car's performance doesn't improve. The customer is very upset and demands that the mechanic put the old fuel pump back.

BELIEFS OR NEGATIVE SELF-TALK ABOUT THE ACTIVATING FACTS OR EVENT

The mechanic says to himself,

He's just a grouch—nothing would please him.

and

Why the hell do I get all the tough jobs?

and

I ought to have figured this out by now.

and, finally,

I'm not much of a mechanic.

CONSEQUENCES: EMOTIONS, SENSATIONS, AND BEHAVIOR

The mechanic feels anger, resentment, and depression, as well as a sense of worthlessness. He feels a knot in his stomach. As the day wears on, he develops a headache. He reluctantly agrees to put in the old fuel pump, but for the rest of the day he is short-tempered with coworkers and then with his family later that night.

The mechanic may later say to himself, *"That guy really made me mad."* But it is not the customer or anything the customer has done that produces the anger—it is the mechanic's own self-talk, his interpretation of reality. Such irrational self-talk can be changed and the stressful emotions, sensations, and behavior that result from this self-talk can be changed with it.

SYMPTOM-RELIEF EFFECTIVENESS

Rimm and Litvak (1969) found that negative self-talk produced substantial physiological arousal. In other words, your body tenses and becomes stressed when you use irrational arguments such as:

People seem to ignore me at parties.

⇩

It's obvious that I'm either boring or unattractive to them.

⇩

How terrible!

The emotional results of irrational negative self-talk are anxiety, depression, rage, guilt, jealousy, low frustration tolerance, shame, and a sense of worthlessness. Rational emotive behavior therapy has been shown to be effective in decreasing the frequency and intensity of these emotions.

TIME TO MASTER

Assessment of your irrational beliefs, plus homework sufficient to refute one of these beliefs, can take approximately twenty minutes a day for two weeks. Rational emotive imagery, the process by which you work directly on changing your emotions, also takes about two weeks if you practice ten minutes a day.

INSTRUCTIONS

Beliefs Inventory

The following Beliefs Inventory will help you uncover some of the irrational ideas that contribute to unhappiness and stress. Take the test now, score it, and note the sections where your scores are highest.

Note that it is not necessary to think over any item very long. Mark your answer quickly and go on to the next statement. Be sure to mark how you actually think about the statement, not how you think you should think.

BELIEFS INVENTORY

Somewhat Agree	Agree	Disagree	Score	Belief
				1. It is important to me that others approve of me.
				2. I hate to fail at anything.
				3. People who do wrong deserve what they get.
				4. When I don't get what I want, I get mad.
				5. Negative feelings are natural consequences of negative events.
				6. I need everyone to like me.
				7. I avoid things I cannot do well.
				8. Too many bad people escape the punishment they deserve.
				9. I'm easily frustrated when things don't go my way.
				10. The best way to avoid pain and be happy is to have control over your environment.
				11. I find it hard to go against what others think.
				12. It is very important to me to be successful in everything I do.
				13. Those who do wrong deserve to be blamed and punished.
				14. I often get disturbed over situations I don't like.
				15. People who are miserable are victims of circumstances beyond their control.
				16. I often worry about how much people approve of and accept me.
				17. It upsets me a lot when I make mistakes.
				18. Immorality should be strongly punished.
				19. I get extremely annoyed when others inconvenience me.
				20. The more problems a person has, the less happy he or she will be.
				21. I worry a lot about what people think about me.

				22. I'm afraid to do things that I cannot do well.
				23. I hold grudges against people who have wronged me.
				24. Things should be different than the way they are.
				25. Inconsiderate people annoy the heck out of me.
				26. I often can't get my mind off some concern.
				27. I usually put off important decisions.
				28. Everyone needs someone he or she can depend on for help and advice.
				29. It is almost impossible to overcome the influences of the past.
				30. To be happy, I would need a lifelong leisurely vacation.
				31. I can't stand to take chances.
				32. I avoid facing my problems.
				33. People absolutely need a source of strength outside themselves.
				34. If I had had different experiences, I could be more like the person I want to be.
				35. I feel most content when I have nothing to do.
				36. I worry a lot about certain things in the future.
				37. I often put things off.
				38. There are certain people upon whom I greatly depend.
				39. I often think of past experiences as affecting me now.
				40. I prefer quiet leisure above all things.
				41. I feel anxious when I think about unexpected dangers or future events.
				42. It is difficult for me to do unpleasant chores even if they benefit me.
				43. I must always seek the advice of others before making any important decision.
				44. Once something strongly affects your life, it always will.

				45. It is only through leisure and relaxation that I can find fulfillment.
				46. If something happened that I was afraid of, it would be terrible, and I couldn't stand it.
				47. I dislike responsibility and avoid it if I can.
				48. I need people in my life whom I can rely upon to feel safe.
				49. People never change basically.
				50. I shouldn't have to work at being happy.

Scoring the Beliefs Inventory:

Give the items you marked as "Disagree" a score of 0, items you marked as "Somewhat Agree" a score of 1 and items you marked as "Agree" a score of 2.

Add up your points for items 1, 6, 11, 16, and 21, and enter the total here: _____ . The higher the total, the more you agree with the irrational idea that *it is an absolute necessity for an adult to have love and approval from peers, family, and friends.*

Add up your points for items 2, 7, 12, 17, and 22, and enter the total here: _____ . The higher the total, the more you agree with the irrational idea that *you must be unfailingly competent and almost perfect in all you undertake.*

Add up your points for items 3, 8, 13, 18, and 23, and enter the total here: _____ . The higher the total, the more you agree with the irrational idea that *certain people are evil, wicked, and villainous, and should be punished.*

Add up your points for items 4, 9, 14, 19, and 24, and enter the total here: _____ . The higher the total, the more you agree with the irrational idea that *it is horrible when things are not the way you would like them to be.*

Add up your points for items 5, 10, 15, 20, and 25, and enter the total here: _____ . The higher the total, the more you agree with the irrational idea that *external events cause most human misery—that people simply react as events trigger their emotions.*

Add up your points for items 26, 31, 36, 41, and 46, and enter the total here: _____ . The higher the total, the more you agree with the irrational idea that *you should feel fear or anxiety about anything that is unknown, uncertain, or potentially dangerous.*

Add up your points for items 27, 32, 37, 42, and 47, and enter the total here: _____ . The higher the total, the more you agree with the irrational idea that *it is easier to avoid than face life's difficulties and responsibilities.*

Add up your points for items 28, 33, 38, 43, and 48, and enter the total here: _____.
The higher the total, the more you agree with the irrational idea that *you need something other or stronger or greater than yourself to rely upon.*

Add up your points for items 29, 34, 39, 44, and 49, and enter the total here: _____.
The higher the total, the more you agree with the irrational idea that *the past has a lot to do with determining the present.*

Add up your points for items 30, 35, 40, 45, and 50, and enter the total here: _____.
The higher the total, the more you agree with the irrational idea that *happiness can be achieved by inaction, passivity, and endless leisure.*

Irrational Ideas

At the root of all irrational thinking is the assumption that things are done to you: "That really got me down.... She makes me nervous.... Places like that scare me.... Being lied to makes me see red." Nothing is done to you. Events happen in the world. You experience those activating events (A), engage in self-talk (B), and consequently experience an emotion (C) resulting from the self-talk. *A does not cause C—B causes C.* If your self-talk is irrational and unrealistic, you create unpleasant emotions.

Two common forms of irrational self-talk are statements that "awfulize" and "absolutize." You awfulize by making catastrophic, nightmarish interpretations of your experience. A momentary chest pain is a heart attack, the grumpy boss intends to fire you, your spouse takes a night job and the thought of being alone is unthinkably terrible. Awfulizing involves exaggerating unwanted events, traits, or behaviors, while almost always ignoring the positive ones. The emotions that follow awfulizing self-talk tend themselves to be awful—you are responding to your own description of the world.

For instance, if you think that a situation is painful, boring, or difficult and you exaggerate these qualities beyond your ability to cope, you'd likely feel overwhelmed. If you define people by their flaws or misdeeds and tell yourself these flaws or misdeeds are horrible, they become terrible people. It becomes easy to justify your anger. Irrational self-statements that absolutize often include words like "should," "must," "ought," "always," and "never." The idea is that other people or things must be a certain way, or you must be a certain way. Any deviation from that particular value or standard is bad. The person who fails to live up to the standard is bad. In reality, the standard is what's bad, because it is inflexible and narrow-minded.

Albert Ellis suggested ten basic irrational ideas, which are listed below. To these we have added some additional common self-statements that are highly unrealistic. Based on your scores on the Beliefs Inventory, and your knowledge of the situations in which you characteristically experience stress, place a check mark next to the ones that seem to apply to you.

—— 1. **It is an absolute necessity for an adult to have love and approval from peers, family, and friends.** In fact, pleasing all the people in your life is impossible. Even those who basically like and approve of you will be turned off by some behaviors and qualities. This irrational belief is one of the greatest causes of misery.

—— 2. **You must be unfailingly competent, successful, and almost perfect in all that you undertake.** The results of believing that you must behave perfectly are self-blame for inevitable failure, lowered self-esteem, perfectionistic standards applied to spouse and friends, and paralysis and fear at attempting anything. Compare this to the belief that you can strive to do your best and learn from your errors.

—— 3. **Certain people are evil, wicked, and villainous and should be punished.** A more realistic position is that they are behaving in ways that are antisocial or inappropriate. They are perhaps stupid, ignorant, or neurotic and may need to change their behavior.

—— 4. **It is horrible when people and things are not the way you would like them to be.** This might be described as the spoiled-child syndrome. As soon as the tire goes flat the self-talk starts: "Why does this happen to me? Damn, I can't take this. It's awful, I'll get all filthy." Any inconvenience, problem, or failure to get your way is likely to be met with such awfulizing self-statements. The result is intense irritation and stress.

—— 5. **External events cause most human misery—people simply react as events trigger their emotions.** A logical extension of this belief is that you must control the external events in order to create happiness or avoid sorrow. The fact is, our control is limited and we are at a loss to completely manipulate the wills of others. Interpreting an event as the reason for your unhappiness can keep you stuck. Although you may have only limited control over others, you do have enormous control over your thoughts, emotions, and behavior.

—— 6. **You should feel fear or anxiety about anything that is unknown, uncertain, or potentially dangerous.** Many describe this as "a little bell goes off and I think I ought to start worrying." They begin to rehearse their catastrophe scenarios. Increasing the fear or anxiety in the face of uncertainty makes coping more difficult and adds to stress. Saving the fear response for actual, perceived danger allows you to enjoy uncertainty as a novel and exciting experience.

—— 7. **It is easier to avoid than to face life's difficulties and responsibilities.** There are many ways of ducking responsibilities: "I should tell him I'm no longer interested—but not tonight.... I'd like to get another job, but I'm just too tired on my days off to look.... A leaky faucet won't hurt anything ...." If this way of thinking applies to you, write down your standard excuses to avoid responsibility:

Area of Responsibility	*Method of Avoidance*
_____	_____
_____	_____
_____	_____
_____	_____

—— 8. **You absolutely need something other or stronger or greater than yourself to rely upon.** This belief becomes a psychological trap in which your independent judgment and your awareness of your particular needs are undermined by a complete reliance on higher authority.

—— 9. **The past has a lot to do with determining the present.** Just because you were once strongly affected by something does not mean that you must continue the habits you formed to cope with the original situation. Those old patterns and ways of responding are just decisions made so many times they have become nearly automatic. You can identify those old decisions and start changing them right now. You can learn from past experience, but you don't have to be overly attached to it.

—— 10. **Happiness can be achieved by inaction, passivity, and endless leisure.** This is called the Elysian fields syndrome. There is more to happiness than perfect relaxation.

OTHER IRRATIONAL IDEAS

—— 1. **People are fragile and should never be hurt.** This irrational belief results in failure to openly communicate important feelings, and in self-sacrifice that gives up what is nourishing and pleasurable (Farquhar and Lowe 1974). Because everything you want seems to hurt or deprive someone else, you feel frustration, helplessness, and depression. Relationships become full of dead space where conflicts developed and nothing was said to resolve them.

—— 2. **Good relationships are based on mutual sacrifice and a focus on giving.** This belief rests on the assumption that it is better to give than to receive. It is expressed in a reluctance to ask for what you want and need and the anticipation that your hidden needs will be divined and provided for. Unfortunately, constant self-denial usually results in bitterness and withdrawal.

—— 3. **If you don't go to great lengths to please others, they will abandon or reject you.** This belief is a by-product of low self-esteem. You usually run less risk of rejection if you offer others your true unembellished self. They can take it or leave it. However, if they get to know the real you, you don't have to worry about slacking off, letting down your guard, and being rejected later.

—— 4. **When people disapprove of you, it invariably means you are wrong or bad.** This extremely crippling belief sparks chronic anxiety in most interpersonal situations (Farquhar and Lowe 1974). The irrationality is contained in the generalization of one specific fault or unattractive feature to a total indictment of the self.

—— 5. **Happiness, pleasure, and fulfillment can occur only in the presence of others, and being alone is horrible.** Pleasure, self-worth, and fulfillment can be experienced alone as well as with others (Farquhar and Lowe 1974). Being alone is growth-producing and, at times, desirable.

—— 6. **There is perfect love, and a perfect relationship.** Subscribers to this belief often feel dissatisfied and resentful of one close relationship after another. Nothing is quite right because they are waiting for the perfect fit, which never comes.

—— 7. **You shouldn't have to feel pain; you are entitled to a good life.** The realistic position is that pain is an inevitable part of human life. Pain frequently accompanies tough, healthy decisions and the process of growth. Life is not fair, and sometimes you will suffer no matter what you do.

—— 8. **Your worth as a person depends on how much you achieve and produce.** A more rational assessment of your real worth would depend on such things as your capacity to experience being fully alive, feeling everything it means to be human (Farquhar and Lowe 1974).

—— 9. **Anger is automatically bad and destructive.** Anger as an act is frequently cleansing and can be an honest communication of current feelings, without attacking the personal worth and security of others (Farquhar and Lowe 1974).

—— 10. **It is bad or wrong to be selfish.** The truth is that no one knows your needs and wants better than you, and no one else has as great an interest in seeing them fulfilled. Your happiness is your responsibility. Being selfish means you are accepting that responsibility. At the same time, you can respect others' right to take responsibility for their own happiness.

—— 11. **You are helpless and have no control over what you experience or feel.** This belief is at the heart of much depression and anxiety. In truth, we have some control over interpersonal situations, and a lot of control over how we interpret and emotionally respond to life events.

You can add other irrational beliefs to this list:

_____

_____

_____

_____

_____

_____

Identifying Elusive Irrational Ideas

Much of the difficulty in uncovering irrational self-talk results from the speed and invisibility of thoughts. They may be lightning quick and barely on the edge of awareness. You will rarely be conscious of a complete sentence, as in the irrational statements above. Because self-talk has a reflexive, automatic quality, it is easy to keep the illusion that feelings arise spontaneously from events. However, once the thoughts are slowed down like a slow-motion film, frame by frame, the millisecond it takes to say "I'm falling apart" is exposed for its malignant influence. The thoughts that create your emotions frequently may appear in a kind of shorthand: "No good ... crazy ... feeling sick ... dumb," and so on. That shorthand has to be stretched out into the original sentence it was extracted from. The sentence can then be challenged with methods you'll learn in the section on refuting irrational ideas.

The best way to uncover your irrational ideas is to reflect on situations in which you experience distressing emotions such as anxiety, depression, anger, guilt, or a sense of worthlessness. Behind each of these emotions, particularly if they are chronic, is irrational self-talk. Ask yourself, **"What am I telling myself about this situation?"** You may be tempted to immediately self-correct with rational self-talk. For instance, in response to the irrational thought "My brother never helps out with our elderly parents; it's just not fair," Amy might have immediately told herself, "Nobody said life was fair." This would have prevented her from exploring the other thoughts that are distressing her.

Instead, she asked herself **"What if that were true? What would it mean to me?"** (Burns 1999). To this, she responded, _He has it easy. I want his easy life. I'm really as selfish as he is. But I have no right to be angry._ By repeatedly asking herself the three questions in bold type, Amy was able to identify many of her other upsetting, irrational thoughts, including these: *It's only right to sacrifice my life—after all, they're family. I love my parents, but they're driving me crazy! I should be stronger. I feel like I'm drowning. What if something happens to me—what will happen to them? I can't stand to think of them all alone. That would be a disaster....* Amy wrote down these thoughts in a notebook to refer to later.

As you can probably imagine, Amy is in an objectively difficult situation. In addition, she has many irrational thoughts that are generating so much distress that she isn't able to problem solve effectively or to make sensible decisions. She can use the Refuting Irrational Ideas technique described next to step back from and challenge the irrational ideas that are bothering her the most.

REFUTING IRRATIONAL IDEAS

There are five steps (A through E) to disputing and eliminating irrational ideas. Begin by selecting a situation that consistently generates stressful emotions in you.

A. **Write the facts** of the event as they occurred at the time you were upset. Be sure to include only the objective facts, not conjectures, subjective impressions, or value judgments.

B. **Write your self-talk** about the event. State all your subjective value judgments, assumptions, beliefs, predictions, and worries. Note which self-statements have been previously described as irrational ideas.

C. **Focus on your emotional response.** Make a clear one- or two-word label such as "angry," "depressed," "felt worthless," "afraid," and so on.

D. **Dispute and change the irrational self-talk** identified at step B. Here's how it is done, according to Ellis:

1. **Select the irrational idea that you wish to dispute.** As an illustration, we will use the irrational idea "It's not fair that I have to suffer with such a problem."

2. **Is there any rational support for this idea?** Since everything is as it should be, given long chains of cause and effect, the answer is no.

   The problem must be endured and dealt with because it happened. It happened because all the conditions necessary to make it happen existed.

3. **What evidence exists for the falseness of this idea?**

   a. There are no laws of the universe that say I should not have pain or problems. I can experience any problem for which the necessary conditions exist.

b. Life is not fair. Life is just a sequence of events, some of which bring pleasure and some of which are inconvenient and painful.

c. If problems occur, it is up to me to try to solve them.

d. Trying to keep a problem from developing is adaptive, but resenting and not facing it once it exists is a dangerous strategy.

e. No one is special. Some people go through life with relatively less pain than I do. This is due to one of two things: the luck of the draw, or decisions I've made that contributed to the necessary conditions for my problems.

f. Just because I have a problem doesn't mean I have to be miserable. I can take pride in the challenge of a creative solution. This may be an opportunity to increase my self-esteem.

4. **Does any evidence exist for the truth of this idea?** No, my suffering is due to my self-talk, how I have interpreted this event. I have convinced myself that I should be unhappy.

5. **What is the worst thing that could happen to me** if what I want to happen doesn't, or what I don't want to happen does?

a. I could be deprived of various pleasures while I deal with the problem.

b. I might feel inconvenienced.

c. I might never solve the problem and experience myself as ineffective in this particular area.

d. I might have to accept the consequences of failure.

e. Others might not approve of how I am behaving or I might be rejected as incompetent.

f. I might feel more stress and tension.

6. **What good things might occur** if what I want to happen doesn't, or what I don't want to happen does?

a. I might learn to tolerate frustration better.

b. I might improve my coping skills.

c. I might become more responsible.

E. **Substitute alternative self-talk**, now that you have clearly examined the irrational idea and compared it with rational thinking.

1. There's nothing special about me. I can accept painful situations when they emerge.

2. Facing the problem is more adaptive than resenting it or running away from it.

3. I feel what I think. If I don't think negative thoughts, I won't feel stressed out. At worst, I will experience inconvenience, regret, and annoyance—not anxiety, depression, and rage.

Homework

To succeed in your war against irrational ideas, you need a daily commitment to doing homework. Make at least 100 copies of the blank Homework Sheet to use, and fill out one copy at least once a day, spending at least twenty minutes on it. Whenever possible, do the homework right after the event has occurred. Use a separate sheet for each event, and save them as a record of your growth.

First read the sample Homework Sheet on the page opposite the blank Homework Sheet. It was completed by a man who had a date with a friend who canceled.

SAMPLE HOMEWORK SHEET

A. Activating event:

A friend canceled a date with me.

B. Rational ideas:

I know she's under a lot of time pressure right now . . . I'll do something by myself.

Irrational ideas:

I'll feel terribly alone tonight . . . The emptiness is setting in . . . She doesn't really care for me . . . No one really wants to spend time with me . . . I'm falling apart.

C. Consequences of the irrational ideas:

I was depressed . . . I was moderately anxious.

D. Disputing and challenging the irrational ideas:

1. Select the irrational idea:

I'll feel terribly alone tonight . . . I'm falling apart.

2. Is there any rational support for this idea?

No.

3. What evidence exists for the falseness of the idea?

Being alone is not as pleasurable as having a date, but I can find pleasure in an alternative activity.

I usually enjoy being alone, and I will tonight as soon as I face the disappointment.

I'm mislabeling frustration and disappointment as "falling apart."

4. Does any evidence exist for the truth of the idea?

No, only that I've talked myself into feeling depressed.

5. What is the worst thing that could happen to me?

I could continue to feel disappointed and not find anything really pleasurable to do tonight.

6. What good things might occur?

I might feel more self-reliant and realize that I do have inner resources.

E. Alternative thoughts:

I'm okay. I'll get out my detective novel. I'll treat myself to a good Chinese dinner. I'm good at being alone.

Alternative emotions:

I feel quiet, a little disappointed, but I'm anticipating a good meal and a good book.

HOMEWORK SHEET

A. Activating event: _____

_____

B. Rational ideas: _____

_____

   Irrational ideas: _____

_____

C. Consequences of the irrational ideas: _____

_____

D. Disputing and challenging the irrational ideas: _____

_____

   1. Select the irrational idea: _____

_____

   2. Is there any rational support for this idea? _____

_____

   3. What evidence exists for the falseness of the idea? _____

_____

   4. Does any evidence exist for the truth of the idea? _____

_____

   5. What is the worst thing that could happen to me? _____

_____

   6. What good things might occur? _____

_____

E. Alternative thoughts: _____

_____

   Alternative emotions: _____

_____

Rules to Promote Rational Thinking

Evaluate your self-statements against these six rules, or guidelines, for rational thinking (adapted from David Goodman's *Emotional Well-Being Through Rational Behavior Training* [1978]).

1. **It doesn't do anything to me.**
   The situation doesn't make me anxious or afraid. I say things to myself that largely produce my anxiety and fear.

2. **Everything is exactly the way it should be.**
   The conditions for things or people to be otherwise don't exist. To say that things should be other than what they are is to believe in magic. They are what they are because of a long series of causal events, including interpretations, responses from irrational self-talk, and so on. To say that things should be different is to throw out causality.

3. **All humans are fallible creatures.**
   This is inescapable. If you haven't set reasonable quotas of failure for yourself and others, you increase the prospects for disappointment and unhappiness. It becomes all too easy to attack yourself and others as worthless, bad, and so on.

4. **It takes two to have a conflict.**
   Before beginning a course of accusation and blame, consider the 30 percent rule. Any party to a conflict is contributing at least 30 percent of the fuel to keep it going.

5. **The original cause is lost in antiquity.**
   Trying to discover who did what first is a waste of time. The search for the original cause of chronic painful emotions is extremely difficult. The best strategy is to make decisions to change your behavior now.

6. **We largely feel the way we think.**
   This is the positively stated principle behind the first statement in this list. This statement reinforces the idea that events don't cause emotions—our interpretations of events cause emotions.

SPECIAL CONSIDERATIONS

If you have difficulty making headway with rational emotive behavior therapy, one of three factors may be influencing your difficulties:

1. You remain unconvinced that thoughts cause emotions. If this is the case, confine your work initially to rational emotive imagery described in the next section. If you then find

that changes in your self-talk can push you toward experiencing less stressful emotions, the statement that thoughts cause emotions may become more believable.

2. Your irrational ideas and self-talk are so lightning-swift that you have difficulty catching them. If this is the case, try keeping a journal of events and situations associated with intense emotions. Put down everything that flows through your mind: scenes, images, single words, vague half-formed thoughts, names, sounds, sentences, and so on.

3. You have difficulty remembering your thoughts. If this is the case, don't wait until after the fact. Use a journal to write everything down just as it is happening.

Rational Emotive Imagery

In 1971, Dr. Maxie Maultsby introduced rational emotive imagery. This technique will help you develop strategies to change stressful emotions. It works as follows:

1. Imagine an event that is stressful and usually accompanied by unpleasant emotions. Notice all the details of the situation: sights, smells, sounds, how you are dressed, what is being said, and so on.

2. As you clearly imagine the event, allow yourself to feel uncomfortable. Let in the emotions of anger, anxiety, depression, worthlessness, or shame. Don't try to avoid the emotion—go ahead and feel it.

3. After experiencing the stressful emotion, push yourself to change it to a healthier negative emotion. You can fundamentally alter these emotions so that anxiety, depression, rage, and guilt are replaced by keenly felt concern, disappointment, annoyance, or regret. If you think you can't do this, you are only fooling yourself. Everyone can push him- or herself to change a feeling, if only for a few moments.

4. Having contacted the stressful feeling and pushed it, however briefly, into a healthier negative emotion, you can examine how you did it. What happened inside your head that altered your original depression, anxiety, or rage? Clearly, you told yourself something different about yourself, or others, or the situation.

5. Instead of saying "I can't handle this ... this will drive me crazy," you might now be saying "I've dealt successfully with situations like this before." You have changed your beliefs, your interpretations of experience. Once you know how you changed the stressful emotion to a healthier negative emotion, you can substitute the new, adaptive beliefs any time you want. Become deeply aware of how the new beliefs lead you away from stress and produce more bearable emotions.

For example, a housewife, who became depressed whenever her husband turned on the television in the evening, practiced rational emotive imagery. During the day, she conjured up the situation in her imagination: her husband wiping his mouth, getting up from the table, taking the plates to the sink, and leaving the room. She could imagine a few moments later the sound of the television coming on, the changing of channels, the voices from his favorite sitcom. As she reviewed the sequence, she sank into despondency and became depressed.

After coming fully in contact with the stressful emotion, she pushed herself to change the feeling of depression into one of disappointment and irritation. This felt like shoving a huge rock single-handed. It took fifteen minutes of effort before she could get even momentary contact with the less stressful emotions. By practicing at hourly intervals, she was soon able to push her depression into irritation or disappointment for several minutes.

She became ready to examine how she had changed her thoughts (self-talk) in order to change her emotions. She found she could change depression into irritation by saying, *I don't have to feel helpless. If he wants to spend his time with TV, I can do something that feels good to me.* Her other thoughts included: "It's his life. He can waste it if he wants to. I'm not going to waste mine. There are people I don't visit because I think I should stay home with him. But I'm going to take care of myself. He may be displeased if I don't stay home, but staying home to watch the tube is not satisfying for me."

Developing Alternative Emotional Responses

Here is a list of sample situations and alternative emotional responses:

Situation	Unhealthy Negative Emotion	Healthy Negative Emotion
Fight with mate	Rage	Annoyance, irritation
Work deadline	High anxiety	Concern
Cruelty to a child	Intense guilt	Regret
Something you enjoy is canceled	Depression	Disappointment
Criticized	Worthless	Annoyance, concern
A public mistake	Shame	Guilt about your act, not self

Now fill in your own stressful situations, including the unhealthy negative emotions you feel and the healthier negative emotions you would like to feel.

Situation	Unhealthy Negative Emotion	Healthy Negative Emotion
_____	_____	_____
_____	_____	_____
_____	_____	_____
_____	_____	_____
_____	_____	_____

You can use rational emotive imagery in each of these situations. If the unhealthy negative emotions do not change right away, let yourself keep feeling them until they do change. You *can* alter these emotions by merely pushing yourself to do so. Afterward, you will isolate the key thoughts and phrases that made the new, healthier emotions possible. Changing your self-talk to include these more adaptive thoughts, beliefs, and ideas will make it increasingly easy for you to change the emotion you're working with. For best results, practice this technique ten minutes a day for at least two weeks.

Insight

Understand that there are three levels of insight necessary for change to take place. They are the following:

1. Knowing that you have a problem, and awareness of some of the events that may have caused the problem.

2. Seeing clearly that the irrational ideas you acquired early in life are creating the emotional climate you live in now, and that consciously or unconsciously you work fairly hard to perpetuate those irrational ideas.

3. Believing strongly that after recognizing the validity of these two prior insights, you will still find no way to eliminate the problem other than working to change your irrational ideas, steadily, persistently, and vigorously.

Without making a commitment to this last insight, you will experience difficulties altering your habitual emotional responses.

If you think this technique could be useful to you but you are unable to master it, contact a rational emotive therapist or center for consultation.

FURTHER READING

Beck, A. T. 1979. Cognitive therapy: Nature and relation to behavior therapy. In *Behavior Therapy* edited by A. Beck. New York: NAL/Dutton.

——. 1989. *Love Is Never Enough: How Couples Can Overcome Misunderstandings, Resolve Conflict, and Solve Relationship Problems with Cognitive Therapy.* New York: HarperCollins.

Burns, D. D. 1999. *Feeling Good Handbook.* Rev. ed. New York: Penguin Books.

Ellis, A., and R. J. Harper. 1975. *A New Guide to Rational Living.* North Hollywood, CA: Wilshire Book Company.

——. 1980. *Growth Through Reason.* Palo Alto, CA: Science and Behavior Books.

——. 1986. *Anger: How to Live with and without It.* New York: Carol Publishing Group.

——. 1988. *Anger: How to Stubbornly Refuse to Make Yourself Miserable about Anything—Yes, Anything.* New York: Carol Publishing Group.

——. 1997. *A Guide to Rational Living,.* 3rd ed. North Hollywood, CA: Wilshire Book Company.

——. 2001. *Overcoming Destructive Beliefs, Feelings, and Behaviors: New Directions for Rational Emotive Behavior Therapy.* Amherst, NY: Prometheus Books.

Ellis, A., and C. MacLaren. 2005. *Rational Emotive Behavior Therapy: A Therapist's Guide.* 2nd ed. Atascadero, CA: Impact Publishers.

Farquhar, W., and J. Lowe. 1974. A list of irrational ideas. In *Youth: Toward Personal Growth; A Rational Emotive Approach,* edited by D. J. Tosi. Columbus, OH: Charles E. Merrill.

Goodman, D. 1978. *Emotional Well-Being Through Rational Behavior Training.* 3rd ed. London: Charles C. Thomas Publisher.

Lazarus, A. A. 1996. *Behavior Therapy and Beyond* (Master Work Series). New York: Jason Aronson.

Maultsby, M. 1971. Rational emotive imagery. *Rational Living* 6:16–23.

Rimm, D. C., and S. B. Litvak. 1969. Self-verbalization and emotional arousal. *Journal of Abnormal Psychology* 74:181–187.

13

Facing Worry and Anxiety

In this chapter you will learn to:

* Use relaxation skills to reduce tension and arousal in general as well as in stressful situations

* Observe objectively the thoughts, feelings, and behaviors associated with anxiety

* Engage in realistic risk assessment

* Face your images of catastrophic events and their accompanying emotions so that they lose their power to frighten you

* Identify and change worry behaviors such as excessive checking and avoiding

* Solve problems effectively

BACKGROUND

A little anxiety and worry can be very useful. Thinking that something bad might happen in the future if you don't take appropriate action motivates you to study for a test, learn your lines for a play, work on solutions to problems, and do your best when you perform. Anxiety's most important function is to prepare you for the possibility of danger in the future. When you are in an anxious state, you're already a little tense and alert, so it's easy to shift into the fight-or-flight response that is your body's natural fear reaction to imminent danger or threat.

For example, when you're driving on a stormy day, you are likely to feel a little anxious and tense. Rather than daydreaming or listening to the radio, you're likely to hold the steering wheel with both hands, sit up straight, and scan the road for possible threat. When you see a large tree falling just ahead of you, your emotion moves from anxious to fearful as your fight-or-flight response is triggered and you respond instantly by braking and steering your car away from the danger.

Anxiety becomes a problem when it is triggered too frequently, is too intense, or you can't turn it off (Craske and Barlow 2006). If you are always anxious and worried, your body is always prepared for the possibility of danger in the future. While you won't go crazy from it, long-term anxiety and worry are likely to cause sleep problems, fatigue, irritability, and poor concentration that can negatively impact your performance and productivity.

Anxiety can be triggered by anything that is perceived as potentially dangerous or threatening, such as the possibility of making a mistake, being rejected, missing a deadline, or not doing well on a test. The danger doesn't even have to be real, because simply thinking it might occur sometime in the future produces anxiety. People create unnecessary anxiety for themselves when they overestimate the danger of a possible future event, as well as overstate the likelihood that it will actually occur. They wonder, "What if this terrible thing happens and I can't cope with it?" Then they think, "It would be a disaster!" Thoughts like these trigger anxiety.

It's Monday morning, and Ana is worried her children will be late for school and get into "big trouble." She's also worried that she isn't prepared to give a five-minute speech at work today, and will therefore blow it, even though she has been working on it for two weeks; and she's worried that her sick brother, at home with a cold, could get pneumonia.

Ana, like most chronically anxious people, does what she can to prevent bad things from happening: she overprepares for work because she is worried she will be criticized and perhaps even lose her job if she makes a mistake. She gets herself and her children to appointments early so as not to impolitely barge in late or miss something important. She's worried that if she doesn't check things repeatedly, disaster might result. Ironically, these "worry behaviors" perpetuate her anxiety because they prevent her from learning that it is highly unlikely that anything catastrophic would happen if she doesn't do these things, and if there were a mishap, that she probably could handle it.

So what if her kids are a few minutes late to school occasionally? She might get a call from the school, but they won't fail or be kicked out. Checking on her sick brother many times a day may provide her with momentary reassurance, but it won't prevent pneumonia.

When they are worrying and engaging in worry behavior, everyone becomes stressed. Ana goes to bed Sunday night worrying about her problems and this makes her feel keyed up rather than sleepy. When she can't sleep, she gets up after tossing and turning for an hour to make her children's lunches, rather than leaving this chore to them as she normally would. She does this because she thinks it might prevent her children from being late to school. She recalls the disapproving look on the school principal's face last week when she arrived late with the kids, and she feels a wave of fear as well as more tension in her shoulders.

She says to herself, *She must think I'm an incompetent mother. Maybe I'm not cut out to work and raise kids on my own.* Her stomach feels queasy. *What if they're not getting enough of my time? What if they start thinking it's okay to be late? What if they start turning their homework in late … maybe not do it at all? I can't handle all this and my job too!* She massages the pain that is spreading across her shoulders and takes an antacid to quell her stomach upset. *"I'm so wired … if I don't get some sleep, I won't be functional tomorrow."* She returns to bed, sets her alarm to go off a half hour earlier than usual, and tosses and turns for another hour before falling asleep. As you can see, worry, worry behavior, and tension interact to escalate and maintain anxiety.

This chapter is based on the work of Michelle G. Craske and David H. Barlow (2006), John White (1999), and Mary Ellen Copeland (1998). It addresses the three components of anxiety that work together to maintain your anxiety and worry over time:

1. Your thoughts that tell you there is a possibility of danger or threat in the future

2. Your body that becomes tense in response to this alert message

3. Your behaviors that are designed to check for danger and avoid it if possible

SYMPTOM-RELIEF EFFECTIVENESS

The skills taught in this chapter will help you reduce your anxiety and worry and lessen the physical symptoms of tension associated with excessive worry, such as feeling restless, keyed up, or nervous; sleep disturbances; tiredness; difficulty concentrating; muscle tension; and irritability. These skills will also lessen the occurrence of your spontaneous fear-provoking images of disaster and cut down on your worry behavior.

TIME TO MASTER

You can learn and apply these skills within a few months. Move at a pace you are comfortable with as you work your way through the exercises in this chapter. Your success will depend on how much you practice these exercises.

INSTRUCTIONS

Relaxation Skills for General and Acute Tension Relief

As you read about in Ana's example above, physical tension both contributes to and results from worry and anxiety. You can use the relaxation skills you've been learning in this book to begin to intervene in your cycle of anxiety and worry. If you haven't already mastered diaphragmatic breathing, turn to chapter 3 and begin with the exercise called How Do You Currently Breathe? then move on to Diaphragmatic or Abdominal Breathing. After you are comfortable with diaphragmatic breathing, use it to practice the exercise Mindful Breath Counting, which, in addition to being relaxing, will help you to become more objective and self-accepting as you observe your thoughts, sensations, and feelings.

Next, turn to chapter 7 and learn the first three stages of Applied Relaxation. That is, practice the exercises from the sections called Progressive Muscle Relaxation, Release-Only Relaxation, and Cue-Controlled Relaxation. Your goal is to be able to relax in two or three minutes using cue-controlled relaxation techniques. As you practice this exercise, be sure to focus on the sensations of relaxation in your body, especially in your chest, abdomen, forehead, and shoulders.

To bring down your general level of arousal and tension associated with anxiety and worry, set aside time once or twice a day to relax for twenty minutes. Use this time to learn and practice Diaphragmatic or Abdominal Breathing, Mindful Breath Counting, and the first three exercises in chapter 7. Keep a log of your level of relaxation before and after you practice your twenty-minute relaxation exercise, using the Record of General Tension in chapter 2, Body Awareness.

Once you have successfully paired the word "relax" in the exercise Cue-Controlled Relaxation with the sensations of deep relaxation, start using cue-controlled relaxation whenever you feel your tension beginning to mount during the day. You will also be using this technique later in this chapter when you practice imagery exposure and change your worry behaviors.

Step Back and Observe Your Anxiety

It's hard to change something until you understand it. So to become more aware of the various components of your own anxiety, you will need to keep a daily record. You will identify your anxious thoughts, sensations of tension, and worry behavior and observe how they interact to cause your anxiety to escalate. According to Craske and Barlow (2006), you will become more detached and objective about your anxiety, worry, and tension when you regularly monitor and record your anxious experiences. You will then use this information to practice the next three techniques presented in this chapter and gain greater control over your anxiety and worry. You can also monitor your improvement, and pinpoint those areas in which you still need to work further, by continuing to fill out the Anxious Episode Record forms.

Make a large number of copies of the blank Anxious Episode Record, adapted from Craske and Barlow's (2006) Worry Record, and use one when you notice a dramatic increase in your anxiety level, when you catch yourself worrying, or when you feel symptoms of physical tension. Following is an example of Ana's Anxious Episode Record Form.

Realistically Assess Risk

If you worry excessively, most likely you don't have the skills to assess risk appropriately. Some people worry excessively every time they plan to fly on an airplane or each time they drive their car on a freeway. Others worry beyond reason about suddenly losing their job, even when there is no external circumstance that would warrant their becoming unemployed. The problem with overestimating risk is that it subtly increases the amount of your worry until the worry itself becomes a bigger problem than the dangers you worry about. Learning accurate risk-assessment skills can make a huge difference in your overall anxiety level.

ANA'S ANXIOUS EPISODE RECORD FORM

Date: *5/5*   Length of episode: *5 hours*

Anxiety Severity Scale:

Put an X at the point on this scale that best describes your maximum level of anxiety during this episode:

0	1	2	3	4	5	6	7	8	9 **X**	10

None   Mild   Moderate   Strong
Extreme

Triggering events: *Five-minute presentation tomorrow at work; children late to school last week; brother sick.*

Worries: *I'm going to blow my presentation tomorrow and my boss will think I'm incompetent and fire me; my kids will be late to school and the principal will think that I'm an incompetent mother. What if my kids start being late about other things like homework? I couldn't handle that! What if my brother's cold turns into pneumonia? He could die! I wouldn't know what to do with such a terrible loss.*

Underline and/or fill in physical symptoms: muscle tension, sleep difficulties, difficulty concentrating, mind going blank, irritability, fatigue, *restlessness, feeling keyed up or on edge.* Other: *upset stomach, pain in shoulders.*

Worry behaviors: *Make children's lunches and set alarm a half hour early to prevent their being late; over-prepare for five-minute presentation; check on sick brother many times a day.*

ANXIOUS EPISODE RECORD FORM

Date: _____ Length of episode: _____

Anxiety Severity Scale:

Put an X at the point on this scale that best describes your maximum level of anxiety during this episode:

0	1	2	3	4	5	6	7	8	9	10
None			Mild			Moderate				Strong

Extreme

Triggering events:

_____

_____

_____

Worries:

_____

_____

_____

Underline and/or fill in physical symptoms: muscle tension, sleep difficulties, difficulty concentrating, mind going blank, irritability, fatigue, restlessness, feeling keyed up or on edge. Other:

_____

_____

_____

Worry behaviors:

_____

_____

_____

PREDICTING OUTCOMES

Most chronic worriers focus their attention on catastrophic outcomes. Regardless of how likely (or unlikely) it is that the event they are worrying about will actually occur, their fear is primarily based on the worst possible consequence. For example, a woman who had worried constantly about being abandoned thought her life would be destroyed when her husband told her he was leaving their marriage. But instead of being lonely and sad and single for the rest of her life, she was very unhappy for only a few months. After some intimate conversations with her friends, she realized that many people went through divorce and ended up happier than they had been before. She soon became very social, physically active, and even fell in love with a more suitable partner—all before her divorce was final. So, although she was very unhappy for a relatively short period of time, the catastrophic outcome she'd expected never came to pass.

When you worry, you tend to forget that your capacity to cope with even the most serious disaster is quite remarkable. People survive—and sometimes even benefit from—situations they originally perceived as catastrophic. In most instances, you, your friends, and your family will find a way to cope with whatever happens.

You will find a Risk Assessment Form below that you can use to lower your anxiety by estimating accurate probabilities and making coping plans for catastrophe. Make a number of copies and fill out one each time you find yourself worrying excessively.

On the first line, record one of your worries in the form of a feared event. Write down the worst possible version of your worry. For example, if you worry about your spouse, who is a traveling salesperson, imagine the very worst: a disastrous plane crash over the Pacific Ocean, months of investigation that lead to no evidence, and none of the bodies ever being recovered. You'll never see your spouse again, and you'll end up financially ruined. On the second line, write the worry thoughts that typically come up for you: "He'll die … the family will never be able to make it …, I'll never sleep again … horrible … a nightmare beyond nightmares…." Jot down whatever comes to mind, even if it is just an image or a fleeting word. On the third line, rate your anxiety when considering this worst-case scenario. Use 0 for no anxiety and 100 for the worst fear you have ever experienced. On the fourth line rate the probability of this worst-case scenario coming to pass—from 0 percent for no likelihood at all to 100 percent for absolute inevitability.

The next five items in the Risk Assessment Form address catastrophic thinking. Assuming your biggest fear actually did occur, predict all the worst possible consequences. Then try to think of specific coping thoughts and actions that might help you manage in the face of the catastrophe. As you do this, consider how long it is likely to last; what resources you can use to help yourself; and how you and/or other people have coped with similar experiences. Once you have some ideas about how you could deal with the worst catastrophe, go ahead and create a revised prediction of the consequences. Some things may now look a little less daunting because you have a coping plan. Rerate your anxiety after this process to see if there's been any change.

The next three items in the Risk Assessment Form address the issue of overestimation. List the evidence against the worst outcome happening. Then list all the alternative outcomes you can think of. Figure the odds of the worst outcome happening as realistically as you can. When you begin to do this, consider how many times you have had this worry versus how many times it has actually happened. If it has happened before, be sure that you are not basing your guess on a limited number of cases. You may want to survey your friends or look up the actual odds. Finally, rerate the probability of the event occurring and your anxiety about the event. You should find that both your probability and anxiety ratings have declined as a result of your making a full and objective risk assessment.

Following is an example of a filled-out Risk Assessment Form from Paul, a student who is afraid of failure in general, and is specifically worried about his entrance examination for law school.

Fill out a Risk Assessment Form each time you are confronted by a significant worry, or whenever you return to a worry more than once. It's important to do this exercise consistently. Each risk assessment helps you change your old habits of catastrophic thinking. When you've completed a risk assessment, keep the form. You may wish to refer to it again when confronting a similar worry. Remember that you've had lots of practice with your old ways of thinking. You are going to have to practice this new fact-based, realistic thinking for some time before it becomes automatic.

SAMPLE RISK ASSESSMENT FORM

1. Feared event: *Performing poorly on my law school entrance exams (LSAT).*

2. Automatic thoughts: *I'll score extremely low. My mind will freeze and I won't know any of the answers.*

3. Rate anxiety from 0 to 100: *95*

4. Rate probability of event from 0 to 100 percent: *90*

5. Assuming the worst happens, predict the worst possible consequences: *I'll score so low that I won't get into any law school. All my undergraduate work will be useless. I'll end up working at a job I detest.*

6. Possible coping thoughts: *If I don't do well the first time, I can take it again and learn from the experience. There are other appealing careers besides law; for example, I'm still very interested in publishing.*

7. Possible coping actions: *Study regularly. Take a class that will help me prepare for the exam. If I need to take the LSAT again, maybe I can find a study partner who is planning to take it at the same time I am.*

8. Revised predictions of consequences: *I won't completely fail. If I do poorly the first time, I'll use that information to help me better prepare for the next opportunity to take the exam. Also, I really can consider an alternative career.*

9. Rerate anxiety from 0 to 100: *70*

10. Evidence against the worst possible outcome: *I am studying diligently and I typically receive higher-than-average scores on my exams. I scored in the eighty-fifth percentile on my SATs.*

11. Alternative outcomes: *I may do just fine. I may do better than I expect. I may not do as well as I need to get into my first-choice law school, but my second choice is also a reputable institution. I may need to take the LSAT again and make a bigger commitment to preparation. In each case, I'd end up being a lawyer.*

12. Rerate probability of event from 0 to 100 percent: *35*

13. Rerate anxiety from 0 to 100: *45*

RISK ASSESSMENT FORM

1. Feared event:

   riding roller coaster

2. Automatic thoughts:

   the ride will come off the track

3. Rate anxiety from 0 to 100: __90__

4. Rate probability of event from 0 to 100 percent: __30__

5. Assuming the worst happens, predict the worst possible consequences:

   death

6. Possible coping thoughts:

   think about how many roller coasters have actually come off track

7. Possible coping actions:

   take some form of medicine

8. Revised predictions of consequences:

   the roller coaster stays on track

9. Rerate anxiety from 0 to 100: __90__

10. Evidence against the worst possible outcome:

    The roller coasters are closely monitored and are tested often.

11. Alternative outcomes:

    The roller coaster runs smoothly

12. Rerate probability of event from 0 to 100 percent: __30__

13. Rerate anxiety from 0 to 100: __90__

Face Your Worst Fears

Have you ever had an image of a terrible event—real or imagined—just pop into your head? Did it trigger a fear response? For instance, if you worry about driving, you might have had the image of a truck plowing into the back of your car when you are stopped at an intersection, which filled you with terror. According to Craske and Barlow (2006), worries are often associated with vivid mental images. Each time you replay such a picture, it's as though the feared incident is really happening, and you experience a fearful fight-or-flight response. Worrying is less distressing than this fear response, and so you are likely to divert your thinking to worrying about "all those bad drivers out there," and take preventive measures such as frequently checking your side and rearview mirrors. Your fearful catastrophic image gives fuel to your worry. Unfortunately, if you try to avoid this fearful image, it is a little like telling yourself not to think of a white polar bear—the image just pops up again.

Craske and Barlow (2006) have observed that if you repeatedly face your feared image on purpose, after a while you'll find that your fear of it has declined. With your fear lessened or even gone, you will be less likely to worry about not being safe and in control. They developed "imagery exposure" as a safe and convenient method to imagine your feared image repeatedly, causing your fear of it to diminish. It incorporates the relaxation, monitoring, and risk-assessment skills that you have been practicing.

GETTING READY FOR IMAGERY EXPOSURE

Before purposefully exposing yourself to your feared images, copy a number of the blank Preparing for Imagery Exposure Form for each of the main topics you worry about most.

Sandy, who had learned from her Navy parents that she must "shape up, keep her home shipshape, or ship out," spent a great deal of her time cleaning and straightening up her house. But no matter how much time she spent cleaning, it was never enough. She rarely had anyone over because she was afraid that others would think she was such a slob they wouldn't want to have anything to do with her.

Sandy's Preparing for Imagery Exposure Form follows:

SAMPLE PREPARING FOR IMAGERY EXPOSURE FORM

1. Write down one of the main topics you worry about most.

    People disapproving of me because of my messy, dirty house and then rejecting me.

2. For this worry, write down the image that pops into your mind that represents the worst thing that could happen. You may have already identified this image on a Risk Assessment Form. This time, instead of concentrating on your anxiety-provoking thoughts, you will focus on the image of the worst thing that could happen. Describe this worst-case image as though it is happening to you right now. Be specific. Include your physical and emotional reactions.

    The neighbors, whom my husband invited over for dinner, arrive early for my husband's birthday dinner. I haven't had time to pick up the house, let alone finish making dinner. My husband lets them in and they look around and shake their heads. My husband says, in a sarcastic tone, that the place looks like a tornado just blew through and he begins picking up clothes, dishes, and newspapers from the living room floor and the dining room table and his wife comes out to the kitchen and starts doing the dishes in the sink, and asks me when did I last wash dishes. I feel a rush of tingling energy through my body, my face is hot, my chest and shoulders are tense, and my stomach churns. I feel embarrassed, ashamed, mad, and nervous. I have a strong urge to flee, but I'm trapped; I'm the hostess and it is my husband's birthday. The next day when I take a walk in the neighborhood, all the people turn away from me and refuse to speak to me. I realize they have been told what a dirty slob I am. My stomach sinks, my chest and arms are tight, and my heart is pounding. I feel ashamed and lonely.

3. What does this image mean to you?

    That if people visit when my house is messy, they will think I'm a dirty slob and they won't want to have anything to do with me and I'll be ashamed and lonely forever.

4. Using the Anxiety Severity Scale on your Anxious Episode Record Form, rate the level of anxiety you experienced as you imagined this image (0 being none and 10 being extreme).

    9

PREPARING FOR IMAGERY EXPOSURE FORM

1. Write down one of the main topics you worry about most.

   _____

   _____

2. For this worry, write down the image that pops into your mind that represents the worst thing that could happen. You may have already identified this image on a Risk Assessment Form. This time, instead of concentrating on your anxiety-provoking thoughts, you will focus on the image of the worst thing that could happen. Describe this worst-case image as though it is happening to you right now. Be specific. Include your physical and emotional reactions.

   _____

   _____

   _____

   _____

   _____

   _____

   _____

   _____

3. What does this image mean to you?

   _____

   _____

4. Using the Anxiety Severity Scale on your Anxious Episode Record Form, rate the level of anxiety you experienced as you imagined this image (0 being none and 10 being extreme).

   _____

   _____

When you have completed a Preparing for Imagery Exposure Form for each of the topics you worry about most, order them from the least anxiety-provoking image to the most distressing image on a scale of 0 (no distress) to 10 (extreme distress).

INSTRUCTIONS FOR IMAGERY EXPOSURE

1. **Beginning with your least distressing image, read your description, and then close your eyes and imagine the scene as clearly as possible, using all of your five senses.** Imagine you are in the situation; you are really experiencing it. Try not only to see the image, imagine its sounds and smells. Imagine what it would feel like to touch something from the image. Imagine your fearful emotions and physical sensations, as well as the meaning you give to the situation in your imagery.

2. **After one minute, use a 0 to 10 point scale to rate the vividness of your imagery, with 0 meaning no image and 10 meaning extremely vivid.** Rate your anxiety on the Anxiety Severity Scale. If your imagery wasn't clear or you rated it as less than 5 and you didn't experience at least a little fear, repeat instruction step 1. Remember that you are a participant and not an observer. Imagine the situation, the meaning you give it, and the fear sensations and emotions that you imagine experiencing. If you still have difficulty imagining the scene, read the first Special Considerations section below before moving to the next item on this list.

3. **When you have a clear image associated with some anxiety, stay focused on it for five minutes.** To do this, you may need to repeatedly reread your description of the image and imagine the event as though it is actually occurring. Let yourself experience any emotions and sensations that are produced by the image. Allow the image, your sensations, and emotions be whatever they will be without trying to change them. The distress and meaning associated with the image will change as you repeatedly expose yourself to the image. Keep bringing your focus back to your image and the accompanying meaning, emotions, and physical sensations.

4. **Relax, using cue-controlled relaxation. If needed, use progressive relaxation. Once you are relaxed, answer these questions:**

    *   Do you think that just because you imaged this event, it might happen?

    *   If this event were to happen, what would you do to handle it?

    *   How are you blowing out of proportion the meaning of this imagined event?

    *   Based on facts and logic, how likely is this imagined event to happen?

Use the strategies that you've been learning, along with your already existing personal resources, to work toward a more realistic interpretation and way of coping with your imagined event.

5. **Read your description again, close your eyes, and imagine the event once more, as if it were really happening, for half a minute.** Rate how vivid the image is on the 0 to 10 scale. Rate your level of anxiety on the Anxiety Severity Scale. Once you have a vivid image associated with some anxiety, then try to imagine it for five minutes. In addition to imagining the event, imagine what happens in the days, weeks, and months ahead. In short, see yourself handling the imagined event. For example, if your imagined event is your house burning down, imagine witnessing that happening. Then imagine the next day when your friends and family come over to commiserate with you and help you salvage what you can. And imagine the next week when you complete the insurance paperwork regarding your losses, and the next month when you meet with an architect to discuss the plans for building your new house.

6. **Repeat instruction step 4, first relaxing and then answering the four bulleted questions again.** Repeat steps 5 and 4 until your anxiety level is 2 or less on the Anxiety Severity Scale, at which point you can move on to exposing yourself to your next image. You may find that as your distress response to the image diminishes, you are less able to imagine the image. This is to be expected and is a natural occurrence.

7. **You can work at your own pace.** As a rule of thumb, you might try three five-minute rounds of imagery exposure a day. Keep a record of your practice with the upcoming Imagery Exposure Log. Apply imagery exposure to all of the catastrophic images you have, one at a time.

SPECIAL CONSIDERATIONS

There are several reasons why you might have difficulty imagining your catastrophic scene:

1. **The first item on your list simply may not be very anxiety-provoking for you.** Typically, emotions cause an image to become more vivid; if the image is neutral for you, it might not be very clear. You may have already realized that your images are of events that are unlikely to happen; or if they did, you could cope with them. You may think, "This is just an image, it's not real." If so, you are ready to move on to the next item.

2. **You may be a novice at using imagery.** If so, practice visualizing more neutral and/or positive scenes before attempting to visualize your catastrophic images. Here is one exercise to get you started:

Without looking up from this page, close your eyes, and imagine your surroundings in as much detail as you can. Use all of your senses. Imagine yourself moving around in this space. What do you see? What do you hear? What do you touch? What do you feel? What do you smell and taste? When you are done, open your eyes and compare your recollection with the real thing.

Then close your eyes again, and imagine yourself in the same place, but this time you see an unfamiliar door. You open this door and imagine walking into a pleasant and safe place. Explore this place, not as an observer, but as a participant. Be sure to use all your senses. Practice this exercise in different settings to improve your observational abilities and imagination. Once you can imagine neutral and/or positive scenes, start doing imagery exposure with your personal catastrophic images again.

3. **The image you are imagining may be too general.** If so, make your image more specific. For instance, instead of imagining your six-year-old disappearing, imagine a specific event such as your child disappearing in your favorite department store filled with a crowd at Christmastime.

4. **Your image may be too anxiety-provoking, and you are trying to avoid anxiety.** If you suspect that this is the case, remember these three facts:

   a. It's just a picture, not reality.

   b. Imagining an image won't make it come true.

   c. The more you expose yourself to the distressing images, the less distressing they will become.

   If necessary, you can make the image feel less threatening by imagining it first as a black-and-white snapshot or a black-and-white moving picture that you are watching from across the room. Work toward imagining yourself in the catastrophic picture. You need to be willing to experience the distress of facing what you are avoiding in order to reduce your fear and anxiety. If you continue to have problems, a cognitive behavioral therapist experienced in using imagery can help you with this.

5. **If you find that your emotional distress does not decrease or actually increases with repeated exposures to the image, observe whether the image is continually changing.** This often happens in everyday worrying. It can actually cause you more distress, because an image can trigger the fearful fight-or-flight response. When you worry, rather than staying with the same image until you get used to it and your distress diminishes, you flit from one distressing picture to the next and your anxiety escalates. When you are practicing this procedure, remember to stick with the same image while you are

repeating the imagery exposure until your distress decreases, and only then go on to the next item on your list.

6. Keep a record of your imagery exposure practice that includes the date, a name for the image you are working on, how vivid the image is, and your maximum anxiety level based on the Anxiety Severity Scale. Use the blank Imagery Exposure Log we've provided to keep your record.

HOW IMAGERY EXPOSURE WORKS

To continue with the last example, Sandy read the description of her image that she had written out on the Preparing for Imagery Exposure Form in which she imagined a neighbor couple disapproving of her messy house, their telling her other neighbors about her slovenly ways, and then all of her neighbors ostracizing her. She was surprised by how easily she could imagine the details of the scene as though she were really in it, and also surprised by how anxious she became. She rated both the vividness of the image and her anxiety as an 8. When she focused on the image for five minutes, she began to sob as she imagined the shame and embarrassment associated with being disapproved of, as well as the painful shame and loneliness of being ostracized by all of her neighbors. When she caught herself blanking out, worrying about something else, or her mind drifting from her original image, she reread her description of the scene a few times. At the end of five minutes, she used cue-controlled relaxation to bring her tension level down. She gave careful thought to the following four questions before she answered them:

- Do you think that just because you imaged this event, it might happen? *No.*

- If this event were to happen, what would you do to handle it? *I would do cue-controlled relaxation as soon as I realized the neighbors were early. I would clarify that I wasn't expecting them for another hour and still have some things to do before I am ready. Since I feel calmer and more in charge giving orders, I would tell my husband to clean up the living and dining rooms and invite the neighbor woman to help me in the kitchen. If they said something that I thought was a sign of disapproval, I would be honest or use humor.*

- How are you blowing out of proportion the meaning of this imagined event? *I have some friends in this neighborhood who have seen my home when it was untidy, and they like me just fine. I see them often and I rarely feel lonely. This couple, based on one visit, may think I'm a lousy housekeeper, but they aren't going to turn the whole neighborhood against me because of one visit.*

- Based on facts and logic, how likely is this imagined event to happen? *Unlikely. Most people are not as particular as my parents are about how a house looks, and they are not likely to condemn anyone based on how her home looks on a single occasion. Certainly the whole neighborhood isn't going to turn against me because of this. I have friends who accept me as I am.*

When Sandy closed her eyes again to imagine her image for a minute, along with the associated emotions, sensations, and meaning, she noticed that the image was still vivid (8), and that her anxiety had come down by two points (6). When she imagined the image for five minutes—including what she would do the following day, week, and month—she could see herself coping, using cue-controlled relaxation, rational thinking, honesty, humor, and her support system of husband and friends. At the end of five minutes, she rated the vividness of her image as an 8 and her anxiety as a 4. When answering the four questions again, she added that she couldn't please everybody and if some people thought she kept a messy house, this didn't make her a bad person.

EXAMPLE OF SANDY'S IMAGERY EXPOSURE LOG

Today's Date	Image (Identifying Phrase)	Vividness 0–10	Maximum Anxiety 0–10
6/1	Messy house	8	8
6/2	Messy house	8	4
6/3	Messy house	6	2
6/4	Job interview	9	8
6/5	Job interview	8	5
6/6	Job interview	7	3
6/7	Job interview	7	2

IMAGERY EXPOSURE LOG

Today's Date	Image (Identifying Phrase)	Vividness 0—10	Maximum Anxiety 0—10

Change Your Worry Behavior

Worry behavior is designed to prevent bad things from happening. It reassures you that you are doing everything you can to keep your world from unraveling. Recall Ana's worry behavior: overpreparing for a five-minute speech, repeatedly checking on her brother, getting up in the middle of the night to make her children's lunches, and setting the alarm clock a half hour earlier in order to get her kids to school on time. Some people even worry about being worried, so they try to avoid activities that might cause them to worry.

As you've learned, worry behavior actually perpetuates your worry and anxiety because it prevents you from finding out that the negative event you are trying to prevent is unlikely to happen; and if something bad did happen, that most likely you could cope with it. For example, you think that you've dodged the bullet of your boss yelling at you for making a mistake by checking and rechecking your work. Unfortunately, checking and rechecking your work keeps you from discovering how likely it is that you will make a mistake significant enough for your boss to soundly criticize you. It also prevents you from learning that, if by chance you did make a big mistake and your boss yelled at you for it, you could handle it. The result: endless worrying, needless tension, and wasted time and effort checking and rechecking.

Worry behavior that reinforces your worry and anxiety needlessly is not the same as actions you take to guard your and your family's safety when the probability of something dangerous happening is relatively high. When you have to leave work alone after dark in a dangerous part of town, it is prudent to have parked your car under a streetlight earlier in the day. When your teenager is out hours past her curfew, it's a good idea to check on his or her whereabouts.

In the next exercise you will be asked to identify your worry behaviors. For each of your worry behaviors, you are to plan an alternative behavior that will allow you to test your negative prediction of what will happen if you don't perform your worry behavior. For example, if you worry that you will miss something crucial if you are late to meetings so you always arrive early for them, your alternative behavior could be to arrive on time or even be a few minutes late.

Here is an example of Owen's Alternatives to Worry Behavior Form:

ALTERNATIVES TO WORRY BEHAVIOR FORM

Worry Behavior	Alternative Behavior	Prediction	Maximum Anxiety
Check 6 times daily on wife	Check once daily on wife	She'll die	10
Stay at work until all work done	Leave work on time with one item incomplete	I'll be seen as unproductive, I'll be fired	8
Wks. of research to buy new appliances	3 hrs. research to buy new appliances	Make a mistake	9
Avoid guests due to messy house	Dinner party with one soiled item left out	Be viewed as slob, Rejection	8
Perfectly groomed for work	Wear soiled, wrinkled, or uncoordinated clothes	They'll think I'm an unprofessional slob	8
Count to 10 before leaving a room	Leave room without counting	I or a family member will get hurt or die	10

You are likely to experience significant anxiety the first time you don't engage in the worry behavior that was designed specifically to protect you from something terrible happening. But you will find that it is actually quite a relief to discover that usually nothing terrible happens; and if something bad does happen, you can handle it. Typically, your anxiety will rapidly diminish with repeated practice of your alternative behavior. Now you are ready to fill out your Alternatives to Worry Behavior Form. Your Alternatives to Worry Behavior Form will serve as a guide when you practice your alternative behaviors in real life. Follow the instructions below.

INSTRUCTIONS

1. **Identify your worry behaviors.** In the first column of the Alternatives to Worry Behavior Form below, write down all your worry behaviors that you know are excessive and based on worry. Review your Anxious Episode Records to help you recall your key worry behaviors.

2. **Plan alternatives to your worry behaviors.** In the second column of the Alternatives to Worry Behavior Form, write down a nonanxiety-based alternative behavior for each of your worry behaviors. You might want to think about what a person would do in the same situation if they didn't have your worry. For example, because Owen worries about being seen as unproductive and losing his job, he stays late to finish his work every night; his coworkers routinely leave work on time with their work incomplete.

3. **Predict what will happen if you don't perform your worry behavior.** In the third column of the Alternatives to Worry Behavior Form, write down your worst-case scenario prediction of what will happen when you practice your alternative behavior in place of your worry behavior.

4. **Estimate the maximum anxiety you will feel when you first do your alternative behavior.** In the fourth column of the Alternatives to Worry Behavior Form, rate on the Anxiety Severity Scale (0 = no anxiety; 10 = extreme anxiety) what you anticipate your maximum anxiety will be the first time you actually do each of the alternative behaviors.

ALTERNATIVES TO WORRY BEHAVIOR FORM

Worry Behavior	Alternative Behavior	Prediction	Maximum Anxiety
_____	_____	_____	_____
_____	_____	_____	_____
_____	_____	_____	_____
_____	_____	_____	_____
_____	_____	_____	_____
_____	_____	_____	_____
_____	_____	_____	_____

PRACTICE YOUR ALTERNATIVE TO WORRY BEHAVIOR

Beginning with the least anxiety-provoking alternative to a worry behavior, practice it daily until your maximum anxiety level when you do it is no more than 2 on the Anxiety Severity Scale. In preparing to do your alternative behavior, you can use the skills you learned earlier in this chapter to realistically judge the odds of something bad happening, evaluate your catastrophic prediction, and plan what you would do if something negative were to happen. You can also use cue-controlled relaxation if you feel tense.

Ideally, you should practice your alternative behavior every day. However, if an alternative behavior can be practiced only once a week (*example*: sitting in the middle of a pew near the front of the church during a service rather than on an aisle seat in the back for easy exit in case of an emergency), it makes sense to work on more than one alternative behavior at a time. This is also true if the alternative behavior depends on circumstances beyond your control (*example*: attending parties to which you have been invited, rather than not going),

Use the Alternative Behavior Practice Log below to record the date on which you practice, what alternative behavior you are practicing, the consequence of doing that behavior, and your maximum anxiety level that day. Compare the consequence of doing your alternative behavior with your prediction of what would happen when you practiced that behavior. Did the consequence of your alternative behavior disconfirm your prediction? Even if something negative did happen when you practiced your alternative behavior, were you able to cope with the consequence? If not, what could you do next time to cope more effectively?

Be on the lookout for subtle worry behaviors you might engage in to avoid the possible consequences of your alternative behavior (for example, attending a party but not talking to anyone or talking only to people you know well to avoid possible rejection). Of course, you have to be the judge of what level of challenge you are ready to take on. As you move through your list practicing your alternatives to worry behaviors, you will discover that you can tolerate more anxiety than you thought you could. This will allow you to take on greater challenges faster.

Owen, a supervisor in a bank, always stayed late to finish all his work every day. He planned as his alternative behavior to leave at least one item incomplete and to leave work on time each day. His prediction was that, if he did this, he would be overwhelmed by the work that would pile up, and that, ultimately, he would be fired for being underproductive.

When evaluating the odds of his negative prediction coming true, he had to admit to himself that his fear was unlikely because he was the only person at the bank besides the bank president who stayed late to finish up his work and the only one who finished all his work every day, yet none of his colleagues had been fired for being underproductive. In the improbable event that he would be fired, he knew that with all of his contacts at other banks he would not be unemployed for very long. In spite of this awareness, he predicted that his anxiety level would score an 8 when he practiced his alternative behavior.

The first day of practice, Owen's maximum level of anxiety was actually a 6 when he left work on time with one small item incomplete. He knew that he had worked hard to get things done during the day so as to not leave anything significant undone. Rather than sabotage his progress, the next day he purposely didn't work very hard and he didn't complete an important item before he left work on time; his maximum level of anxiety for the day was an 8. He resisted the temptation to stay late, and instead he practiced cue-controlled relaxation at his desk before he went home. He did the same over the next three days. By the middle of the second workweek, Owen's maximum anxiety level was a 2; he had learned he could leave work on time, confident that if something important had to wait until the next day he could manage it.

Here's an example of Owen's Alternative Behavior Practice Log:

ALTERNATIVE BEHAVIOR PRACTICE LOG

Date	Alternative Behavior	Consequence	Maximum Anxiety
7/10	Leave work on time with one item not done	Nobody noticed; able to complete item	6
7/11	"	Nobody noticed; able to complete 7/10 item	8
7/12	"	Client wanted 7/11 item not done; able to deliver by end of day, acceptable to customer	7
7/13	"	Nobody noticed; able to complete 7/12 item	4
7/14	"	Boss wanted 7/13 item but agreed to wait until item complete	5
7/17	"	Nobody noticed; unable to complete 7/14 item	3
7/18	"	Nobody noticed; able to complete 7/14 and 7/17 undone items today	3
7/19	"	Nobody noticed; chose not to complete 7/18 item today	2
7/20	Wore wrinkled shirt to work	Nobody noticed	7
7/21	"	Coworker joked about it	6

Make copies of the Alternative Behavior Practice Log to keep a record of your practice of alternative behaviors.

ALTERNATIVE BEHAVIOR PRACTICE LOG

Date	Alternative Behavior	Consequence	Maximum Anxiety

Other Factors to Consider

If you experience little or no anxiety when you practice behavioral alternatives, you may have learned to think more realistically. If this is the case, completing the behavior alternatives exercise will confirm your new way of thinking. Be careful not to engage in subtle forms of checking, preventing, and avoiding to keep your anxiety low. For instance, if as an alternative to micromanaging you choose to delegate responsibilities to others, don't go around checking on them and making improvements on what they have done.

If you think that it would be too anxiety-provoking to practice this exercise, remember that your anxiety will be short-lived compared to the ongoing anxiety you will experience if you don't change your behavior. Remember that it's not unusual to experience the greatest anxiety the first time you practice an alternative behavior; stick with it because with repeated exposures to the new behavior your anxiety will quickly diminish.

If your anxiety level doesn't come down with repeated practice of your alternative behavior, examine your thoughts and use the realistic thinking skills you learned at the beginning of this chapter. You may be interpreting the consequences of practicing your alternative behavior in a way that supports your old negative prediction. For example, Caleb, a realtor, who was always at least ten minutes early to his appointments no matter how rushed he was, practiced being at least two minutes late to his appointments.

After a week of no one commenting on his tardiness, Caleb still felt anxious. He realized that he was telling himself that people were just being polite and that they were going to stop doing business with him if he kept it up. He reminded himself that he wasn't a mind reader or a fortune-teller, and that he needed to focus on his clients' behavior in response to his tardiness. He decided to persevere in practicing his alternative behavior, and at the end of two weeks, he had lost only one client who found a house through another realtor. He was able to handle this and his anxiety level regarding being tardy with his clients was a 1.

TURN WORRY INTO PROBLEM SOLVING

In this chapter, so far you've learned how to deal more realistically with exaggerated worries, not to get rid of appropriate concerns about real threats. But what can you do to keep your worry from getting out of hand when you have a life crisis or genuine problem? There are three practical steps you can take to minimize your worry and anxiety. They are: (1) clearly define the problem; (2) use brainstorming to find solutions; and (3) make a contract with yourself to follow through on your solutions.

This step-by-step model for turning worry into problem solving was adapted from the *Worry Control Workbook*, by Mary Ellen Copeland (1998). Each step, written in bold, is followed by an example of how a young entrepreneur used the problem-solving process to deal with worries about starting her business.

1. **Write down one situation that is really worrying you. Be specific about what the problem is.** *I really want to start a business of my own, but my financial resources are very limited. I'm worried that I don't know enough to avoid the pitfalls and I'll end up losing everything.*

2. **Brainstorm for solutions.** Make a list of possible things you can do to improve or correct the situation.

   - *Talk to other entrepreneurs about their experiences in starting their businesses.*

   - *Research organizations that support entrepreneurial efforts and people.*

   - *Research the possibility of acquiring a small-business loan or other capital available for small start-up businesses.*

   - *Join a couple of small-business and entrepreneurial organizations.*

   - *Find investors among friends and family.*

   - *Start the business out of my home to save overhead and protect me financially.*

   - *Work an extra job for a couple of years to earn more money.*

   - *Stay at current job while starting my own company part-time.*

3. **Evaluate each idea.** Which ideas are not possible? Put an X next to those. Which ones would be difficult to implement? Put a question mark next to those. Which ideas could you implement right now? Put a Y next to those.

Talk to other entrepreneurs about their experiences in starting their businesses.	Y
Research organizations that support entrepreneurial efforts and people.	Y
Research the possibility of acquiring a small-business loan or other capital available for small start-up businesses.	Y
Join a couple of small-business and entrepreneurial organizations.	?
Find investors among family and friends.	Y
Start the business out of my own home to save overhead.	?
Work an extra job for a couple of years to earn more money.	X
Stay at current job while starting the company part-time.	X

4. **Set specific dates.** Make a contract with yourself to do all the things that you've marked with a Y.

By April 1, I will talk to other entrepreneurs about their experiences in starting their businesses.

By April 15, I will research organizations that support entrepreneurial efforts and people.

By May 1, I'll have canvassed family and friends for possible investors.

By May 15, I will research the possibility of acquiring a small-business loan or other capital available for small start-up businesses.

5. **When you have completed all of the items marked with a Y, go on to the more difficult things marked with a question mark.** Make a contract with yourself to do those.

By June 15, I will join a couple of small-business and entrepreneurial organizations.

By July 1, I'll decide whether I should clear out a back bedroom to create a home-based business office.

By July 15, I will apply for all available capital that I find during my initial research.

6. **Now maybe some of the items marked with an X don't look so hard.** If there are any you think you could manage, make a contract with yourself to take that action.

By August 15, if other options have not worked out, I will start my company part-time while continuing to work full-time at my job.

PROBLEM-SOLVING WORKSHEET

Use this space to apply the problem-solving technique to one of your worries.

1. Write down one situation that is really worrying you.

   <u>passing all exams</u>

   _____

   _____

   _____

2. Brainstorm for solutions. Make a list of possible things you can do to improve or correct the situation.

   Y <u>start studying now.</u>

   Y <u>make a study plan</u>

   Y <u>devote library time</u>

   Y <u>meet w/ classmates to study</u>

3. Evaluate each idea. Which ones are not possible? Put an X next to those. Which ones would be difficult to implement? Put a question mark next to those. Which ones could you do right now? Put a Y next to those.

4. Set specific dates. Make a contract with yourself to do all the Y items.

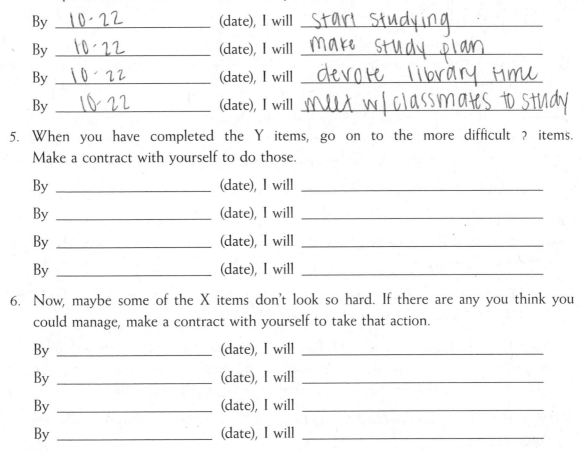

By __10·22__ (date), I will __start studying__

By __10·22__ (date), I will __make study plan__

By __10·22__ (date), I will __devote library time__

By __10·22__ (date), I will __meet w/ classmates to study__

5. When you have completed the Y items, go on to the more difficult ? items. Make a contract with yourself to do those.

By _____ (date), I will _____

By _____ (date), I will _____

By _____ (date), I will _____

By _____ (date), I will _____

6. Now, maybe some of the X items don't look so hard. If there are any you think you could manage, make a contract with yourself to take that action.

By _____ (date), I will _____

By _____ (date), I will _____

By _____ (date), I will _____

By _____ (date), I will _____

Note that three other chapters in this workbook can help you deal with life problems. They are Goal Setting and Time Management, Work-Stress Management, and Assertiveness Training.

FINAL THOUGHTS

Facing your worry and anxiety will become progressively easier as you regularly practice the skills presented in this chapter. Consider these goals for yourself: Each time you choose to use your relaxation skills, you will feel less tense. Each time you successfully challenge your worry, you will experience more peace of mind. Each time that you systematically confront your catastrophic images, you become a little less fearful. Each time you tackle situations you worry about in real life and don't experience negative consequences that you can't cope with, you will become a little more self-confident and resilient. Each time you focus on problem solving, you will become more aware of the many resources you have to accomplish your goals. Just be patient with yourself as you work through this chapter, because it takes a while to overcome old habits of thinking and behaving and to develop new ones.

FURTHER READING

Barlow, D. H. 2002. *Anxiety and Its Disorders: The Nature and Treatment of Anxiety and Panic.* New York: Guilford Press.

Brown, T. A., R. M. Hertz, and D. H. Barlow. 1992. New developments in cognitive-behavioral treatment of anxiety disorders. In *American Psychiatric Press Review of Psychiatry*, vol. 2, edited by A. Tasman. Washington, DC: American Psychiatric Press. Out of print.

Copeland, M. E. 1998. *Worry Control Workbook.* Oakland, CA: New Harbinger Publications. Out of print.

Craske, M. G., and D. H. Barlow. 2006. *Mastery of Your Anxiety and Worry.* 2nd ed. New York: Oxford University Press.

McKay, M., M. Davis, and P. Fanning. 2007. *Thoughts and Feelings: Taking Control of Your Moods and Your Life.* 3rd ed. Oakland, CA: New Harbinger Publications.

O'Leary, T. A., T. A. Brown, and D. H. Barlow. 1992. The efficacy of worry control treatment in generalized anxiety disorder: A multiple baseline analysis. Paper presented at the annual meeting of the Association for Advancement of Behavior Therapy, Boston.

White, J. 1999. *Overcoming Generalized Anxiety Disorder: Client Manual.* Oakland, CA: New Harbinger Publications.

14

Coping Skills Training for Fears

In this chapter you will learn to:

✳ Feel calmer and more capable when anticipating stressful events

✳ Relax before and during stressful situations

✳ Counteract irrational anxious thoughts in stressful situations

BACKGROUND

Donald Meichenbaum (1977), one of the principal developers of coping skills training, suggests that the fear response involves the interaction of two main elements: (1) physiological arousal and (2) thoughts that interpret your situation as threatening or dangerous and attribute your physiological arousal to the emotion of anxiety or fear. The actual stressful situation has little to do with your emotional response. Your evaluation of the danger and how you label your body's reaction are the real forces that determine what emotional response you will have. This accounts for why the same person who loves the "feelings of exhilaration" he experiences when skydiving leaps to a chair shaking and screaming in mortal terror when he sees a pet mouse on the floor.

In both situations he is experiencing the fight-or-flight response. In the first case, he views jumping out of an airplane as a thrilling adventure and he labels his physical sensations as excitement; they actually serve to heighten the pleasure of his experience. In the second situation he sees the mouse as his mortal enemy because of some prior adverse learning, and he interprets his physiological arousal as fear, which further confirms to him that the situation is dangerous.

With coping skills training, you learn to relax at the first sign of the stress response and counter your anxious thoughts with coping thoughts when faced with a challenging situation. This training doesn't assume that you will master anxiety so that it will never come back. Rather, it gives you effective coping strategies so you develop confidence in your ability to handle any situation, no matter how upsetting it may feel at first.

THE FIVE STEPS OF COPING SKILLS TRAINING FOR FEARS

1. **Relaxation skills.** You've probably already begun to master the relaxation procedures described in the earlier chapters in this book that you will need for coping skills training: diaphragmatic breathing, progressive relaxation, release-only relaxation, and cue-controlled relaxation.

2. **Stressful-events hierarchy list.** In order to apply coping skills training to your life, you will construct a personal hierarchy, or list, of your stressful situations, ranging from the least distressing to most distressing situation.

3. **Coping thoughts.** You will create your own list of coping thoughts. These will be used to get you through times when you feel anxious and are likely to be saying to yourself something like, "This is impossible ... I can't do this ... I'm overwhelmed ... it's too much. ..."

4. **Imagery exposure coping skills.** Using your imagination, you can call up each stressful situation in your hierarchy, feel the tension and distressing emotions associated with it, and then relax away the tension and counter your stressful thoughts with coping thoughts. This rehearsal in imagination prepares you to reverse the stress response when you're under fire in real life.

5. **Real life coping skills.** When you've completed the first four steps, you begin to apply them to challenging situations in your daily life. Eventually, self-relaxation procedures and stress-coping thoughts become automatic in any stressful situation.

SYMPTOM-RELIEF EFFECTIVENESS

Coping skills training has been shown to be effective for reducing anxiety in specific situations, such as before and during interviews, speeches, and tests. It is useful in the treatment of phobias, particularly for the fear of heights. The control of specific and generalized anxiety has long-term effects: two-year follow-ups of hypertense, postcardiac patients showed that 89 percent were still able to achieve general relaxation using coping skills training, and 79 percent were able to fall asleep sooner and sleep more deeply (Goldfried 1973).

TIME TO MASTER

You can master the key relaxation techniques for coping skills training within a month. Writing out a stressful-events hierarchy list takes a few hours; typically, you can spread your writing over a few days. You can successfully go through your stressful-events hierarchy in your imagination using your relaxation procedures and coping thoughts in a week or less. With regular practice for two to six months in real life, these coping skills can become automatic and be used whenever you feel anxious or angry.

INSTRUCTIONS

Step 1: Learn to Relax Efficiently

The foundation stone of coping skills training is knowing how to relax. The skills you will need are all in this book:

- Diaphragmatic Breathing (chapter 3)

- Progressive Relaxation (chapter 4)

- Release-Only Relaxation (chapter 7)

- Cue-Controlled Relaxation (chapter 7)

- Creating Your Special Place (chapter 6)

You will need to overlearn these relaxation techniques so that (1) you can use them at a moment's notice and (2) you can achieve deep relaxation in a minute or two. You want to be able to relax with the same unconscious coordination with which you ride a bike or write your name. Begin practicing these relaxation techniques immediately. You can complete steps 2 and 3 while you are learning to relax, but don't go beyond step 3 until you have mastered each of these relaxation techniques.

Step 2: Make a Stressful-Events Hierarchy List

Pick a theme in your life you feel anxious about (for example, participating in groups, driving, heights, health, family, deadlines). On a piece of paper, list all the things you would like to do that might trigger anxiety about this theme. Try to include only stressful situations that you are likely to encounter in the relatively near future. Be specific, including the setting and the people involved. Get as close to twenty items on your list as possible, and let them run the full gamut from very mild discomfort to your most dreaded experiences. These items should be things you don't do because of your anxiety or you do only with significant anxiety.

At the top of another piece of paper write the least anxiety-provoking item you imagined. At the bottom of the page write the item that would make you the most anxious. Now select between six to eighteen items of graduated intensity that you can fill in between your lowest- and highest-anxiety scenes. As you move down your list, each item should represent an increase in stress over the preceding item, and the increases should be in approximately equal increments.

For help with this, you can use the Wolpe and Lazarus (1966) rating system called subjective units of distress, or SUDs. Total relaxation is 0 SUDs, while the most stressful situation on your hierarchy should be rated at 100 SUDs—the highest stress you can imagine. All the other items on your hierarchy should fall somewhere between 5 and 99 SUDs. Assign SUDs scores to each of your items, based on your subjective impression of where each situation falls relative to your most relaxed or most anxious states.

For instance, Ann has a fear of heights and her most stressful item is "A five-hour flight to New York for my daughter's wedding," which she ranks at 100, while her least stressful item is "standing on a low stool," which she rates as a 5. "Driving over a suspension bridge" she ranks up at 70, and "walking over an overpass" she ranks at 45.

You are the expert on how you react to each situation, and you therefore must decide where each stressful event fits, relative to the others. For a list of twenty items, try to separate them all by increments of five SUDs. In that way, the items on your hierarchy will progress in relatively equal steps from one to twenty.

Zack, a college student, constructed the following hierarchy for his social anxiety:

ZACK'S STRESSFUL-EVENTS HIERARCHY WORKSHEET

Theme: Social Anxiety

SUDs Rank	Item
5	Make eye contact and smile at classmates I happen to see around campus.
10	Make eye contact, smile, and say "hello" to classmates I see around campus.
15	Make small talk for five minutes before class.
20	Join a classmate during a break in the cafeteria and make small talk.
25	Join a small group of classmates during a break in the cafeteria and make small talk.
30	Attend a family Fourth of July picnic.
35	Ask a classmate to work on a class project with me.
40	Call on the phone to inquire about a summer job.
45	Attend a party with friends and strangers.
50	Volunteer to answer the teacher's questions in class.
55	Ask questions in class.
60	Volunteer my opinion during a class discussion.
65	Make eye contact, smile, and say "hello" to a very attractive woman.
70	Join a very attractive woman in the cafeteria and make small talk.
75	Give a five-minute presentation in class.
80	Give a twenty-minute presentation in class.
85	Invite a very attractive woman to join me for coffee after class.
90	Ask a very attractive woman out to dinner.
95	Interview for a summer job.
100	Be best man at a friend's wedding and toast the bride and groom.

Now, here is a blank Stressful-Events Hierarchy Worksheet. Make several copies of it to work on in the future.

STRESSFUL-EVENTS HIERARCHY WORKSHEET

Theme: _____

SUDs Rank	Item

Step 3: Create Stress-Coping Thoughts

Stress-coping thoughts can put a stop to or at least soften painful emotions. To understand how they work, consider the four components of an emotional response, continuing with the example of Zack, the socially anxious college student:

1. **The stimulus situation:** He is giving a five-minute presentation in front of his class.

2. **Physical reactions:** His aroused autonomic nervous system produces dry mouth; cold, clammy, tremulous hands; butterflies in his stomach; tightness in his throat; sweaty armpits; rapid heartbeat; and light-headedness.

3. **Behavioral response:** He fights the impulse to bolt out of the room, gets up, and gives a stiff presentation that he reads very softly and quickly, avoiding eye contact.

4. **Thoughts:** How he interprets the situation, what his self-evaluations are, and what he predicts will happen are what create his emotions. He says to himself: "I can't do this ..." (*prediction*); "I'm a nervous wreck ..." (*self-evaluation*); "My mind is going to go blank and nothing is going to come out of my mouth ..." (*prediction*); "Everyone will look at me and think I'm a complete idiot ..." (*interpretation*).

Zack's emotional response is high anxiety and his behavior is inhibited. The feedback loop from thoughts to physical reactions to behavioral choices to more negative thoughts can spiral on and on. Fortunately, your thoughts don't have to intensify your fear response. Instead, they can serve to calm your body and neutralize your feelings of high anxiety. According to McKay, Davis, and Fanning (2007), the feedback loop can work for you as well as against you. Stress-coping thoughts tell your body there is no need for arousal—it can relax. Before and during any stressful situation, you can begin saying to yourself a series of fear-conquering statements such as, "Take a deep breath and relax.... You've given lots of successful class presentations before.... Calm down.... It's natural to be a little nervous.... Nobody is going to think less of you for it...."

The more attention you give to your coping monologue, the faster you will experience relief from the fight-or-flight response.

Meichenbaum and Cameron (1974) suggest four situations when you can use stress-coping statements:

1. When you are preparing to do something that provokes anxiety and you are having thoughts that trigger anticipatory anxiety

2. When you confront the stressful situation and you are having anxiety-provoking thoughts that interfere with your ability to concentrate and cope comfortably in the moment

3. When you feel tension or fear and need to be reminded to relax

4. When you have completed an anxiety-provoking activity and you want to acknowledge that you succeeded in getting through the stressful event by using your coping skills

EXAMPLES OF STRESS-COPING THOUGHTS

1. **Preparing to cope**

   There's nothing to worry about.

   I'm going to be all right.

   I've succeeded with this before.

   What exactly do I have to do?

   I know I can do each one of these tasks.

   It gets easier once I get started.

   I'll jump in and be all right.

   Tomorrow I'll be through it.

   Don't let negative thoughts creep in.

2. **Confronting the stressful situation**

   Stay organized.

   Take it step by step; don't rush.

   I can do this, I'm doing it now.

   I can only do my best.

   Any tension I feel is a signal to use my coping exercises.

   I can get help if I need it.

   If I don't think about fear, I won't be afraid.

   If I get tense, I'll take a breather and relax.

   It's okay to make mistakes.

3. **Coping with fear**

   Relax now!

   Just breathe deeply.

There's an end to it.

Keep my mind on right now, on the task at hand.

I can keep this within limits I can handle.

I can always call _____.

I am afraid only because I decided to be. I can decide not to be.

I've survived this—and worse—before.

Once I'm doing something, my fear gradually lessens.

4. **Reinforcing success**

I did it!

I did all right. I did well.

Next time I won't have to worry so much.

I am able to relax away anxiety.

I've got to tell _____ about this.

It's possible not to be scared. All I have to do is stop thinking I'm scared.

HOW TO CREATE YOUR OWN STRESS-COPING THOUGHTS

Although many of the stress-coping thoughts listed above can work for you, the ones you create yourself will probably fit you best. For each one of the items on your hierarchy, select or create two or three stress-coping thoughts that will relax your body and reassure your mind.

● Visualize an item on your hierarchy in detail.

● Notice how you feel.

● Listen to what you are saying to yourself that is anxiety-provoking.

● Write down these stressful thoughts for each item on your hierarchy.

● Examine each of your stressful thoughts. Typically, anxious thoughts are not completely accurate or rational. Questioning your anxious thoughts will tend to lead to stress-coping thoughts. Here are seven questions to ask when evaluating your anxious thoughts:

1. Can I really read people's minds?

2. Can I really predict the future?

3. Am I exaggerating how bad it is or will be?

4. If what I fear does happen, how long will I really have to endure it?

5. How likely is it that what I fear will actually happen?

6. What are some other more probable things that could happen?

7. What coping skills can I use to handle what I fear might happen (relaxation skills, ways to reassure myself, people I can call on to help me, things I can do, a plan I can make)?

For example, here are some of the distressing thoughts that the anxious college student, Zack, had when he contemplated doing a few of the activities he listed on his hierarchy. He used the seven questions listed above to challenge his anxious thoughts.

- Make eye contact and smile at classmates I happen to see around campus.

    They'll think I'm weird and they won't want to have anything to do with me.

    1. I can't read minds.

    2. I can't predict the future.

    3. I'm exaggerating. The worst thing that will happen is that they'll ignore me or make a rude remark.

    4. If someone responds negatively, I can endure a few moments of rejection.

    5. It's extremely unlikely. Most people are pretty friendly. Smiling at people is usually considered a friendly gesture. They'll probably think I'm just another friendly guy.

    6. Most likely, most people will respond positively.

    7. If someone responds negatively, I don't have to take it personally. Maybe he's just having a bad day. I'll just relax, make eye contact, and smile. I can keep track of how many people respond positively versus how many don't.

- Call on the phone to inquire about a summer job.

  I'll go blank because I'm so nervous, and really blow it!

  1. (Not applicable to this situation)

  2. I can't predict the future.

  3. I'm exaggerating. I've never gone blank in my life. If it really happened, I'd excuse myself and call back later or call some other company.

  4. I'd only have to endure it intensely for a few minutes at the most.

  5. It is highly unlikely since I'm well prepared, am using coping skills, and I have everything I want to ask written out in the event I forget something.

  6. I'll do just fine. I'll make a few mistakes but I'll still get the information I'm seeking in spite of being a little nervous.

  7. I can relax before and during the call. I can refer to my notes if I need to. It's okay not to be perfect.

- Give a five-minute presentation in class.

  I will feel panicky; I can't stand that.

  1. (Not applicable to this situation)

  2. I can't predict the future.

  3. I'm exaggerating. I don't like high anxiety, but I have handled it before and I survived.

  4. My anxiety level will be high for no more than five minutes and drop as soon as I sit down after my presentation is finished.

  5. I know that I'll be able to handle my anxiety and give my presentation using coping skills.

  6. As I continue practicing my coping skills, I might even enjoy giving presentations.

  7. Anxiety is my cue to relax and breathe. My notes are there if I need them. I can look forward to basketball practice after class.

EXERCISE

On a piece of paper, write down the first item on your hierarchy. Then write down one of your anxious thoughts about that item. Finally, write down the number of the question(s) that you are answering along with your answer(s). Follow this format for each item on your hierarchy:

SUDs Rank _____ Item _____

Anxiety-Provoking Thought: _____

Question Number   My Answer

1.

2.

3.

4.

5.

6.

7.

Select two or three stress-coping thoughts for each of the items on your hierarchy. To do this, review your answers to question 7 and put an asterisk next to the answers that are most effective in helping you to feel relaxed and reassured. Particularly powerful stress-coping thoughts are brief, accurate, realistic, believable, and positive. While they probably won't eliminate all your anxiety, they will lessen your tension and make you feel more confident that you can cope with the situation you're facing. If you have difficulty coming up with your own stress-coping thoughts, refer to the general list of stress-coping statements under the heading "Examples of Stress-Coping Thoughts."

Step 4: Imagery Exposure Coping Skills

A. Relax for five or ten minutes or until you feel deeply relaxed, calm, and safe. Now briefly review your coping statements for the situation you plan to work with next.

B. Imagine you're in the situation. Try to make the scene come alive in your imagination. See the situation. Hear what is going on. Feel the mounting tension in your body. Remember your anxiety-provoking thoughts. When you can really feel the anxiety, proceed to step C.

C. Start to cope. As soon as the imagined scene is clear in your mind and you can feel its effects, begin relaxing and using coping thoughts. Cue-controlled relaxation is the fastest stress reduction technique and therefore is best-suited to this step. Keep saying your coping thoughts to yourself and relaxing while you continue to imagine the anxiety-provoking scene for about one minute.

D. Rate your anxiety. On a scale from 0 (no anxiety) to 10 (the most anxious you have ever felt), rate the anxiety you experienced in the scene just before you closed it down. If your anxiety is a 1 or 0, you can relax (step E) and move on to the next situation in your hierarchy. If your anxiety is 2 or more, relax (step E) and then repeat steps B and C using the same situation. Review your coping thoughts. If any of them are ineffective, replace them with new ones of your own or go back to the general list of stress-coping statements and try one or two others. Keep in mind that the ones you create yourself are likely to be the most powerful for you.

E. Always relax deeply between scenes. Use cue-controlled relaxation and spend time calming yourself in your special place. If you are having difficulty relaxing using these two techniques, use progressive relaxation or release-only relaxation before reentering the scene.

Continue imagining and coping with scenes until you've finished the most difficult item in your hierarchy. Practice daily for best results. Your first practice session should be about fifteen to twenty minutes. Later, you may want to extend your session to as long as thirty minutes. If you get tired and have trouble visualizing a scene, it's better to postpone practice until you are more alert. Expect to master one to three hierarchy items during each practice session. When starting a new practice session, always go back to the last scene you successfully completed. This helps consolidate your gains before you face more anxiety-provoking items.

When you have mastered all the items on your hierarchy using imagery and coping skills, you will have a better awareness of how and where tension builds in your body. You will be able to use the early signs of tension as your signal to relax. Mastery of those items with the highest SUDs provides a degree of confidence that stress reduction is possible—even in the most threatening situations.

EXAMPLE

Zack, the socially anxious college student, began his imagery exposure coping skills sessions with ten minutes of relaxation. When he tried to visualize his first stressful situation (5 SUDs), he had difficulty recalling the details of the scene and he didn't experience any anxiety. Since learning to relax in the face of fear requires that each scene be vivid and real, he waited until the following morning just before class to study the sights, sounds, and smells of the busy halls of his college. He closed his eyes and described the scene to himself, using all of his senses. Then he opened his eyes and added to his description the things that he had missed the first time.

He described to himself how he felt and what he was thinking as he imagined himself making eye contact and smiling at his classmates hurrying by. That night he began his practice again with ten minutes of relaxation before he visualized the first item on his hierarchy. This time it was easy to imagine himself in the scene and he experienced some tension in his throat, chest, and stomach. He then used cue-controlled relaxation and coping thoughts as he continued to imagine being in the stressful scene for about one minute. He rated his level of anxiety at the conclusion of one minute as 0.

He took a couple of minutes to relax in his special place, using cue-controlled relaxation, then went on to imagine the next item on his hierarchy.

Sometimes, Zack had to visualize a situation six or more times before the image produced no anxiety. He scheduled his practice for mornings and evenings at about fifteen to twenty minutes. On the average, he was able to successfully relax away tension in three scenes per day, and in a week he completed his hierarchy.

Step 5: Real-Life Coping Skills

When you encounter stress in real life, your body tension is a cue to begin to relax. At that time, repeat to yourself your stress-coping thoughts as you prepare for and confront the situation and begin to limit the fear you feel. Remember to praise yourself for meeting the challenge. Using coping skills in real life will probably be more difficult than relaxing away stress in imagined scenes. Some setbacks are inevitable. Practice, however, will make relaxation and stress-coping thoughts so natural that, eventually, they will automatically begin at the first symptom of tension.

Zack was preparing for a job interview the next morning. Rather than staying up late worrying, he wrote down his stress-coping thoughts to use before, during, and after the interview.

Then he spent twenty minutes practicing his stress-coping skills, using the coping thoughts that he found most powerful, just as when he was practicing his hierarchy.

1. **Preparing to cope**

    I've succeeded with this before.

    I know what to do to succeed this time.

    I'm prepared.

    I can relax and get a good night's sleep.

2. **Confronting the stressful situation**

    Focus on my goal.

    It's okay to not know something.

    Answer the questions so that the interviewer can see my strengths.

3. **Coping with fear**

    I can use my anxiety as a cue to relax.

    Keep breathing from the belly and let go of the tension.

    I can feel anxious and still deal with this situation.

    I'll feel great when this is over.

4. **Reinforcing success**

    I did it!

    I was able to cope with my anxiety and do a good job.

    It's getting easier to calm down and relax.

    I can really relax now.

Zack typed the phrase "Take a deep breath and let go of the tension" onto a file card and taped it to the top of his computer monitor. Other signs were taped on the front page of his notebook, his refrigerator, and his car visor. On the way to the interview he practiced deep breathing and repeated the coping thoughts listed under "Preparing to cope." While he waited in the lobby to be called in by the interviewer, he continued to relax and slowly read over all of his coping thoughts. He memorized several of them. In spite of all this preparation, when the interviewer came out for him, he thought, "Oh no, here we go!" and he felt his heart beat hard in his chest, his stomach knotted up, and his mouth went dry. He remembered the coping thought "I can use my anxiety as a cue to relax" and immediately began consciously deep breathing and focusing on relaxing his jaw, shoulders, and stomach. As the interviewer began to question him, he repeated to himself, "Talk about my strengths … I can be anxious and still deal with this. …" When he was asked a question that he didn't know the answer to, his mind momentarily froze, until he thought, "It's okay not to know something … take a deep breath and relax." By the end of the interview, he was actually enjoying himself. When he left the interviewer's office, his first thought was "I did it! I was actually able to cope with my anxiety and do a good job!"

When it came to dealing with spontaneous social interactions, at first he often forgot his training and was overwhelmed by the intensity of a situation. In time, he discovered that the key to real-life practice was to start using cue-controlled relaxation and stress-coping thoughts the moment he noticed any tension or anxiety. He gradually learned to spot stress coming, tune in to his early warning signs of physical tension, and start working his coping skills early.

SPECIAL CONSIDERATIONS

1. If you have difficulty relaxing at the beginning of the session, you may want to record your relaxation routine and play it.

2. If you have difficulty imagining your scenes, reread chapter 6, Visualization. Be sure to use all of your senses. You might also try going to the real setting of one of your scenes to gather images and impressions and practice remembering the details. Close your eyes and describe the scene to yourself and then open your eyes and see what you missed. Keep this up, gradually adding sounds, textures, smells, and temperatures until you have a vivid sense picture in your imagination.

3. If you can visualize your scenes clearly yet experience little or no anxiety, your first items need to be more challenging, or perhaps you need more variety in the content of your scenes. In either case, you may need to rewrite your hierarchy.

4. If you can visualize your scenes clearly and experience erratic levels of tension, you may need to rearrange your hierarchy. You also may need to rewrite some of your scenes so that you have a more even increase in the level of distress as you move down your hierarchy.

FURTHER READING

Goldfried, M. R. 1973. Reduction of generalized anxiety through a variant of systematic desensitization. In *Behavior Change through Self-Control*, edited by M. R. Goldfried and M. Merbaum. New York: Holt, Rinehart and Winston.

McKay, M., M. Davis, and P. Fanning. 2007. *Thoughts and Feelings: Taking Control of Your Moods and Your Life*. 3rd ed. Oakland, CA: New Harbinger Publications.

Meichenbaum, D. 1977. *Cognitive Behavior Modification.* New York: Plenum.

————. 1992. Self-instructional methods. In *Helping People Change*, edited by F. K. Kanfur and A. P. Goldstein. New York: Pergamon Press.

Meichenbaum, D., and R. Cameron. 1974. Modifying what clients say to themselves. In *Self-Control: Power to the Person*, edited by M. J. Mahoney and C. E. Thoresen. Monterey, CA: Brooks/Cole. Out of print.

Suinn, R. M., and F. Richardson. 1971. Anxiety management training: A non-specific behavior therapy program for anxiety control. *Behavior Therapy* 2:498–510.

Wolpe, J., and A. A. Lazarus. 1966. *Behavior Therapy Techniques.* New York: Pergamon Press.

15

Anger Inoculation

In this chapter you will learn to:

* Relax rather than tense up in anger-provoking situations

* Develop coping thoughts to control anger-triggering cognitions

* Use provoking images to rehearse new coping skills and to inoculate yourself against anger

* Develop situation-specific anger coping plans

BACKGROUND

Anger inoculation (McKay and Rogers 2000) is based on the anger management protocol developed by Jerry Deffenbacher (Deffenbacher and McKay 2000). The idea behind anger inoculation is that if you progressively expose yourself to memories of more and more provocative anger situations—while using coping skills—you will learn to manage the anger response. Raymond Novaco (1975) was the first to utilize this technique, and his research showed that it worked to reduce anger-driven aggression. Deffenbacher et al. (1987) confirmed Novaco's original findings, showing that combining relaxation and coping thoughts can significantly control anger. With anger inoculation, you learn to relax at the first sign of provocation, and to counter your anger-triggering thoughts with thoughts intended to calm you and disconnect you from the upset. This training doesn't prevent you from feeling anger; but it gives you effective coping strategies so you'll have the confidence that you can face a provocation without flying off the handle and damaging your relationships.

Anger inoculation involves four steps. They are as follows:

1. **Relaxation skills.** The specific relaxation training you'll need is available in other chapters of this book: diaphragmatic breathing, progressive relaxation, release-only relaxation, cue-controlled relaxation, and special place visualization.

2. **Coping thoughts.** You will create your own anger coping thoughts that will help you combat distorted thinking that triggers upsets.

3. **Inoculation.** You'll practice relaxation and cognitive coping skills while visualizing anger-evoking memories at five levels of intensity.

4. **Real-life coping.** You'll combine your most effective coping skills into an anger management plan designed for specific provocations.

SYMPTOM-RELIEF EFFECTIVENESS

Novaco (1975), Hazaleus and Deffenbacher (1986), Deffenbacher et al. (1987), and Deffenbacher and Sabadell (1990) have demonstrated across numerous studies that the anger inoculation protocol you'll learn here works to control the anger response. Significant reductions in both trait anger and anger incidents were achieved with this program.

TIME TO MASTER

You can master the key relaxation techniques in three to four weeks. Developing coping thoughts for specific anger situations would likely take several hours. The anger inoculation process in which you visualize provocative memories uses five levels of intensity with two anger images at each level. This work could take three to four weeks. Developing real-life coping plans may take an hour or two for each specific plan.

INSTRUCTIONS

Step 1: Learn to Relax

The fight-or-flight response is an important component of anger. Although angry thoughts may trigger the response, often you are already at a high level of sympathetic nervous system arousal when something happens that provokes angry thoughts and further stimulates your physiological arousal. This then, of course, produces more angry thoughts. An all too common example of this occurs when you are driving home in heavy traffic after a long day at work, suffering from a tension headache, and someone does something reckless. Already tense, you may lash out.

One way to intervene in your cycle of anger is to lower your overall sympathetic nervous system arousal through regular practice of deep relaxation techniques. But it also helps to use quick, breath-based relaxation strategies as soon as you start to feel upset. So, instead of shouting or blowing your car's horn and going crazy, you take several diaphragmatic breaths to release your pent-up tension.

The core relaxation skills you'll need to manage anger are all in this book. They are listed here—in the order you should learn them. It's hard to master cue-controlled relaxation without first learning progressive relaxation and release-only relaxation, so follow the sequence.

In provocative situations, some relaxation skills can be used quickly to get fast relief. Others are useful only as general stress relievers, and won't help you at the moment you're angry. Each technique is labeled as either "quick relief" or "general stress relief."

The skills you'll need are as follows:

- Diaphragmatic breathing (chapter 3)—*quick relief*

- Progressive relaxation (chapter 4)—*general stress relief*

- Relaxation without tensing or release-only relaxation (chapter 7)—*general stress relief*

- Cue-controlled relaxation (chapter 7)—*quick relief*

- Special place visualization (chapter 6)—*general stress relief*

You will need to master or overlearn these relaxation techniques so that the quick relief strategies are available to you at a moment's notice. The general stress relief techniques provide you with deep release in two to three minutes. You must be able to relax with the same unconscious coordination with which you type or drive your car. Begin practice immediately. Do not go to step 3—anger inoculation—until you have mastered each of these relaxation skills.

Step 2: Develop Anger Coping Thoughts

Your thoughts have an enormous impact on your anger and your ability to defuse your anger. Anger-triggering thoughts are built on the following assumptions:

1. The belief that you have been harmed and/or victimized

2. The belief that the provoking person harmed you deliberately

3. The belief that the provoking person was wrong to harm you, and should have behaved differently (McKay and Rogers 2000)

During stressful experiences, thoughts that paint you as a victim of deliberate and heedless harm will instantly ignite an anger reaction. And the more you think such thoughts, the angrier you will get.

Anger Distortions

Anger-triggering thoughts often distort reality. There are six key cognitive distortions that typically inflame anger, and one or more of them are likely to be factors in many of your anger experiences. Here are the six distortions:

1. **Blaming.** This is the belief that someone else is responsible for your pain, and there is nothing you can do about it. By blaming others, you forget that you have the power to make choices that will change the situation. You end up feeling helpless and stuck— waiting for someone else to fix things that will stay exactly as they are—until you do something. Another problem with blaming is that people are moving through life, trying to make the best choices they can to meet their own needs. When you blame others for their actions, you are blaming them for taking care of themselves in the best way they know how.

2. **Magnifying.** This is the tendency to take what is uncomfortable or unpleasant and frame it as so much worse. Words like "disgusting," "awful," "terrible," or "horrible" set you up to be angry because they exaggerate the impact of the provoking situation.

3. **Global labels.** These distortions use sweeping global judgments to inflame your anger. They paint the other person as totally bad, utterly worthless. Epithets such as "loser," "jerk," "bitch," "selfish pig," "bastard," and so forth are typical global labels. Their danger lies in ignoring the full reality of who the human being is with whom you are angry, and reducing that person to a single negative term.

4. **Misattributions.** This distortion involves jumping to conclusions and mind reading. You assume malicious intent; you think you know people's motives and feelings toward you. You imagine that you can peer into others' hearts, seeing exactly why they do what they do. You don't ask questions or get direct feedback because that's too embarrassing, so you go on guessing and trying to read people, and a good part of the time you guess wrong.

5. **Overgeneralization.** This distortion uses words like "never," "always," "nobody," "everybody," and so on. "She's *always* late." "He's *never* willing to help." Overgeneralization makes an occasional occurrence feel like an ongoing event. The exaggeration makes everything feel intolerable and serves only to crank up your anger response.

6. **Demanding/commanding.** This distortion turns your personal needs or preferences into immutable laws—and when people ignore your preferences, you may feel as though they've broken one of the Ten Commandments. This gives you the right, it often seems, to really blast them. But there's one big problem with demanding/commanding. Often,

other people don't agree with our definition of appropriate rules of conduct. They have their own rules, or at least their own interpretation of the rules, that leaves them feeling blameless while you think they've done wrong. Demanding/commanding is really nothing more than your values and needs imposed on others who may have very different values and needs.

Coping Thoughts

Each anger-provoking distortion requires a coping thought specifically designed to neutralize its effect. Here are some basic guidelines for developing these coping thoughts (adapted from McKay and Rogers 2000):

1. **Blaming**

   - Make a coping plan to solve the problem yourself.

   - Remind yourself that people are mostly doing the best they can to meet their own goals and needs.

   Example coping thoughts:

   Blaming only makes me feel helpless—what can I do to change the situation?

   My plan to change the situation is _____.

   I'm upset about this, but he/she is doing the best they can in the situation.

   They're doing what they need to do. I'll do what I need to do.

2. **Magnifying**

   - Be realistically negative (for example, the situation is disappointing or frustrating, not awful or horrible).

   - Answer this question: How bad is it really?

   - Restate using extremely accurate language.

   - Remind yourself of the whole picture—notice the positives as well as the negatives.

   Example coping thoughts:

   In the grand scheme of things, this is no big deal.

   This is a molehill-size problem. I don't have to make it bigger than it is.

   This is irritating, but it'll be history next week.

3. **Global Labels**

- Be specific.

- Describe the behavior, not the person as a whole.

Example coping thoughts:

Specifically what bothers me is _____.

Don't make it ugly, just state what the problem is.

Stick to the facts.

It's nothing more than a problem. I don't have to make him/her into a monster.

4. **Misattributions**

- Remind yourself that you're guessing about motives—you don't know.

- Find alternative explanations for the problem behavior.

- Make a plan to check out your assumptions with the person who provokes you.

Example coping thoughts:

I'm guessing one possibility, but there are probably other reasons for _____ 's behavior.

Getting angry won't help me figure out what's going on. I need more facts.

Some other possible reasons for this behavior are _____.

5. **Overgeneralization**

- Revise your trigger thoughts so they don't include words like "always," "all," "every," and "never."

- Use only specific and accurate descriptions.

- Look for exceptions—recall how people sometimes behave very differently from their tendencies.

Example coping thoughts:

I'll just focus on the facts and I'll get through without blowing up.

Be accurate—how often does this really happen?

It doesn't *always* happen this way. There are lots of exceptions.

6. **Demanding/Commanding**

- Focus on your desires and preferences—not "shoulds." Think "I prefer," not "You should."

- Figure out what needs the other person is meeting with his/her behavior.

Example coping thoughts:

I'm not getting what I want but it's not the end of the world.

I'd rather things were different but I'll get through it.

People do what they want to do, not what I need them to do.

I wish this wasn't happening but I can live with it.

If you find it difficult to develop your own coping thoughts, here's a list of coping thoughts for dealing with anger that may help. Many of these coping statements were developed in an anger management program that proved to be very effective (Novaco 1975).

GENERALIZED COPING THOUGHTS LIST

- Take a deep breath and relax.

- Getting upset won't help.

- Just as long as I keep my cool, I'm in control.

- Easy does it—there's nothing to be gained by getting mad.

- I'm not going to let him/her get to me.

- I can't change him/her with anger; I'll just upset myself.

- I can find a way to say what I want to say without anger.

- Stay calm—no sarcasm, no attacks.

- I can stay calm and relaxed.

- Relax and let go. There's no need to get my knickers in a twist.

- No one is right, no one is wrong. We just have different needs.

- Stay cool, make no judgments.

- No matter what is said, I know I'm a good person.

- I'll stay rational—anger won't solve anything.

- Let them look upset and foolish. I can act calm and in control.

- His/her opinion isn't important. I won't be pushed into losing my cool.

- Bottom line, I'm in control. I'm out of here rather than say or do something dumb.

- Take a time-out. Cool off, then come back and deal with it.

- Some situations don't have good solutions. Looks like this is one of them. No use getting all bent out of shape about it.

- Break it down. Anger often comes from lumping things together.

- Got angry, but kept the lid on saying dumb things. That's progress.

- Anger means it's time to relax and cope.

- If they want me to get angry, I'm going to disappoint them.

- I can't expect people to act the way I want them to.

- I don't have to take this so seriously.

- This is funny if you look at it that way.

Step 3: Anger Inoculation

Now it's time to get to work. Think back and write down five anger situations you've struggled with over the past few weeks. List them in a journal or on a sheet of paper. Beneath each anger event you name, leave room to identify the following:

1. Your anger-triggering thoughts

2. Any anger distortions that might be embedded in your trigger thoughts

3. Counterresponse strategies (see previous section on coping thoughts) that might neutralize the distortion

4. One or more helpful coping thoughts—including revising the trigger thought to become more accurate

EXAMPLE

Nancy, a forty-year-old schoolteacher, listed anger-provoking events in both her home and classroom. Here are three of them:

Situation 1. Julian pulls out Rebecca's chair just when she's about to sit down—she falls on her back.

Anger-triggering thought: He always does crap like this. He's a mean kid.

Anger distortions: Overgeneralization, global labeling.

Counterresponse plan: Stop using the word "always," be specific; look for exceptions; focus on behavior, not the kid.

Coping or revised trigger thought: "Julian gets in trouble maybe once a day. It's mostly silly stuff where he doesn't hurt anybody. And he's actually pretty sweet to the boy with cerebral palsy. I'm not gonna let his pranks get to me."

Situation 2. I'm assigned yard duty for the second week in a row.

Anger-triggering thought: They're always taking advantage of me because I don't complain. They're making this job unbearable.

Anger distortions: Overgeneralization, misattribution, blaming, magnifying.

Counterresponse plan: Stop using the word "always"; be specific; find alternative explanations; how bad is the job really?

Coping or revised trigger thought: "This is only the second time in a year I've had to do two weeks in a row. It happens to other teachers, not just me. Maybe it's because Hilda was absent this week and they're shorthanded. It's just a hassle, nothing more, nothing less."

Situation 3. Bill takes off for his poker night and leaves the dishes in the sink.

Anger-triggering thought: He's so damned thoughtless. If you're going to go off and play, you'd better finish your work first.

Anger distortions: Global labeling, demanding/commanding.

Counterresponse plan: Focus on the behavior, not the person; stay with my desires and preferences, not "shoulds."

Coping or revised trigger thought: "Bill sometimes forgets to do what he promised. I'd prefer he wouldn't leave a stack of dishes, but it's not the end of the world—he can do them when he gets home."

On the next page is a worksheet for creating your own coping thoughts. Make copies of it and you can follow the steps for creating coping thoughts in any anger situation. Anger-triggering thoughts are those thoughts that set off your anger response.

CREATING A COPING THOUGHTS WORKSHEET

1. Trigger thoughts that inflame my anger:

   a. _____

   b. _____

   c. _____

2. Anger distortions that underlie my trigger thoughts:

   a. _____

   b. _____

   c. _____

2. Counterresponse plan for each of my trigger thoughts (for example, looking for exceptions, alternative explanations, preferences not shoulds, and so on). Revised trigger thought based on each counterresponse plan.

   a. Counterresponse plan: _____

   _____

   Revised trigger thought: _____

   _____

   b. Counterresponse plan: _____

   _____

   Revised trigger thought: _____

   _____

   c. Counterresponse plan: _____

   _____

   Revised trigger thought: _____

   _____

2. Helpful coping thoughts (see Generalized Coping Thoughts List earlier in this chapter):

   a. _____

   b. _____

   c. _____

Developed by McKay and Rogers (2000).

Visualizing Your Anger Scenes

Now it's time to practice your new coping skills (relaxation and anger coping thoughts) while visualizing anger scenes of increasing intensity. Let's start by selecting ten typical anger events that will help you rehearse what you've been learning.

To establish a hierarchy of gradually more provocative anger scenes, you can use a scale called Anger Units (AU), where 100 AUs is the worst rage you've ever felt in your life and 0 AUs is no anger at all. In the spaces provided below, write:

- Two mild to moderate anger scenes (40 to 50 AUs)

- Two moderate anger scenes (50 to 60 AUs)

- Two moderate to high anger scenes (60 to 75 AUs)

- Two high anger scenes (75 to 85 AUs)

- Two extreme anger scenes (85 to 100 AUs)

As you write descriptions of your anger scenes, include details from the physical environment and what the provoking people are saying or doing. Also describe your trigger thoughts, feelings, and physical reactions. Here's an example of one of Nancy's moderate to high anger scenes:

"The school principal is presiding over a faculty meeting. It's hot, and I'm feeling flushed. She announces that I need to switch classrooms next year to something that's about the size of a broom closet. She's smiling in a phony, apologetic way. I'm thinking that she's taking my room away because I wouldn't do that demonstration reading project. What a bitch! I'm perspiring and my stomach's in a knot. I'm so angry, I want to let her have it, but I smother down the words."

YOUR HIERARCHY OF ANGER SCENES

Mild to Moderate (40 to 50 AUs)

Scene 1: _____

_____

_____

Scene 2: _____

_____

_____

Moderate (50 to 60 AUs)

Scene 1: _____

_____

_____

Scene 2: _____

_____

_____

Moderate to High (60 to 75 AUs)

Scene 1: _____

_____

_____

Scene 2: _____

_____

_____

High (75 to 85 AUs)

Scene 1: _____

_____

_____

Scene 2: _____

_____

_____

Extreme (85 to 100 AUs)

Scene 1: _____

_____

_____

Scene 2: _____

_____

_____

Anger Inoculation Protocol for Mild to Moderate and Moderate Anger Scenes

1. Create a Coping Thoughts Worksheet. Develop several anger coping thoughts prior to visualizing each scene.

2. Relax using cue-controlled relaxation and special place visualization. If there are specific areas of your body that remain tense, try progressive muscle relaxation or release-only relaxation.

3. Once you've relaxed, visualize the first anger scene at the mild to moderate level. Try to see as much detail as possible and hear whatever is being said. Intensify your anger response with some of your trigger thoughts. Keep at it, letting your anger rise as much as possible. Hold the scene in your mind for thirty seconds.

4. Now erase the scene and use your relaxation skills again. Also recall your anger coping thoughts. Keep this up until you feel calm again (0 AUs).

5. Repeat the whole sequence again, visualizing the second anger scene (at the mild to moderate level).

6. Alternate back and forth between these two scenes for four to six repetitions each. Then, using these same two scenes, have a second practice session a few days later.

7. Now move on to the two moderate anger scenes.

Anger Inoculation Protocol for Moderate to High Through Extreme Anger Scenes

For these higher-level anger scenes, you will make one important change in the procedure. Instead of erasing the scene after thirty seconds and beginning to cope (with relaxation and coping thoughts), *you'll use your coping skills while you continue to visualize the anger scene.* You will hold onto the provocative image while at the same time practicing cue-controlled relaxation, and perhaps releasing tension in specific areas of your body. You will maintain the image while using your new coping thoughts or revised versions of trigger thoughts. Stay with the process until you feel completely calm (0 AUs).

After you've gotten down to 0 AUs in the first scene of a particular anger level, switch off the scene, do some cue-controlled breathing, and start imaging the second scene. Switch back and forth between each scene four to six times, always waiting to get to 0 AUs before changing scenes. You are encouraged to do two practice sessions, switching scenes four to six times each, for each anger level.

It's hard to do two things at once (stay locked on an anger scene and, at the same time, cope). But with practice you can learn to do it. You'll soon be able to balance visualization with relaxation and anger management thoughts. Remember this: coping with real-life provocation is going to require this same balancing act. You'll need to deal with what's going on at the moment *and* use your coping skills. So all the practice you do now will put you in a far better position to handle real upsets.

EXAMPLE

Let's go back to Nancy's anger scene with her principal—where she was being assigned to a "broom-closet" size classroom. Nancy begins by relaxing with her special place visualization (Tuolumne Meadows in Yosemite) and some cue-controlled relaxation. She notices any places in her body that feel tense and deliberately relaxes those areas. Now she begins to visualize the scene in the faculty meeting. She remembers her principal's phony smile as she told Nancy about her new classroom assignment. She recalls how hot the room felt and the flushed feeling in her body. She thinks, "What a bitch," and assumes that the principal is taking revenge for Nancy's refusal to do the demonstration project.

Now Nancy feels really steamed; this room assignment was a deliberate slap in the face. As her anger reaches the moderate to high level, Nancy begins to cope. She takes a cue-controlled breath; she reminds herself that her principal has done her favors as well as disappointed her.

She thinks that the smaller room might reflect that her third-grade class is expected to have fewer students next year. While holding onto the scene of the faculty meeting and her principal's phony smile, Nancy reminds herself that "getting upset won't change anything—stay cool." She takes several more cue-controlled breaths.

Only when her anger is completely gone does Nancy switch off the scene. Now she returns for a few moments to her Yosemite Meadows before beginning her second moderate to high anger scene. Nancy continues to switch back and forth between her two moderate to high anger scenes four to six times.

Step 4: Real-Life Coping

Although you can't schedule real-life practice with provocations, you can prepare for them. You can have well-rehearsed coping thoughts ready, and you can stay alert for early warning signs of anger in your body and mind. The sooner you intervene with cue-controlled relaxation and coping thoughts, the more likely you are to maintain control.

If you know you are going to be in a situation that is likely to spark your anger, prepare your coping thoughts ahead of time and commit yourself to using them along with cue-controlled relaxation. With practice this will be easier to do, and in time it will become more automatic. If you forget to use your coping skills, or you start to use them and then give up in the heat of the moment, visualize the scene later and practice coping just as you did when you were doing the anger inoculation exercises.

In addition to relaxation and coping thoughts, it's always helpful to plan your best coping behaviors. What can you say or do to defuse the situation and get through it without blowing up?

Your Anger Plan

For each provocation where you forget to use your new skills, make a written anger plan.

ANGER COPING PLAN WORKSHEET

Precipitating event:

_____

_____

_____

Anger-triggering thoughts:

_____

_____

_____

Anger distortions:

_____

_____

_____

Coping thoughts/revised distortions:

_____

_____

_____

Relaxation strategy (Check for body tension? Cue-controlled breath? Diaphragmatic breath?):

_____

_____

_____

Coping behavior (Count to ten? Excuse yourself from the situation? Suggest a compromise? Validate both points of view?):

_____

_____

_____

SPECIAL CONSIDERATIONS

1. If you have difficulty following the relaxation protocol, you may want to record your relaxation routine and practice with that.

2. If you have difficulty forming images of anger scenes, include more sense impressions. For example, if your images are primarily visual, try to bring in sounds, smells, or the sense of touch. Add as many of these additional sensory elements to the scene as possible.

3. If you can image clearly, but it produces little or no anger, focus more on anger-triggering thoughts. If that doesn't work, dump the scene and develop one that is more anger-provoking. Or bring in a higher-level anger scene to work with.

4. If you are interested in learning more about irrational ideas that trigger unnecessary distress, refer to chapter 12, Refuting Irrational Ideas.

FURTHER READING

Deffenbacher, J. L., and M. McKay. 2000. *Overcoming Situational and General Anger.* Oakland, CA: New Harbinger Publications.

Deffenbacher, J. L., and P. M. Sabadell. 1990. A combination of cognitive, relaxation, and behavioral coping skills in the reduction of general anger. *Journal of College Student Development* 31:351-358.

Deffenbacher, J. L., D. A. Story, R. S. Stark, J. A. Hogg, and A. D. Brandon. 1987. Cognitive-relaxation and social skills interventions in the treatment of general anger. *Journal of Counseling Psychology* 34(2):171-176.

Hazaleus, S., and J. L. Deffenbacher. 1986. Relaxation and cognitive treatments of anger. *Journal of Psychological Record* 15:501-511. Out of print.

McKay, M., and P. D. Rogers. 2000. *The Anger Control Workbook.* Oakland, CA: New Harbinger Publications.

Novaco, R. 1975. *Anger Control: The Development and Evaluation of an Experimental Treatment.* Lexington, MA: D. C. Health.

Goal Setting and Time Management

In this chapter you will learn to:

✳ Understand the limits of multitasking

✳ Clarify values, define your goals, and develop a plan to reach your goals

✳ Assess how you are currently spending your time

✳ Reorganize your time to fit your priorities

✳ Combat procrastination

✳ Use shortcuts for time management

BACKGROUND

Most people approach the subject of time management with one major question: "How can I get more done in less time?" If you are one of these people, you are probably wondering how you are going to fit some of the exercises described in the other chapters of this book into your already overloaded schedule. You may feel so pressured to take care of the many demands and all the details in your life that you rarely have guilt-free time to do as you please. Or you may have loads of free time, yet you never get around to doing the things that would give you the most satisfaction. Other problems associated with ineffective time management include the following:

- Constant rushing
- Frequent lateness
- Low productivity, energy, and motivation
- Frustration
- Impatience

- Chronic vacillation between alternatives

- Difficulty setting and achieving goals

- Procrastination

- Lack of focus and purpose

- Unproductive multitasking

How is it that although each one of us has twenty-four hours in a day, some of us feel as though we have no time at all, while others manage to get their work done and still have enough time left over to enjoy themselves? People who manage their time effectively have learned to structure their lives so that they focus most of their time and energy on what is most important to them; they minimize the time they spend on activities they do not value. They realize that the quality of their lives is enhanced when they do a few things well, instead of trying to find time to do a little of everything.

In order to realize the goals of effective time management, it is also important to look at how you can achieve balance in your life. Effective time management is a powerful way to lower your stress level, particularly when you use it to create balance in your life.

LIMITS OF MULTITASKING

In today's business world people often think they can juggle phone calls, e-mails, text messages, and computer work to get more done. It is not uncommon to hear a prideful "I was multitasking." In the December 2004 issue of *Scientific American Mind*, an article entitled "The Limits of Multitasking" by Klaus Manhart reported that in "a study done by the Families and Work Institute in New York City, 45 percent of U.S. workers believe they are asked or expected to work on too many tasks at once."

They may have a legitimate complaint. In a June 2006 article called "A Multitasking Brain—Doing Everything at Once" on the website www.netbull.org, this statement appeared: "[S]cientists have tested the brain's ability to do two things at once by mapping its activity as a task was performed alone and then with another task. When people try to do two tasks, scans show that the amount of brain activity devoted to each task decreases." Another way to say this is that when the brain must process two things at once, it doesn't do either task at full power.

"Multitasking is going to slow you down, lose time and increase chances of mistakes," says David Mayer, a cognitive scientist at the University of Michigan. This is particularly true when you are trying to process or analyze complex information or to learn new information.

In their 2004 book *The Power of Full Engagement*, the authors, Schwartz and Loehr discuss the importance of balance in an age of overload. They state, "being fully engaged means being able to immerse yourself in the mission you are on, whether it is grappling with a creative challenge at work, managing a group of people, spending time with loved ones, or simply having fun (p. 5)."

So are you really being productive and safe when you

- Talk on your cell phone while driving?

- Read e-mail on your computer while you are talking to an important client on the phone?

- Plan a trip while using a skill saw?

- Respond to instant messages on your laptop while attending a meeting?

- Allow yourself to be interrupted while you are preparing an important report or focusing on an important decision?

The answer to these scenarios is an unequivocal No. Multitasking can be effective only for brief periods of time and usually with tasks that are habitual or routine. You cannot multitask effectively when you are learning something new, focusing on a complex task, or planning a new strategic direction. The real key to time management is setting priorities and focusing on what you need to accomplish in the moment. This requires knowing what part of the day you have the most energy and planning your day around it. This includes doing routine tasks, for example, e-mailing or gardening, during low-energy periods and planning, writing, leading meetings, and learning new skills or content during higher energy periods.

The 80–20 Principle

If you are thinking "All of my responsibilities are important. I can't simply drop some of them to do what I please," consider the 80–20 principle. Vilfredo Pareto, an Italian economist, noted that 80 percent of what we gain comes from 20 percent of our effort; conversely, 80 percent of our effort produces only 20 percent of value. Empirical studies have shown this to be true time and again. This principle can be applied to many areas of life. For example, about 20 percent of the newspaper is worth your while to read. You are better off just skimming the rest of it. A good 80 percent of most people's mail is junk and best not read at all. The same applies to e-mail; usually 20 percent requires your immediate response. Just about 80 percent of your housework can wait almost indefinitely, while 20 percent of it, if not done, would soon make your home uninhabitable.

In a 2007 article on the Internet called "Managing Your Time When You Don't Have the Time," Barry J. Izsak listed the following tactics for effective time management:

1. Focus on your priorities.

2. Be proactive, not reactive, with your time.

3. Plan your day.

4. Schedule your tasks.

5. Schedule appropriate tasks to the time and energy you have.

6. Don't procrastinate.

7. Don't be a perfectionist.

SYMPTOM-RELIEF EFFECTIVENESS

Effective time-management skills can help with minimizing deadline anxiety, lack of focus, procrastination, and job fatigue.

TIME TO MASTER

You can begin to clarify what is most important in your life in as little time as an hour and then, as additional ideas come to you, return later to this important task. Defining your goals will take at least a few more hours. However, you can create an action plan for one of your goals in an hour. You will need at least three days to complete the time log.

Take at least several hours to evaluate how you actually spend your time—in terms of your priorities and goals—and decide how you want to change the way you spend your time, so that it more closely matches your ideals and goals. Although you can begin using the tips to combat procrastination and organize your time more efficiently within a week, you'll probably need several months of conscious effort before these techniques become habitual. If all this seems like a huge investment of your time, consider that the time you spend now will give you a lot more energy and free time in the future.

INSTRUCTIONS

In this chapter you will be asked to do six tasks:

1. Clarify your values.

2. Set goals.

3. Develop an action plan.

4. Evaluate how you spend your time.

5. Combat procrastination.

6. Organize your time.

Since each step builds on the previous ones, start with step 1 and work your way through to the last step.

CLARIFYING YOUR VALUES

The first step toward effective time management is deciding what is most worthwhile or desirable to you. People typically have priorities involving such things as career, health, home, family, spirituality, finances, leisure, learning, creativity, happiness, peace of mind, and communication. Knowing what is most valuable to you gives you direction in life. You can focus the majority of your time and energy on these values, rather than on those that are less important to you. When you have to choose between alternatives, you can look to your priorities to help you make your decision.

Identify Your Highest Priorities

The following two brief guided fantasies can be done alone or with a family member or friend. They will help you identify your highest priorities.

1. Close your eyes, take a few deep breaths, and relax. Imagine yourself in a favorite place where you can take a few minutes to think. The time is many years from now. You have lived a long and full life. Reflect upon your life from this mature vantage point. What did you most enjoy experiencing and doing? What did you most appreciate accomplishing or having? Write your answers in this space or on a separate sheet of paper.

_____

_____

_____

_____

_____

2. Return to your relaxed position and imagine yourself again in your favorite place. This time, you are still your current age. You have just learned that you have a rare illness that has no symptoms but will kill you in six months. Given only half a year to live, what

do you want to experience, change, do, accomplish, and have? Write your answers in this space or on another sheet of paper.

_____

_____

_____

_____

_____

Compare your two sets of answers. Are they the same or different? Most people actually faced with a life-threatening illness find that their priorities change. Things once believed to be crucial seem less important, and things once overlooked take on new meaning.

Order Your Values

Take the list that you developed doing the two previous exercises and order your values from the most to the least important. You'll find that this list will come in handy when you have trouble choosing between two or more alternatives.

Here's how Alice, a single working parent, listed her values in order of importance.

1. Family	5. Nice home
2. Financial security	6. Friends
3. Health	7. Travel
4. Creativity	8. Honesty

Alice was troubled because her bosses were pressuring her to sign off on incomplete drafts of her designs. When she refused, they simply bypassed her signature. She vacillated between reporting her company's infractions to a government regulatory agency and remaining silent to avoid reprisal. When she examined her values, she realized that not speaking out was a form of dishonesty. But she also realized that although honesty was important to her, it had the lowest priority of all her values, and that all her other values were being successfully fulfilled by her job. With this insight, she stopped criticizing herself and waited until she had found a job in another company to report her former employer's misconduct. In that way she didn't jeopardize the other important aspects of her life.

Now, rank your values from the most to least important for you. Use only single words to describe your values.

1.	5.
2.	6.
3.	7.
4.	8.

SETTING GOALS

The second step to effective time management involves setting goals. Values are ideals. They are the things, experiences, qualities, and principles that you would most like to have in your life. Goals are real and specific. Goals are objectives that you want to achieve, given the constraints of your time and other resources. For example, your fondest hope might be to become a champion race-car driver. Your goal might be to cross the Indianapolis 500 finish line in first place three years from now. To bring your life into closer alignment with what you consider most worthwhile, use your list of values to guide you in defining your goals.

Designing Effective Goals

Here are five crucial questions to ask yourself when designing effective goals:

1. **Is this a goal that you really want to devote a lot of time and energy to accomplish?** Or is it simply a dream of what you would like to have fall in your lap, but are not willing to work for? Many people think that they would like to travel around the world, but they aren't willing to save the money this would require.

2. **Is this goal consistent with your highest values?** One reason you may not accomplish a goal is because it doesn't fit in with what is most important to you. If you value education and your goal is to finish college in the next year, but your highest priorities are family

and socializing with friends, you may want to give yourself more time to complete your college goal so that you won't have to neglect your family and friends.

3. **Is this goal achievable?** Is it specific enough so that you will know when you have achieved it? Is it achievable within a definite time frame that you can set for yourself? Do you have access to the resources necessary to achieve it? Instead of saying that you want to "retire on a comfortable income," set a date for retirement and specify an amount of money that you know you can realistically earn and save to support the lifestyle that you want when you retire. Note that you can modify your goals as you obtain more information.

4. **Is this goal positive?** You are far more likely to achieve goals you are moving toward, rather than away from. For example, instead of setting the negative goal of no longer overeating, give yourself the positive objective of eating three sensible, nutritious meals a day.

5. **Are your goals in balance?** Do most of your goals involve your career and finances, while none or almost none of your goals have to do with health, relationships, or fun? Lack of balance is a major source of stress. If you spend your workday alone in front of a computer terminal, a useful, not too hard to achieve, short-term goal might be to get regular exercise outdoors with other people.

Balancing Your Goals

Do you have about an equal number of short-term, medium-term, and long-term goals? Some people plan on waiting until they retire to live their lives the way they really want to. Others can enjoy the here and now, but are handicapped when it comes to achieving goals that involve delayed gratification. A mixture of short-term, medium-term, and long-term goals can provide you with satisfaction in the here and now, as well as give you objectives that you will find meaningful to work toward.

Are your short-term and medium-term goals compatible with your long-term goals? If you want to live to a ripe old age to travel the world with old friends, your short-term and medium-term goals need to include taking care of your health, cultivating friendships, and making money.

Do you periodically reassess your goals to make sure that they are still what you want? As you work toward your goals, you gain new information and insights. Part of balancing your goals involves adapting them to the changes that invariably will take place in your life. Be flexible and allow yourself time both to reflect on and renew your goals.

Here's how Eric, a forty-one-year-old manager in an electronics firm, used his list of values to guide him in setting his life goals. First he listed his values:

1. *Family:* To enjoy, take care of, and provide for them.

2. *Health:* To preserve the good health I enjoy into my eighties.

3. *Financial security:* To have enough money to take care of family, leisure, travel dreams, and retirement.

4. *Professional success:* To become a vice president with my company.

5. *Nature:* To spend time in the wilderness every year; to learn more about animal behavior.

6. *Friends:* To enjoy them by spending quality time with them and to help out.

7. *Spiritual:* To maintain my connection with my higher power and give my children an opportunity for this, too.

8. *Travel:* To go abroad as often and as far as my time and money permit.

9. *Communication:* To be open and honest with others and to know and feel that they are open and honest with me.

10. *Self:* To allow time to reflect on my life and to renew my focus on what is important to me.

Here are the goals that Eric developed, based on his list of values.

Long-term goals (over five years):

1. Own and live in a house on the lake where I spent my summers as a child.

2. Optimize my health with regular exercise, diet, rest, and medical checkups.

3. Raise my three children and provide each of them with an education.

4. Save and invest enough money so that I can retire at fifty-five-years old, live at the lake, and travel.

5. Publish a book on hiking based on my wilderness experience.

Medium-term goals:

1. Become a vice president for the company in four years.

2. Buy a new house to accommodate our growing family within two years.

3. Find a church that the whole family can agree on and become an active participant.

4. Listen to audiotapes on personal financial planning and investing when commuting.

5. Go on a backpacking trip with friends to the Lost Coast a year and a half from now.

Short-term goals:

1. Go camping with my partner alone for a long weekend in the next month.

2. Set up a weekly family night starting this Thursday.

3. Have a fun evening with friends at least once a week.

4. Jog three mornings a week and take a hike with family and friends at least once a month.

5. Meditate for fifteen minutes before leaving the office to go home.

6. Remember to take a few deep breaths and relax my muscles when faced with a stressful event.

7. Take at least one week off from work once a quarter for renewal and to spend time hiking with my family and friends, or alone.

Write down one or more specific goals for each of your priorities. You may find it helpful to list your various goals under the following three categories:

1. Your long-term goals (goals that will take you over five years to accomplish).

    _____

    _____

    _____

    _____

2. Your medium-term goals (goals that will take you between one and five years).

    _____

    _____

    _____

    _____

3. Your short-term goals (goals that will take from one week to less than one year).

    _____

    _____

    _____

    _____

DEVELOPING AN ACTION PLAN

Your third step is to identify the specific steps you need to take to achieve each of your goals. The most common reason that people do not attain their objectives is that they don't have an action plan that describes step by step how they are going to get from where they are now all the way to their goal. Without an action plan, your goal may seem too big and too remote. Without knowing what to do first, you may never get beyond the dreaming stage.

An effective action plan includes:

- A well-thought-out and specific goal

- A description of all the resources that you will need and how you will access them

- Each step you must take, in the correct order

- How you will monitor your progress

- The most likely reasons you might procrastinate and how you will deal with this

- What rewards you will use to motivate yourself

Here are two alternative strategies for creating an action plan.

1. **Imagine that you've already achieved your goal**. How would you feel, look, behave, and sound? How would the people around you respond to you? Once you have a clear picture of what you want and are in touch with the good feelings that picture generates for you, begin to work backward from that fantasized image. Ask yourself what steps you must have taken to achieve your objective. Notice which resources you used. Did you need to develop new skills? Did you use outside resources or did you simply rely on your personal ones? How much time did it take? How did you deal with obstacles like your fears and excuses and other people's demands on your time? How did you motivate yourself to keep going? Run a mental movie from where you are now all the way through to achieving your goal. Write down, in order, the steps you took.

   Tom, a student in a college English class, used the following approach. His goal was to receive an A on a paper for his creative writing class. First he visualized getting his paper back from his professor with an A on its cover. After relishing his pleasure and excitement and enjoying the imaginary congratulations of his friends, he went on to think through the steps he could have taken to reach that goal. Here's the original list of steps that he generated:

   a. I take a walk by myself just to come up with a topic for my paper.

b. While walking, I come up with a great idea about writing a short story about salmon fishing in Alaska, which is how I earned money last summer. I reminisce about my experiences. I get excited about writing the paper.

c. I write an outline of my story.

d. I write a rough draft of my story.

e. I look over the rough draft and write a more polished version.

f. I ask my friend to read my paper. I'm encouraged by her positive comments.

g. I review and incorporate many of my friend's suggestions.

h. I make the final copy of my paper.

i. I turn my paper in on time.

After thinking about his action plan, Tom realized that it didn't deal with one very familiar obstacle: his tendency to get sidetracked by his family and friends. He decided that his best strategy would be to reward himself with some time off once he had written a rough draft to hang out with his friends. Then he would bring himself back to his project by again visualizing accomplishing his goal.

2. **Brainstorm.** A second way to create an action plan would be to write your goal at the top of a blank sheet of paper and then randomly ask yourself questions about everything you need to know and do in order to achieve your objective. When you are finished brainstorming, rewrite the specific steps you need to take from where you are now all the way through to achieving your goal.

Angela's goal was to establish an ongoing aerobic exercise program for herself. She began by asking herself the following questions, and then answering them.

Why do I want to exercise?

I want to feel and look healthy, fit, trim, and strong. One of my long-term goals is to be healthy into my old age.

How often and how long do I need to exercise aerobically to get the results I want?

I need to do more research about exercise to answer these questions. I can talk to my friends about their experiences with exercise. I can read more. I want to start out gradually and set more challenging goals as I become stronger.

What kind of exercise do I like? What kind am I capable of doing and have the time and resources to do consistently?

Walking, swimming, jogging, biking, and working out to an aerobic dance video are all good candidates.

What do I need in order to exercise safely and have a hassle-free time?

I need a form of exercise that I can do without having to get in my car and deal with traffic. (That rules out swimming and biking!) There's a safe trail near my house. I have a DVD player and I can buy an aerobic dance video. Except for shoes, I already have plenty of clothes I can dance, walk, and jog in.

Which exercise video should I buy?

I can ask my friends for recommendations, or rent some videos and see which I like best. I can then go to a store and buy the ones I like best.

What kind of shoes should I get and where do I find them?

Go to the local sports store and ask the salesperson for help. I could read up on shoes, but I'd rather talk to my friends.

When am I going to exercise?

After work, when I arrive home, before I do anything else.

How am I going to motivate myself to stick with this program?

I can jog with a friend. I can participate in local races. I can pay attention to how much better I feel and look when I have been exercising regularly for a while. I can reward myself with new exercise clothes and videos and gold stars. I can always do aerobic dance, even when the weather is bad or it's dark outside because it's so enjoyable.

How am I going to monitor my progress?

I will keep track of my progress by reviewing the gold stars on my calendar every other week with my friend Stacey, who knows what I am trying to accomplish and is very supportive of me.

Here's the action plan that Angela developed after she read through and reorganized her answers:

1. Define my specific exercise goal and keep in mind my purpose in exercising regularly.

2. Read more about aerobic exercise to find out how often and how long I need to exercise.

3. Talk to my friends about jogging, proper shoes, and aerobic dance videos.

4. Find a jogging partner. (This is an optional step: not essential for me to start my program.)

5. Consult with a salesperson at local sports store and buy a comfortable pair of shoes to fit my exercise needs.

6. Try out aerobic videos by renting or borrowing them first.

7. Buy favorite aerobic videos at local record, book, or video store.

8. Jog or work out to an aerobic dance videos when I get home right after work.

9. Monitor my progress by putting a gold star on the days of the week I exercise. I'll use the calendar in my kitchen, since I look at it every day.

10. Evaluate my progress with Stacey.

11. Reward myself by buying new exercise clothes, participating in local races, and buying new videos. I can look and feel great!

Evaluating Your Progress

Identifying a way to keep track of your progress should be a part of your action plan. One powerful approach is to plan to go over what you have accomplished toward your goal with a support person every couple of weeks. Choose a support person who understands and appreciates what you are trying to do. This person should be able to give you positive suggestions and encouragement, as well as point out when you may be fooling yourself.

By the time of your second two-week progress evaluation, you should begin to see some positive results. Success can serve as a powerful reinforcer to continue your program, but don't let your first gains trick you into slacking off. Old habits don't die easily, and it can take three or more months to develop new ones.

If you are not seeing positive results, or you catch yourself making excuses for not following through on your plan, don't be too hard on yourself. Instead, reassess your original goal. Is this what you really want? If not, modify your goal. If it is something you want, consider how you can modify your action plan so that you can start moving toward your goal.

EVALUATING HOW YOU SPEND YOUR TIME

Now you can begin the fourth step toward effective time management by keeping a daily log of your time. Do this in real time, rather than at night trying to estimate how much time you spent on the various activities that filled your day. Most people tend to grossly underestimate how long it takes them to do their various tasks, and they also tend to overlook or forget the unplanned activities that pop up during the day.

If you really want to learn something new about yourself, stop once an hour during your waking day to record how long it took you to do each activity that you were involved in during that hour. At the very least, get out your notebook after lunch and dinner and before bed and write down every activity you engaged in. Note the amount of time each one took. When you're through, the total amount of time for all activities should be fairly close to the total number of hours you were awake. A sample time log you can use is included on the next page.

Keep recording all of your activities for this time inventory for at least three days. Categories of activities at work might include: paperwork, e-mail or instant messaging, phone calls, socializing face-to-face, meetings, multitasking, low-priority work, focused productive work, interruptions, eating, and/or conference calls. Typical activities not related to work are: personal hygiene, grooming, dressing, cooking, eating, naps, daydreaming, child care and parenting, shopping, household chores and maintenance, commuting, travel for errands, personal telephone calls, face-to-face conversations, watching television, engaging in hobbies or reading, participating in sports, exercising, and other recreation. Modify or add categories to suit yourself.

Keep in mind that this time log is designed to help you break down and examine as carefully as you need to the various ways that you use your time, so that you can decide later whether you want to spend more or less time engaged in each of these activities.

Samantha, a radio public-affairs interviewer, kept the following record on the first day of her three-day time assessment.

After the sample time log that follows, you'll find a record that Samantha, a radio public-affairs interviewer, kept on the first day of her three-day assessment.

SAMPLE TIME LOG

Activity	Time
Waking through lunch	
After lunch through dinner	
After dinner until sleep	

SAMANTHA'S TIME LOG

Activity	Time
Waking through lunch	
Lying in bed trying to get up	20 minutes
Shower	20 minutes
Grooming and dressing	25 minutes
Cooking breakfast	5 minutes
Eating breakfast and reading paper	10 minutes
Phone call (family)	10 minutes
Commute and listen to news	45 minutes
Morning staff meeting (10 minutes late)	40 minutes
Routine work—review and respond to:	60 minutes
Phone messages	
Electronic mail	
Written memos	
Mail	
Daydreaming	5 minutes
Socializing (friend)	15 minutes
Meeting (15 minutes late)	45 minutes
Productive work (preparing for interview)	40 minutes
Lunch with friend (15 minutes late)	75 minutes
After lunch through dinner	
Productive work (preparing for interview)	95 minutes
Phone call (friend)	5 minutes
Daydreaming	10 minutes
Low-priority work (helping coworker)	65 minutes
Socializing with coworker	15 minutes
Phone call (work related)	30 minutes
Commute and listen to news	45 minutes
Shopping	40 minutes
Mail	10 minutes
Phone call (personal)	25 minutes

Activity	Time
Neighbor visits	20 minutes
Phone call (work related)	30 minutes
Cook while listening to news on TV	60 minutes
Eat	20 minutes
After dinner until sleep	
Clean up kitchen	15 minutes
Phone call (personal)	10 minutes
Television (documentary)	60 minutes
Reading novel	25 minutes
Turn off light (30 minutes late)	

Evaluating Your Time Log

Now that you know how you are actually spending your time, you are ready to compare the inventory you made with your real priorities. From there, you'll be able to decide what changes you want to make to bring your current schedule into closer alignment with your most important values and goals. Here are some questions that will guide you in making this comparison.

1. **Which of the activities on your daily log are in line with your values and goals?** Mark these activities with a star.

    Samantha starred "reading paper" and "listen to news," since these activities reflected her priority of staying current with the news. She starred her productive time at work preparing for radio interviews because this reflected her priority to be a successful radio interviewer. She starred "phone call (personal)" since one of her priorities was to spend time with friends.

2. **Which of the activities on your daily log are not in line with your values and goals?** Circle these activities.

    Samantha was amazed to find that on this day she had spent three hours and ten minutes preparing, eating, and cleaning up after meals. She felt that two hours on the phone and reading and responding to e-mail and text messages for work was excessive. She also realized that she had wasted a half hour in the morning with extra time in bed and a long shower. She recognized that she allowed unexpected calls and socializing to get in the way of being on time. When she analyzed her work patterns, it became obvious that her most productive hours were at midday—and that lunch was a big interruption right in the middle of this time.

Look at the circled items on your list and write down how you would be willing to reschedule, reduce, or eliminate low-priority activities in your day.

_____

_____

_____

_____

_____

3. **Are any of your values being violated by any of the activities on your daily log?**

Mark these activities with an X.

Engaging in activities that run counter to your values can cause you to feel guilty, ashamed, anxious, depressed, resentful, or exhausted. Samantha's problem with tardiness ran counter to her priorities of peace of mind and being a successful radio interviewer. She felt rushed, anxious, guilty, and embarrassed when she arrived at meetings late.

Look at the items that you've marked with an X and write down how you would be willing to change your behavior so that it no longer violates your values.

_____

_____

_____

_____

_____

4. **Are some of your values and goals being neglected or ignored?**

Activities that reflect these neglected values and goals may be the very ones that you need to expand or increase to bring balance into your life. On the other hand, these neglected values actually may have a lower priority at this time in your life than your other values, and you may realize that you feel okay about postponing activities associated with them.

Samantha noticed that her priorities having to do with friends, family, and health were underrepresented in how she spent her time. Except for brief phone calls, she didn't talk with her family. Since her parents and sisters lived in another state and she had recently visited them, this limited contact was okay with her for right now.

She did want to spend more time with friends and take better care of herself physically. Her sedentary lifestyle and eating habits had caused her to gain weight.

Write down how you would be willing to change your behavior so that it would be consistent with the values and goals that you have been neglecting.

_____

_____

_____

_____

_____

Samantha decided that she was willing to make the following immediate changes in her use of time:

1. Eat a quick breakfast that does not require cooking.

2. Prioritize being on time over answering unexpected phone calls and other low-priority activities.

3. Limit reading and responding to e-mail to twice a day.

4. Limit lunch to an hour and take it later in the day to take advantage of my most productive time of day.

5. Prepare simple dinners in half an hour.

6. Limit most work-related calls to ten minutes.

7. Skim written communication for "must know" and "must respond" information.

8. Prioritize going to sleep on time over watching TV and reading.

9. Get up with the alarm and limit shower to ten minutes.

10. Go to the gym and work out with my friends four nights a week.

Although it is unlikely that you would want to try to do something that reflects each one of your values and goals every single day, you can integrate all of your values and most of your goals into your activities if you plan your time on a weekly or even monthly basis. Continue using the tools you learned earlier in this chapter to clearly define your goals and prepare an action plan that lets you evaluate and reward yourself for the progress you've made.

COMBATING PROCRASTINATION

The fifth step toward managing your time more effectively is to get yourself unstuck. What distasteful activity are you avoiding? Compare it with your values. Does it violate one of your priorities? If it does, are you ready to take a stand and declare that you are not going to do it? If not, what can you do to change your circumstances in the future so that you will no longer violate one of your values? If you are avoiding an activity that is tied to one of your goals, review the section in this chapter on setting effective goals. If you don't know where to start, create an action plan. If you simply need to get better organized, refer to the sixth and final step in this chapter, which deals with organizing your time.

Here are ten additional suggestions to use when you find yourself procrastinating.

1. **Stop worrying.** You probably spend more time worrying about chores that you do not want to do than you would spend by simply doing them. To illustrate this point to yourself, keep track of how much time it takes you to complete each distasteful task.

2. **Start small.** Once you start doing an unpleasant task, you may find that it isn't as bad as you anticipated. Lead yourself into the cold water with a small but related task. For example, if you have to mow the lawn, decide to go as far as filling the gas tank on the mower and wheeling it out to the edge of the lawn.

3. **Count the cost.** Make a list of all the unpleasant aspects of doing the activity you are avoiding and then make a second list of the consequences of putting it off. Look squarely at the discomfort of doing it versus the cost of delay and ask yourself which list contains the greater degree of unpleasantness. Use this information to create enthusiasm for getting the job done.

4. **Look for the hidden rewards.** Look for any payoffs you may be receiving for not getting the distasteful job done. For example, by procrastinating you may be avoiding feeling anxious or facing the possibility of failure. Also examine the advantages of avoiding whatever changes might follow from completing the task. For example, success might mean that you lose the attention that you now get from people who nag you or sympathize with your predicament.

5. **Confront negative beliefs.** Read chapter 12, Refuting Irrational Ideas, to confront beliefs that may be interfering with doing what you need to do. Are you making statements to yourself like "No way am I going to do this, it just isn't fair," "I must do it perfectly," "Life should be easy," "I can't stand the thought of giving a speech in front of a group of strangers," "What if I succeed? They'll expect even more out of me," or "I'll fail, so why even try?"

6. **Double your resistance.** Exaggerate and intensify whatever you are doing that puts off beginning a task. If you stare at yourself in the mirror in the morning instead of getting to work, draw that stare out. Really examine all of your pores and go over each quadrant of your face minutely. Keep it up until you are really bored and getting to work seems like a more attractive alternative.

7. **Take responsibility for each delay.** You are the one wasting your precious time. Make a list of each procrastination or escape activity and note how long each took. Add up the total and list all the positive things you could have done with that time if you'd simply begun and finished the job.

8. **Tie a distasteful activity to an activity that you know you will do.** For example, if you dislike exercise, find a gym you can visit on your way home from work or plan to exercise by walking to lunch at a restaurant twenty minutes from your office.

9. **Reward yourself for doing activities that are unpleasant to you.**

10. **Finish things.** Avoid beginning a new task until you have completed a specific segment of your current task. The experience of finishing something is itself a great reward.

ORGANIZING YOUR TIME

The sixth and final step toward more effective time management is to become better organized. Here are eleven suggestions to structure your time and focus your attention on creating the life of your choice.

1. **Purchase an organizer (PDA [personal digital assistant]), computer or notebook version).** Find one that includes a daily, weekly, and monthly calendar and use it.

2. **Make sure that your list of daily goals and your calendar reflect your long-term, medium-term, and short-term goals.** You can schedule time each day for exercise and for practicing relaxation techniques. If spending quality time with a loved one is a high priority, block off regular time on your calendar to do this and include that time on your daily to-do list. If you arrange your schedule of activities on a weekly or even monthly basis, you will find that you have time to work on all of your important goals.

3. **Plan for efficiency.** Combine activities that can be done at the same time, such as watching your favorite TV show while exercising, ironing, or washing dishes. Use a video or digital recorder to record favorite TV shows and watch them at a time that is convenient for you. You can sequence activities to save time. Match tasks to your varying energy

levels. Although you can usually predict your energy level at different points during the day and plan accordingly, occasionally you will run out of steam earlier than anticipated. If so, you may want to reschedule activities that require energy and alertness to a time when you can perform them with maximum efficiency.

4. **Minimize time wasters.** Cut back on TV, time spent on the Internet, telephone interruptions, drop-in visitors, unproductive meetings, ineffective delegation of responsibilities, crises, activities that lack direction, and overly ambitious goals. Plan ways to avoid as many predictable time wasters as possible, but be realistic enough to schedule some time for unexpected interruptions.

5. **Learn to say no.** Set limits on how much you are willing to do for others. If you have difficulty with this, see chapter 17, Assertiveness Training.

6. **Make a list of things to do when you're waiting.** Good candidates include doing a relaxation exercise, planning tomorrow's list of goals, reviewing your priorities and goals, reading a book, or filing your nails.

7. **Set aside several short periods each day for quiet time.** Use this time to practice your deep relaxation techniques. This will help you stay in touch with what is most important to you, rather than rushing faster and faster in response to others' demands.

8. **When you are performing a high-priority activity, focus your full attention on it.** Make a list of your usual distractions and plan how you can block each one of them. For instance, if you often find yourself daydreaming when you should be working, schedule in a visualization session or some other way of using your imagination during one of your quiet times.

9. **Arrange your environment to support your values and goals.** If your priorities require focus and concentration, make sure that you have a quiet room or corner available for reading, writing, practicing deep relaxation, or just thinking through your plans.

10. **Don't waste time on decisions that involve equally attractive or inconsequential alternatives.** If you find yourself in a quandary over choices like this, just flip a coin and go with the winning call.

11. **Reward yourself for improving your time management.** One of the greatest rewards of effective time management comes from not having to rush to accomplish the important things in your life. By prioritizing and planning your activities, you can choose to move through your day at a more leisurely pace.

Organizing Your Day

Managing your time on a daily basis requires setting immediate priorities and sticking to them. At the beginning of each day, develop a to-do list that reflects your goals as well as the necessary tasks. Each day's list should be prioritized by sorting activities into the following categories:

1. *Top drawer.* These are the most essential and most desired items.

2. *Middle drawer.* You could put these activities off for a while, but they are still important.

3. *Bottom drawer.* You can easily put these tasks off indefinitely with no harm done.

Go through your list and mark each item TD, MD, or BD according to its status.

Now, when you start your day, you have a blueprint for how to apportion your time. Start with the top-drawer items first and then work your way down the list. Move on to the middle drawer only when all of your top-drawer items have been completed. If you have too many top-drawer tasks to finish in a day, then you've given too many things a high priority. Assign top-drawer status only to tasks that absolutely cannot be put off and would result in negative consequences if they were.

Banish the bottom-drawer items from consideration unless you have completed all your higher priority items for the day. The definition of bottom-drawer items is that they can wait. Unless it's your boss who's asking, keep away from commitments that force you to spend time in the bottom drawer. Be prepared to say "I don't have the time" to these requests. If circumstances force you to take on a bottom-drawer task, try to delegate it. Give it to your assistant, your housecleaner, or your children.

As you move through your day, stay focused on the high-priority tasks and make sure that you limit your opportunities for procrastination. Block off any escape routes that turn up by scheduling daydreaming for a later time, and putting off socializing until a chunk of work is done. Avoid getting caught up in busywork or less important errands, and resist the impulse to run out for coffee or any other tempting indulgences.

At the end of the day, review your to-do list. Check off the items that you completed as planned and give yourself a mental pat on the back. Add anything you did that was not on your original list. Note whether it was a high-, medium-, or low-priority item. Important things you did not finish can be moved to the next day. A good time to prepare a day's list of goals is the preceding evening or first thing in the morning. Either way, you start out fresh, on top of things, and in tune with your priorities.

Track and Manage Interruptions

How often do you allow yourself to be interrupted by others? How often do you take on a new task not on your top-drawer list? Interruptions may be phone calls, people who drop by your office or home, or letting yourself get involved in someone else's agenda or priority for the day.

To see how often you let yourself be distracted by daily interruptions, keep a notebook handy and when this happens, begin to track how you react and what you could do differently in the future.

Here are several tips on how to manage interruptions in your day:

- Schedule time during your day to take care of e-mail, voice mail, phone calls, and receiving visitors.

- Be proactive in reaching out to personal or business relationships to check in to assess and anticipate needs before those needs become priorities; for example, get regular status reports from important clients, employees, or an aging parent. These check-ins can be done by telephone, e-mail, or in face-to-face meetings.

- When you are interrupted, make it clear that you have only a few minutes, and that you would be able to get back to the person at a later, specific time.

You will discover that balance, focus, and renewal energy are but three of the benefits of clarifying your values, priorities, and goals. Managing your time efficiently is a path that will help you regain a sense of control and purpose in your life. Enjoy your new journey!

FURTHER READING

Brinkman, R. 1993. *Life by Design: Making Lifestyle Choices That Contribute to Better Physical and Emotional Health.* Boulder, CO: Career Track Publications. (This is an audiotape and workbook set.)

Covey, S. R. 2004. *The 7 Habits of Highly Effective People.* New York: Simon & Schuster.

Griessman, B. E. 1994. *Time Tactics of Very Successful People.* New York: McGraw-Hill.

Loehr, J., and T. Schwartz. 2004. *The Power of Full Engagement: Managing Energy, Not Time, Is the Key to High Performance and Personal Renewal.* New York: Free Press.

Manhart, K. 2004. The limits of multitasking. *Scientific American Mind,* December.

McCorry, K. J. 2005. *Organize Your Work Day In No Time.* New York: Que.

Morgenstern, J. 2005. *Never Check E-Mail In the Morning: And Other Unexpected Strategies for Making Your Work Life Work.* New York: Fireside.

Schwartz, T. 2004. *The Power of Full Engagement: Managing Energy Not Time Is the Key to High Performance and Personal Renewal.* New York: Simon & Schuster.

Stautberg, S. S., and M. L. Worthing. 1992. *Balancing Acts! Juggling Love, Work, Family, and Recreation.* New York: Midea Master.

RECORDINGS

Epstein-Shepherd, B. 1993. *Creating More Time in Your Life* (Audiotape). Boulder, CO: Career Track Publications.

Morgenstern, J. 2004. *Making Work Work: New Strategies for Surviving and Thriving at the Office* (Abridged Audio CD). New York: Harper Audio.

Richardson, C. 2001. *Take Time for Your Life* (Audio CD). New York: Sounds True.

Scott Decker, D. 1997. *How to Put More Life in Your Time: Practical Tools to Sharpen Your Thinking, Focus Your Priorities, and Simplify Your Life* (5 Audiotapes). New York: New American Library.

17

Assertiveness Training

In this chapter you will learn to:

✻ Evaluate your current patterns of communication

✻ Differentiate between aggressive, passive, and assertive styles of communication

✻ Examine mistaken traditional assumptions and your assertive rights

✻ Express your feelings and opinions, set limits, and initiate change

✻ Use nonverbal assertive communication

✻ Listen assertively

✻ Avoid manipulation

BACKGROUND

Andrew Salter (1949) initially described assertiveness as a personality trait. It was thought that some people had it, and some people didn't, just like extroversion or stinginess. But Wolpe (1958) and Lazarus (1966) redefined assertiveness as "expressing personal rights and feelings." They found that nearly everybody could be assertive in some situations, and yet be totally ineffectual in others. The goal of assertiveness training is to increase the number and variety of situations in which assertive behavior is possible, and decrease occasions of passive collapse or hostile blowup.

You are assertive when you stand up for your rights in such a way that the rights of others are not violated. Beyond just demanding your rights, assertiveness implies that you can: express your personal likes and interests spontaneously; talk about yourself without being self-conscious; accept compliments comfortably; disagree with someone openly; ask for clarification; and you can say no. In short, when you are an assertive person, you can be more relaxed in interpersonal situations.

Some people think that assertiveness training turns nice people into irascible complainers or calculating manipulators. Not so. It's your right to protect yourself when something seems unfair. You are the one who best understands your discomfort levels and your essential needs.

How you interact with people can be a source of major stress. Assertiveness training can reduce that stress by teaching you to stand up for your legitimate rights, without bullying others or allowing them to bully you. You can use assertive communication to reduce conflict and build strong, supportive relationships.

Before reading any further, write down how you would typically respond to the following problem situations:

1. You finish shopping in the market, and after you walk out you discover that the change is three dollars short.

   I would:

   _____

   _____

   _____

2. You order a rare steak and it arrives medium-well done.

   I would:

   _____

   _____

   _____

3. You're giving a friend a lift to a meeting. The friend keeps puttering around for half an hour and you realize that you will arrive late for the meeting.

   I would:

   _____

   _____

   _____

4. You've been looking forward all week to seeing a particular movie, and your companion informs you that he or she wants to see a different movie.

   I would:

   _____

   _____

   _____

5. You're relaxing watching TV after a long, hard day. Your spouse pops in, list in hand, and says, "I thought you'd never get here. Quick, go out and pick up these things from the store."

I would:

_____

_____

_____

6. While you wait for the clerk to finish with the customer ahead of you, another customer comes in and the clerk starts to wait on him before you.

I would:

_____

_____

_____

After you have written down what you would do in these problem situations, set your responses aside. They will be put to use shortly.

Investigators such as Jakubowski-Spector (1973) and Alberti and Emmons (1995) have demonstrated that people who show relatively little assertive behavior do not believe that they have a right to their feelings, beliefs, or opinions. In the deepest sense, they reject the idea that we are created equal and are meant to treat each other as equals. As a result, they can't find grounds for objecting to exploitation or mistreatment. Most likely such people learned as children some traditional assumptions that implied their perceptions, opinions, feelings, and wants were less important or less correct than those of others. They grew up doubting themselves and looking to others for validation and guidance.

When you were a child, you didn't have much choice about which traditional assumptions you were taught. Now, however, you have the option of deciding whether to continue behaving according to assumptions that keep you from being an assertive adult. Each of the following mistaken assumptions violates one of your legitimate rights as an adult:

Mistaken Traditional Assumptions	Your Legitimate Rights
1. It is selfish to put your needs before others' needs.	You have a right to put yourself first sometimes.
2. It is shameful to make mistakes. You should have an appropriate response for every occasion.	You have a right to make mistakes.
3. If you can't convince others that your feelings are reasonable, then the feelings must be wrong, or maybe you are going crazy.	You have a right to be the final judge of your feelings and accept them as legitimate.
4. You should respect the views of others, especially if they are in a position of authority. Keep your differences of opinion to yourself. Listen and learn.	You have a right to have your own opinions and convictions.
5. You should always try to be logical and consistent.	You have a right to change your mind or decide on a different course of action.
6. You should be flexible and adjust. Others have good reasons for their actions and it's not polite to question them.	You have a right to protest unfair treatment or criticism.
7. You should never interrupt people. Asking questions reveals your stupidity to others.	You have a right to interrupt in order to ask for clarification.
8. Things could get even worse, don't rock the boat.	You have a right to negotiate for change.
9. You shouldn't take up others' valuable time with your problems.	You have a right to ask for help or emotional support.
10. People don't want to hear that you feel bad, so keep it to yourself.	You have a right to feel and express pain.
11. When someone takes the time to give you advice, you should take it very seriously. They are often right.	You have a right to ignore the advice of others.

Mistaken Traditional Assumptions	Your Legitimate Rights
12. Knowing that you did something well is its own reward. People don't like show-offs. Successful people are secretly disliked and envied. Be modest when complimented.	You have a right to receive formal recognition for your work and achievements.
13. You should always try to accommodate others. If you don't, they won't be there when you need them.	You have a right to say no.
14. Don't be antisocial. People will think you don't like them if you say you'd rather be alone than spend time with them.	You have a right to be alone, even if others would prefer your company.
15. You should always have a good reason for what you feel and do.	You have a right not to have to justify yourself to others.
16. When someone is in trouble, you should help them.	You have a right not to take responsibility for someone else's problem.
17. You should be sensitive to the needs and wishes of others, even when they are unable to tell you what they want.	You have a right not to have to anticipate others' needs and wishes.
18. It's always a good policy to stay on people's good side.	You have a right not to always worry about the goodwill of others.
19. It's not nice to put people off. If questioned, give an answer.	You have a right to choose not to respond to a situation.

As you continue working through this chapter, keep in mind that assertive communication is based on the assumption that you are the best judge of your thoughts, feelings, wants, and behavior. Nobody is better informed than you are regarding how your heredity, history, and current circumstances have shaped you into a unique human being. Therefore, you are the best advocate for expressing your positions on important issues. Because of your uniqueness, there are many times when you differ with significant people in your life. Rather than overpowering the meek or giving in to the aggressive, you have the right to express your position and try to negotiate your differences.

SYMPTOM-RELIEF EFFECTIVENESS

Assertiveness training has been found to be effective in dealing with depression, anger, resentment, and interpersonal anxiety, especially when these symptoms have been brought about by unfair circumstances. As you become more assertive, you begin to lay claim to your right to relax and take better care of yourself.

TIME TO MASTER

Some people master assertiveness skills sufficiently for symptom relief with just a few weeks of practice. For others, several months of step-by-step work are needed to experience significant change.

INSTRUCTIONS

Step 1: Three Basic Interpersonal Styles

Assertiveness is a skill that can be learned, not a personality trait that some are born with and others are not. The first step in assertiveness training is to identify the three basic styles of interpersonal behavior.

- **Aggressive style.** In this style, opinions, feelings, and wants are honestly stated, but at the expense of someone else's feelings. The underlying message is "I'm superior and right, and you're inferior and wrong." The advantage of aggressive behavior is that people often give aggressive individuals what they want in order to get rid of them. The disadvantage is that aggressive individuals make enemies, and people who can't avoid them entirely may end up behaving dishonestly toward them in order to avoid confrontations.

- **Passive style.** In this style, opinions, feelings, and wants are withheld altogether or expressed indirectly and only in part. The underlying message is "I'm weak and inferior, and you're powerful and right." The advantage of passive communication is that it minimizes responsibility for making decisions and the risk of taking a personal stand on an issue. The disadvantages are a sense of impotence, lowered self-esteem, and having to live with the decisions of others.

- **Assertive style.** In this style, you clearly state your opinions, feelings, and wants without violating the rights of others. The underlying assumption is "You and I may have our differences, but we are equally entitled to express ourselves to one another."

The major advantages include active participation in making important decisions, getting what you want without alienating others, the emotional and intellectual satisfaction of respectfully exchanging feelings and ideas, and high self-esteem.

To test your ability to distinguish interpersonal styles, label person A's behavior in the following scenes as aggressive, passive, or assertive:

SCENE 1

A: Is that a new dent I see in the car?

B: Look, I just got home, it was a wretched day, and I don't want to talk about it now.

A: This is important to me, and we're going to talk about it now.

B: Have a heart.

A: Let's decide now who is going to pay to have it fixed, when, and where.

B: I'll take care of it. Now leave me alone, for heaven's sake!

A's behavior is ☐ Aggressive ☐ Passive ☐ Assertive

SCENE 2

A: You left me by myself at that party … I really felt abandoned.

B: You were being a party pooper.

A: I didn't know anybody—the least you could have done was introduce me to some of your friends.

B: Listen, you're a grown-up. You can take care of yourself. I'm tired of you nagging to be taken care of all the time.

A: And I'm tired of your inconsiderateness.

B: Okay, I'll stick to you like glue next time.

A's behavior is ☐ Aggressive ☐ Passive ☐ Assertive

SCENE 3

A: Would you mind helping me for a minute with this file?

B: I'm busy with this report. Catch me later.

A: Well, I really hate to bother you, but it's important.

B: Look, I have a four o'clock deadline.

A: Okay, I understand. I know it's hard to be interrupted.

A's behavior is ☐ Aggressive ☐ Passive ☐ Assertive

SCENE 4

A: I got a letter from Mom this morning. She wants to come and spend two weeks with us. I'd really like to see her.

B: Oh no, not your mother! And right on the heels of your sister. When do we get a little time to ourselves?

A: Well, I do want her to come, but I know you need to spend some time without my relatives underfoot. I'd like to invite her to come in a month, and instead of two weeks, I think one week would be enough. What do you say to that?

B: That's a big relief to me.

A's behavior is ☐ Aggressive ☐ Passive ☐ Assertive

SCENE 5

A: Boy, you're looking great today!

B: Who do you think you're kidding? My hair is a fright and my clothes aren't fit for the Goodwill box.

A: Have it your way.

B: And I feel just as bad as I look today.

A: Right. I've got to run now.

A's behavior is ☐ Aggressive ☐ Passive ☐ Assertive

SCENE 6

While at a party, A tells her friends how much she appreciates her boyfriend taking her out to good restaurants and to the theater. Her friends criticize her for being such an old-fashioned, unliberated woman.

A: Not so. I don't make nearly as much at my job as he does at his. I couldn't afford to take us both out or pay my own way to all the nice places we go. Some traditions make sense, given the economic realities of both of our lives.

A's behavior is ☐ Aggressive ☐ Passive ☐ Assertive

Now that you have labeled person A's responses in these scenes as aggressive, passive, or assertive, compare your assessment with ours:

Scene 1. A is aggressive. A's seemingly innocent question is actually an accusation in disguise. A's insistence on immediate action with total disregard for B's state of mind sets up a polarized conflict in which B is likely to withdraw, and feel wrong and defensive.

Scene 2. A is aggressive. The tone is accusing and blaming. B is immediately placed on the defensive and no one wins.

Scene 3. A is passive. A's timid opening line is followed by complete collapse. The file problem must now be dealt with alone.

Scene 4. A is assertive. The request is specific, nonhostile, and open to negotiation.

Scene 5. A is passive. A allows the compliment to be rebuffed and surrenders to B's rush of negativity.

Scene 6. A is assertive. She stands up to the prevailing opinion of the group and achieves a clear, nonthreatening statement of her position.

Step 2: The Assertiveness Questionnaire*

The second step in assertiveness training is to identify those situations in which you want to be more effective. Having clarified the three interpersonal styles, now reexamine your responses to the six problem situations presented at the beginning of this chapter. Label your responses as falling primarily in the aggressive, passive, or assertive style. This is a start in objectively analyzing your behavior and finding out where assertiveness training can most help you.

To further refine your assessment of the situations in which you need to be more assertive, complete the following questionnaire. Put a check mark in column A by the items that are applicable to you and then rate those items from 1 to 5 in column B:

* Adapted from Sharon and Gordon Bower's 2004 book *Asserting Yourself: A Practical Guide for Positive Change*. New York: Da Capo Press.

1. Comfortable

2. Mildly uncomfortable

3. Moderately uncomfortable

4. Very uncomfortable

5. Unbearably threatening

(Note that the varying degrees of discomfort can be expressed whether your inappropriate reactions are hostile or passive.)

	A Check here if the item applies to me	B Rate from 1–5 for discomfort
WHEN do I behave nonassertively?		
Asking for help	_____	_____
Stating a difference of opinion	_____	_____
Receiving and expressing negative feelings	_____	_____
Receiving and expressing positive feelings	_____	_____
Dealing with someone who refuses to cooperate	_____	_____
Speaking up about something that annoys me	_____	_____
Talking when all eyes are on me	_____	_____
Protesting a rip-off	_____	_____
Saying no	_____	_____
Responding to undeserved criticism	_____	_____
Making requests of authority figures	_____	_____
Negotiating for something I want	_____	_____
Having to take charge	_____	_____
Asking for cooperation	_____	_____
Proposing an idea	_____	_____
Asking questions	_____	_____
Dealing with attempts to make me feel guilty	_____	_____
Asking for service	_____	_____
Asking for a date or appointment	_____	_____
Other _____	_____	_____

WHO are the people with whom I am nonassertive?

Parents   _____   _____

Fellow workers, classmates   _____   _____

Strangers   _____   _____

Old friends   _____   _____

Spouse or mate   _____   _____

Employer   _____   _____

Relatives   _____   _____

Children   _____   _____

Acquaintances   _____   _____

Salespeople, clerks, hired help   _____   _____

More than two or three people in a group   _____   _____

Other _____   _____   _____

WHAT do I want that I have been unable to achieve with nonassertive styles?

Approval for things I have done well   _____   _____

To get help with certain tasks   _____   _____

More attention, or time with my mate   _____   _____

To be listened to and understood   _____   _____

To make boring or frustrating situations more satisfying   _____   _____

To not have to be nice all the time   _____   _____

Confidence in speaking up when something is important to me   _____   _____

Greater comfort with strangers, store clerks, mechanics, and so on   _____   _____

Confidence in asking for contact with people I find attractive   _____   _____

To get a new job, ask for interviews, raises, and so on   _____   _____

Comfort with people who supervise me or work under me   _____   _____

To not feel angry and bitter a lot of the time   _____   _____

To overcome a feeling of helplessness and the sense that nothing ever really changes   _____   _____

	A Check here if the item applies to me	B Rate from 1–5 for discomfort
To initiate satisfying sexual experiences	_____	_____
To do something totally different and novel	_____	_____
To have time by myself	_____	_____
To do things that are fun or relaxing for me	_____	_____
Other _____	_____	_____

WHY am I hesitant to be assertive?

If I'm assertive, I am concerned that I might appear to be:

Selfish	_____	_____
Imperfect or foolish	_____	_____
Wrong or crazy	_____	_____
Disrespectful	_____	_____
Illogical or inconsistent	_____	_____
Inflexible	_____	_____
Stupid	_____	_____
A troublemaker	_____	_____
A complainer	_____	_____
Unappreciative	_____	_____
A show-off	_____	_____
Uncooperative	_____	_____
Uncaring	_____	_____
Insensitive	_____	_____
Unfriendly	_____	_____
Rude	_____	_____
Weak*	_____	_____
Other _____	_____	_____

* Aggressive people worry about being taken advantage of, not getting what they want, and not being obeyed if they are perceived as weak.

Evaluating your responses. Now, examine your answers and analyze them for an overall picture of what types of situations and people threaten you. How does nonassertive behavior contribute to the specific items you checked on the *What* list? In constructing your assertiveness program, initially focusing on items you rated as falling into the 2–3 range will be useful. These are the situations that you will find easiest to change. Items that are very uncomfortable or threatening can be tackled later.

If you checked off any of the items on the *Why* list that address your concerns about appearing in a negative light if you are assertive, review the Mistaken Traditional Assumptions and Your Legitimate Rights from which the items on the *Why* list were derived. Remember that you are your own best advocate, and that you have a responsibility to take care of yourself even when you don't have the full approval or support of others.

It's natural to feel anxious when you are doing something new. With practice, you will feel more comfortable behaving assertively. You may not always get what you want when you are assertive, inasmuch as other people also have the right to disagree and say no; but you are much more likely to achieve your goals when you behave assertively rather than passively or aggressively. Chapter 12, Refuting Irrational Ideas, is another resource that can help you examine unhelpful self-talk that contributes to your discomfort with being assertive.

Step 3: Describing Your Problem Scenes

The third step in assertiveness training, according to Sharon and Gordon Bower (2004), is to describe your problem scenes. Select a mildly to moderately uncomfortable situation that suggests itself from items on the Assertiveness Questionnaire. Write out a description of the scene, being certain to include *who* the person involved is, *when* it takes place (time and setting), *what* bothers you, *how* you deal with it, your *fear* of what will take place if you are assertive, and your *goal*. Always be specific! Generalizations will make it difficult later on to write a script that will make assertive behavior possible in this situation. The following is an example of a poor scene description.

> I have a lot of trouble persuading some of my friends to listen to me for a change. They never stop talking, and I never get a word in edgewise. It would be nice for me if I could participate more in the conversation. I feel that I just let them run over me.

Notice that the description doesn't specify *who* the particular friends are, *when* this problem is most likely to occur, *how* the nonassertive person acts, what *fears* are involved in being assertive, and a specific *goal* for increased involvement in the conversation. This scene might be rewritten as follows:

My friend Joan (*who*), when we meet for a drink after work (*when*), often goes on and on—nonstop—about her marriage problems (*what*). I just sit there and try to be interested (*how.*) If I interrupt her, I'm afraid she'll think I just don't care (*fear*). I'd like to be able to change the subject and talk sometimes about my own life (*goal.*)

Here is a second poor scene description:

A lot of times I want to strike up a conversation with people, but I worry that maybe they don't want to be disturbed. Often I notice someone who seems interesting, but I can't imagine how to get his or her attention.

Once again there is a lack of detail. No clear statement is made as to *who* these people are, *when* the experience takes place, *how* the nonassertive person behaves, or the specific *goal*. The described scene will become much more useful by including the following elements:

There is an attractive girl (*who*) who always brings a bag lunch and often sits at my table in the cafeteria (*what, where*) at lunch (*when*). I just eat in silence and read my book (*how*). I would like to start a conversation by asking about her boss, who has a very hard-to-get-along-with reputation (*goal*), but she looks so intent on her book I'm afraid she will think that I was rude and be annoyed if I interrupt her (*fear*).

As you write three or four problem scenes, you will likely recall the thoughts and feelings you actually experienced. You might notice, for example, that in each problem scene you shoot yourself down with negative thoughts ("I can't do it … I'm blowing it again … boy, do I look stupid"), or you usually feel tense in the stomach and seem to be breathing way up in your chest. Some of the strategies in other chapters of this workbook that will help you cope with distressing habitual thoughts and physical reactions when you act assertively are: Refuting Irrational Ideas, Facing Worry and Anxiety, Coping Skills for Anxiety, Anger Inoculation, Applied Relaxation Training, and Breathing (diaphragmatic breathing). This chapter, however, primarily focuses on changing your habitual way of behaving in these problematic interpersonal situations.

Step 4: Your Script for Change

The fourth step in assertiveness training is writing your script for change. A script is a working plan for dealing with the problem scene assertively. There are five elements in a script:

1. **Arrange a time and place to discuss your problem that is convenient for you and for the other person.** For example, "After we have dinner tonight in the living room, I will ask my roommate if she would be willing to talk about keeping the living room tidy. If she doesn't want to do it then, I'll ask her to name a more convenient time." This step

may be excluded when dealing with spontaneous situations in which you choose to be assertive, such as when a person cuts ahead of you in a line of waiting people.

2. **Define the problem situation as specifically as possible.** This is essential for focusing the discussion. Here is your opportunity to state the facts as you see them and share your opinion and beliefs without attacking the other person. For example: "I notice that your clothes, books, and papers are left out in the living room for days at a time. We live in a small apartment, and when one person doesn't clean up after herself, the place gets messy fast."

3. **Describe your feelings so that the other person has a better understanding of how important the issue is to you.** Once your feelings are expressed, they can often play a major role in helping you get what you want, especially when your opinion differs markedly from that of your listener. If nothing else, the listener may be able to relate to and understand your feelings about an issue even when she or he totally disagrees with your perspective. When you share your feelings, you become less of an adversary.

    There are three useful rules to remember when assertively expressing your feelings:

    a. Do not substitute an opinion for a feeling ("I feel that you're a lazy, immature slob!"). More accurate feeling statements are "I hate living in a messy house. I resent having to clean up after you in order to have a neat living room."

    b. Use "I messages" that express your feelings without evaluating or blaming others. Rather than saying "You are inconsiderate" or "You piss me off," you would say "I'm annoyed and frustrated."

    c. Use "I messages" to connect the feeling statement with specific behaviors of the other person. For example, "I feel angry and frustrated when you leave your things in the living room for days at a time." Contrast the clarity of this message with this vague blame statement: "I feel pissed off because you are so inconsiderate."

4. **Express what you want in one or two easy-to-understand sentences.** Be specific and firm. Instead of expecting others to read your mind and magically meet your needs, as in the case of the passive individual, clearly state your wishes and needs. Rather than assuming that you are always right and entitled to getting your way, as an aggressive person might, state your wants as preferences, not as commands. For example, "I would like you to not leave clothes, books, and papers in the living room when you are not using them."

5. **Reinforce the other person to give you what you want.** The best reinforcement is to describe positive consequences. "We will have a neater living room.... We'll save money.... We'll have more time together.... I'll give you a backrub.... My mother will

stay only one week.... I'll be less tired and more fun to be with.... I'll be able to get my work in on time.... Little Julia will do better in school," and so on.

In some cases, describing positive consequences may be ineffective. If the person you're dealing with seems resistant or if you feel that you're having trouble motivating him or her to cooperate with you, consider describing some negative consequences for failure to cooperate. The most effective negative consequences are descriptions of the alternative way you will take care of yourself if your wishes aren't accommodated.

- If we can't leave on time, I'll have to leave without you. Then you'll have to drive over later by yourself.

- If you can't clean the bathroom, I'll hire someone to do it once a week and add it to your rent.

- If you won't fold and put away your clothes, I'll just leave them in this box. I guess you can sort through it whenever you need something.

- If you keep talking in this loud, attacking way, I'll leave. We can talk again tomorrow.

- If you get drunk at the party, I'm driving home.

- If your check bounces again, we'll have to work on a cash-only basis.

- If you keep talking during the movie, I'm going to ask the manager to come over here and deal with the problem.

- If you can't give me an accurate idea of when you'll be home, I'm not going to cook dinner and keep it warm for you.

Notice that these examples are different from threats. The consequence of noncooperation is that the speaker takes care of his or her interests. The consequences are not designed to hurt, merely to protect the speaker. Threats usually don't work because they make people so angry. If you do make a threat ("You won't go to my sister's wedding? I won't go to your family reunion!"), be sure you are willing and able to back it up before you make the threat. Even then, it will often do more harm than good.

As an example of a script for change, let's say that Jean wants to assert her right to have half an hour every day of uninterrupted peace and quiet while she does her relaxation exercises. Frank often interrupts with questions and attention-getting maneuvers. Jean's script goes like this:

Arrange a time and place to discuss the situation.

I'll ask Frank if he's willing to discuss this problem when he gets home tonight. If he isn't, we'll set a time and place to talk about it in the next day or two.

Define the problem specifically.

At least once, and sometimes more often, I'm interrupted during my relaxation exercises—even though I've shut the door and asked for the time to myself. My concentration is broken and I find that relaxing deeply is harder.

Describe your feelings using "I messages."

I feel angry when my time alone is broken into and I feel frustrated that the exercises are then made more difficult.

Express what you want simply and firmly.

I would like not to be interrupted when my door is closed, except in a dire emergency. As long as it is closed, assume that I am still doing the exercises and want to be alone.

Reinforce the other person to give you what you want.

If I'm not interrupted, I'll come in afterward and chat with you. If I am interrupted, I will take more time to do the exercises.

In the next example, Nick demonstrates how to use the assertive script for change to say no. Nick has felt very reluctant to approach his coworker to tell her he has changed his mind about helping her with her new project. Nick's script is as follows:

Arrange a time and a place to discuss the situation:

I'll send her an e-mail tomorrow morning requesting a time to talk about this problem.

Problem:

Clara, I know that I agreed to help you with your new project, but I have discovered that it's taking much more time than I anticipated. I'm finding that I'm not getting my own work done, and that's going to cause me big problems with my boss.

Feelings:

I feel guilty about changing my mind and letting you down. I'm also feeling pressured and anxious about falling behind in my own work when a deadline is looming.

Wants:

I'm going to have to take myself off your project sometime in the next week. Is Friday too soon?

Reinforcement:

I might be available to help you in a smaller capacity after the end of the fiscal year next month. In the meantime, consider asking Jeff to help you out since he is between projects now.

(Note: Nick doesn't have to offer a reinforcement to make his withdrawal from the project more acceptable to Clara, but he chooses to because he is willing to help her as long as his own work doesn't suffer, and he wants to maintain a good working relationship with her.)

Now, here is an example of how you can use a script for change when a situation suddenly presents itself and you want to be assertive. You skip arranging a time. Before you speak, think of a sentence or two to complete the three essential elements of the script for change. Offer a reinforcement, if you like.

Crystal is watching TV in the family room when her little brother comes into the room, grabs the remote, and starts channel surfing. Crystal stifles her first response to call him "an inconsiderate little creep" and wrestle the remote away from him. After thinking about the four basic elements of her script for change, she says:

> *Lenny, I was watching my favorite program when you came in here and started channel surfing.* (Problem)
> *I'm really annoyed that you turned off the program I was watching without consulting with me first.* (Feeling)
> *I want you to turn back to my program right now.* (Want) *If you do that, I'll leave the TV to you for the rest of the evening when my program is over in fifteen minutes.* (Positive reinforcement)

Exercise: Read the following script for change, write down what you think is wrong with it, and then rewrite it on the blank Script for Change Form below, based on what you've learned about good scripts for change.

For the past two semesters, Julie has wanted to take a night class in ceramics. Each time, her husband had an excuse about why he could not watch the children on the night of the class. Here's Julie's script for change:

Arrange a time and a place to discuss the situation:

When Kevin gets home tonight.

Problem:

You've made it impossible for me to take my ceramics class for a whole year. I've been pushed around for too long.

Feelings:

I'm sick and tired of you being such a selfish, inconsiderate son of a gun.

Request:

You're just going to have to suffer through babysitting while I take my class.

Reinforcement:

If you don't like it, you can kiss this marriage good-bye.

Problems with this script for change:

1. _____

   _____

2. _____

   _____

3. _____

   _____

4. _____

   _____

5. _____

   _____

Compare your ideas with the following problems we found in Julie's script for change:

1. She didn't get an agreement on the time and place for the discussion.

2. She used nonspecific and blaming phrases such as "made it impossible" and "pushed around."

3. She failed to specify exactly what her husband was doing that was a problem.

4. She accused her husband of being a selfish, inconsiderate son of a gun rather than expressing her feelings about his specific undesirable behaviors.

5. She did not specify which nights during the semester she needed her husband to do the child care or how long the semester would last. Instead, she made a very unappealing demand.

6. She threatened negative consequences that she probably would not be willing to carry out.

Now, rewrite Julie's script for change so that she is assertive:

Arrange a time and a place for discussion:

_____

_____

Problem:

_____

_____

Feelings:

_____

_____

Request:

_____

_____

Reinforcement:

_____

_____

Here is an example of how Julie might make her request:

Arrange a time and a place:

I'll ask Kevin if he would be willing to talk about doing the child care during my ceramics night class after breakfast Saturday morning. If he's not, I'll ask him to name a time in the immediate future when he is.

Problem:

I've missed two previous ceramics classes because you weren't available for child care on class night. I've waited a year and I would like to enroll this time.

Feelings:

I feel frustrated that I haven't been able to explore something that really excites me. I also feel hurt and angry when you do other things rather than help me take the class.

Request:

I'd like you to look after the children on Wednesday nights between 6:30 and 9:00. The class starts January 25th and ends June 2nd.

Reinforcement:

If you're willing to do this for me, I'll cook your favorite meatloaf for you on Wednesdays, but if you're not, we'll have the expense of a babysitter.

In the new and improved script for change, the time to talk is agreed upon, the described problem behavior has become specific, the expressed feelings are now nonthreatening "I messages" tied to specific behaviors, and the request is simple and concrete. Julie's reinforcements are realistic and explicit. Note that negative reinforcement is often not necessary, and that positive reinforcement may require no more than the assurance that you will feel good if a certain behavior change is made. Elaborate promises usually can be avoided.

Exercise: Now, you can write your own scripts for change. Make several copies of the blank Script for Change Form so that you can write out different scripts for change.

SCRIPT FOR CHANGE FORM

Arrange a time and a place to discuss the situation (if appropriate):

_____

_____

_____

Define the problem specifically:

_____

_____

_____

Describe your feelings using "I messages":

_____

_____

_____

Express your request simply and firmly:

_____

_____

_____

Reinforce the other person to give you what you want (if you like):

_____

_____

_____

Step 5: Assertive Nonverbal Communication

The fifth step in assertiveness training is to learn to use your body and tone of voice to support your assertive words. Practicing your assertive scripts for change in front of a mirror or with a friend will help you master the following five basic rules:

1. Maintain direct eye contact. Note that it is natural to blink and look away occasionally.

2. Maintain an erect body posture.

3. Speak clearly, calmly, and firmly.

4. Don't whine or use an apologetic or hostile tone of voice.

5. Use gestures and facial expressions for emphasis that are congruent with what you have to say. *Example:* Use a serious look rather than a smile when you are saying no to a door-to-door salesperson.

Exercise: Rehearse your written scripts in front of a mirror, using assertive nonverbal communication. Be your own coach: observe what you are doing well and what you might improve next time.

Exercise: Record your rehearsals to further refine your assertive voice.

Exercise: Practice your script with a friend who can play the role of the other person. Afterwards, ask your friend's opinion on what you did well and what you might do to improve when you express your script for change in real life.

Exercise: Use your script for change in a real-life situation. Afterwards, ask yourself what you did well, and how you could do better if you were to do it again. Did you get the response you wanted from the other person? If you didn't, give yourself credit for trying to stand up for yourself. Continue to rehearse and then use your scripts for change in real life, adding in new assertiveness skills as you learn them.

Step 6: Assertive Listening

The sixth step of assertiveness training involves learning how to listen. As you practice being assertive in real-life situations, you will find that sometimes you need to deal with an issue that is important to the other person before he or she will be able to focus on what you have to say. This is especially true when what you want directly conflicts with long unspoken and unmet needs of the listener.

For example, if your spouse responds to your request for change with, *"You want an hour of silence when you get home from work? Well, I haven't said this before because you're working so hard, but I'm ready to tear out my hair after spending the entire day with the kids. I have needs too, you know,"* it might be wise to practice assertive listening at this point.

In listening assertively, you focus your attention on the other person so that you can accurately hear the speaker's opinions, feelings, and wishes. Assertive listening involves three steps:

1. **Prepare.** Become aware of your feelings and needs. Are you ready to listen? Are you sure that the other person is really ready to speak?

2. **Listen and clarify.** Give your full attention to the other person; listen to the speaker's perspective, feelings, and wants. If you are uncertain about one of these three elements, ask the speaker to clarify with more information: *I'm not quite sure how you view the situation ... could you say more about it? How do you feel about this? I don't understand what you want ... could you be more specific?*

3. **Acknowledge.** Communicate to the other person that you heard his or her position. For example, you might say, *I hear you don't want to take on this new project because you're feeling overwhelmed with your current responsibilities and want to catch up.* Another way to acknowledge the other person's feelings is to share your feelings about what has already been said: *I'm feeling overwhelmed too, and I feel terrible about having to ask you to do more work.*

Assertive listening and assertive expressing go together. Here is a sequence in which both people use assertive listening and expressing skills to solve a problem. John is unhappy about the way Carmen communicates her needs to him.

John: Is this a good time to talk about something that's bugging me a little? (*Arrange*)

Carmen: Okay.

John: Yesterday you told me you were feeling cut off and kind of abandoned by me. (*Problem*) I felt like I was doing something horrible to you. I felt very wrong, but totally confused about what exactly I was doing. (*Feelings*) Rather than making such generalized complaints like that, could you say what I'm not doing that you need, or what I could change? (*Request*) I think I could be a lot more responsive that way. (*Reinforce*)

Carmen: What was it you needed more information about? (*Clarify*)

John: What you needed me to do, at that moment, to feel closer.

Carmen: Okay, so what you're saying is that when I talk about my feelings without making any specific requests for change, that leaves you feeling confused and responsible. (*Acknowledge*)

John: Right.

Carmen: Well, sometimes I'm just telling you how I feel. I don't know why I feel that way or what to do about it. Telling you is an attempt to open the discussion. (*Redefining problem*)

John: I see. So you really aren't sure what I could do at that point. (*Acknowledge*) How about just saying you aren't sure and asking what we could do about it together? Making it "we" instead of just me would help a lot on my end. (*New request*)

Carmen: That sounds right. I like it.

Notice that Carmen clarifies and acknowledges before attempting any further explanation of the problem from her point of view. Then, in a nonblaming way, she explains why she can't go along with John's request. John, in turn, acknowledges what Carmen has said. He then uses this new information to make a second proposal that works better for Carmen.

But here's the rub: You can't always expect the other person to play by the rules. There are times when you'll have to both express and listen assertively in the face of defensive or hostile reactions. Consider Hal and Sara's case:

Sara: I have a problem with the cash projections. Can we talk? (*Arrange*)

Hal: Whatever.

Sara: Currently you're only running them out for the next three months, and I can't see how sales, inventory, and costs are going to interact six to eight months down the line. (*Define*) I'm getting pretty nervous about the big printing bills because we don't know if the money will be there. (*Describe feeling*) Could you run out the cash projection for at least six months? (*Express request*) I think we'd all breathe easier. (*Reinforce*)

Hal: Forget it, Sara. There's no time. I haven't got the bodies in my department to do stuff like that. Take a Valium and cool out.

Sara: How much extra work would it take? (*Clarify*)

Hal: Forget it, Sara. (Loudly) Forget it, okay?

Sara:	I hear you. You're overworked and haven't the staff to take on anything extra. (*Acknowledge*) But I'm wondering, how many extra hours of work are involved? (*Clarify*)
Hal:	At least twenty. Keep pushing, Sara. I'm up to here with everybody's demands.
Sara:	I hear how stressed you are. (*Acknowledge*) If once a month I got a twenty-hour bookkeeper from the pool for you, could you handle it? (*New request*)
Hal:	Probably. Let me see the body first, Sara.

In the face of sarcasm and anger, Sara continues to clarify and acknowledge until she understands Hal's problem. Hostile resistance doesn't sidetrack her. She keeps working to understand Hal's stresses and needs so she can make a new, more acceptable proposal.

Exercise: Role-play assertive listening with a friend. Have your friend play the role of a real person in your life who isn't ready to hear your script because he has issues of his own that are getting in his way. Use assertive listening to help him express his problems, feelings, and wants. Alternatively, write out a dialogue as you imagine it taking place between you (the assertive listener) and the other person (the expresser).

Exercise: Practice assertive listening in everyday life with or without combining it with a script for change. Be sure the other person wants to express the issue.

Step 7: Arriving at a Workable Compromise

The seventh step of assertiveness training is learning how to arrive at a workable compromise. When two people's interests are in direct conflict, a fair compromise that totally satisfies both parties is difficult, if not impossible, to achieve. Instead, look for a workable compromise you both can live with, at least for a while. Although a compromise might emerge naturally in your discussion, sometimes you and the other person might have to make a list of all the alternative solutions you can think of. Cross off the list those that aren't mutually acceptable. Finally, decide on a compromise you can both live with. This brainstorming process is most effective if you let your imaginations run wild while you are generating ideas. It's best to agree to review a workable compromise in a specified length of time, such as a month. At that time, you can examine the results of your changed behavior. If you aren't both sufficiently satisfied, you can renegotiate and fine-tune your compromise.

Typical compromise solutions include the following:

- My way this time, your way next time.

- I get part of what I want and you get part of what you want.

- Meeting halfway.

- If you'll do _____ for me, I'll do _____ for you.

- We'll do this one my way, but we'll do _____ your way.

- We'll try my way this time, and if you don't like it, you can veto it next time.

- We'll try your way this time, and if I don't like it, I can veto it next time.

- My way when I'm doing it, your way when you're doing it.

If you feel resistant to brainstorming and making lists of alternatives, try this simpler approach. When someone doesn't want to give you what you want, ask for a counterproposal. If the counterproposal isn't acceptable to you, make a new one of your own. But first do a little assertive listening to uncover the other person's feelings and needs in the situation. Keep going back and forth with counterproposals until something works for both of you.

A second route to compromise asks this question: *What would you need from me to feel okay doing this my way?* The answer may surprise you and offer solutions you never thought of.

Exercise: Plan how you will use a workable compromise in a situation where you are in conflict with another person. Combine it with your script for change and assertive listening.

Step 8: Avoiding Manipulation

The eighth and final step to becoming an assertive person is learning how to avoid manipulation. Inevitably, you will encounter blocking gambits from those who seek to ignore your assertive requests. The following techniques are proven ways to overcome the standard blocking gambits.

Broken record: When you find that you are dealing with someone who won't take no for an answer or refuses to grant you a reasonable request, you can carefully choose a concise sentence to use as your broken-record statement that you'll say over and over again. For example, you could say to your insistent four-year-old, "Jeff, I am not going to give you any more candy." You might say to the aggressive used-car salesman, "I am not going to buy a car today; I'm just looking." You could say to the uncooperative store clerk, "I want you to give me back my money for this defective radio." Briefly acknowledge that you have heard the other person's point, and then calmly repeat your broken-record statement without getting sidetracked by irrelevant issues. "Yes, but.... Yes, I know, and my point is.... I agree, and.... Yes, and as I was saying, ... Right, but I'm still not interested."

Content-to-process shift. Shift the focus of the discussion from the topic to an analysis of what is going on between the two of you. "We're getting off the point now." "We've been derailed into talking about old issues." "I realize I'm doing all the talking. I get the impression you don't feel comfortable talking to me about this right now. Am I right?"

Defusing. Ignore the content of someone's anger, and put off further discussion until she has calmed down. "I can see that you are very upset and angry right now. Let's discuss it later this afternoon."

Assertive delay. Put off a response to a challenging statement until you are calm, have more information, or know exactly how you want to respond. "Yes ... very interesting point.... I'll have to reserve judgment on that.... I need more time to think about the issue.... I don't want to talk about it at this time."

Assertive agreement. Acknowledge criticism you agree with. You don't need to give an explanation unless you wish to. "You're right. I did botch the Sudswell account." "Thanks for pointing out that I was smiling when I was trying to say no to that salesman. No wonder I couldn't get rid of him." "You're right, boss, I am half an hour late ... my car broke down."

Clouding. When someone puts you down as a person, acknowledge something in the criticism you can agree with, and ignore the rest. *Agree in part:* "You're right. I am late with the report." *Agree in the probability:* "You may be right that I am often late." *Agree in the principle (agreeing with the logic without agreeing with the premise):* "If I were late as often as you say, it certainly would be a problem." When clouding, rephrase the critic's words so that you can honestly concur. By giving the appearance of agreeing without promising to change, you soon deplete the critic of any reasons to criticize you.

Assertive inquiry. Invite criticism to find out what is really bothering the other person. "I understand you don't like the way I chaired the meeting last night. What was it about my behavior that bothered you? What is it about me that you feel is pushy? What is it about my speaking out that bothers you?"

Prepare yourself against a number of typical blocking gambits that will be used to attack and derail your assertive requests. Some of the most troublesome blocking gambits include the following:

Laughing it off. Your assertion is responded to with a joke. "Only three weeks late? I've got to work on being less punctual!" Use the content-to-process shift ("Humor is getting us off the point") and/or the broken record ("Yes, but...," "As I was saying ...").

Accusing gambit. You are blamed for causing the problem. "You always cook dinner so late, I'm too tired to do the dishes afterward." Use clouding ("That may be so, but you are still breaking your commitment") or simply disagree ("Eight o'clock is not too late to do the dishes").

The beat-up. Your assertion is responded to with a personal attack. "Who are you to worry about being interrupted—you're the biggest loudmouth around here." The best strategies to use are assertive irony ("Thank you") in conjunction with the broken record or defusing ("I can see you're angry right now; let's talk about it after the meeting").

Delaying gambit. Your assertion is met with "Not now, I'm too tired," or "Another time, maybe." Use the broken record, or insist on setting a specific time when the problem can be discussed.

"Why" gambit. Every assertive statement is blocked with a series of "why" questions, such as, "Why do you feel that way.... I still don't know why you don't want to go ... why did you change your mind?" The best response is to use the content-to-process shift (*"Why* isn't the point. The issue is that I'm not willing to go tonight") or the broken record.

Self-pity gambit. Your assertion is met with tears and the covert message that you are being sadistic. Try to keep going through your script using assertive agreement ("I know this is causing you pain, but I need to get this resolved").

Quibbling. The other person wants to argue with you about the legitimacy of what you feel, or the magnitude of the problem, and so forth. Use the content-to-process shift ("We're quibbling now and we've gotten off the main concern") with the assertion of your right to feel the way you do.

Threats. You are threatened with statements such as, "If you keep harping at me like this, you're going to need another boyfriend." Use assertive inquiry ("What is it about my requests that bothers you?") as well as content-to-process shift ("This seems to be a threat") or defusing.

Denial. You are told, "I didn't do that," or "You've really misinterpreted me." Assert what you have observed and experienced, and use clouding ("It may seem that way to you, but I've observed....").

Exercise: Write out at least one example from your life for each type of manipulation listed above. Make up or borrow examples if you need to. Following each example of manipulation, write an assertive response to it.

Exercise: Allow yourself to imagine or role-play with a friend the worst possible response that could be made to your scripts for change that you are most reluctant to express in real life. Become desensitized to the possible "nightmare" response by facing it, and then prepare your countermeasures. When you are ready, follow up by expressing your script in real life.

Exercise: Continue writing out, rehearsing, and expressing your scripts for change in real life on a frequent basis. In time, the writing and rehearsing can be eliminated, except in the most challenging situations. Combine or use separately the other assertiveness skills you learned in this chapter. As with all learned behavior, your assertiveness skills will improve and your confidence will grow with practice.

FURTHER READING

Alberti, R. E., and M. Emmons. 1995. *Your Perfect Right.* 7th ed. San Luis Obispo, CA: Impact Publishers.

Bower, S. A., and G. H. Bower. 2004. *Asserting Yourself: A Practical Guide for Positive Change.* New York: Da Capo Press.

Butler, P. E. 1992. *Self-Assertion for Women.* New York: HarperCollins.

Gabor, D. 1994. *Speaking Your Mind in 101 Different Situations.* New York: Simon & Schuster.

Jakubowski-Spector, P. 1973. Facilitating the growth of women through assertiveness training. *Counseling Psychologist* 4:75–86.

Lazarus, A. 1966. Behavioral rehearsal vs. nondirective therapy vs. advice in effecting behavior change. *Behavioral Research and Therapy* 4:209–212.

McClure, J. S. 2003. *Civilized Assertiveness: Communication with a Backbone, Not a Bite.* Denver, CO: Albion Street Press.

Paterson, R. J. 2000. *The Assertiveness Workbook: How to Express Your Ideas and Stand Up for Yourself at Work and in Relationships.* Oakland, CA: New Harbinger Publications.

Phelps, S., and N. Austin. 2002. *The Assertive Woman.* San Luis Obispo, CA: Impact Publishers.

Salter, A. 1949/2002. *Conditioned Reflex Therapy: The Classic Book on Assertiveness That Began Behavior Therapy.* Gretna, LA: Selfhelpbook.com (A Division of the Wellness Institute, Inc.).

Smith, M. J. 1985. *When I Say No, I Feel Guilty.* New York: Bantam Books.

Wolpe, J. 1958. *Psychotherapy by Reciprocal Inhibition.* Stanford, CA: Stanford University Press.

18

Work-Stress Management

In this chapter you will learn to:

    ✳ Identify how you currently respond to work stress

    ✳ Set goals to take control of your stress at work

    ✳ Counter stressful thinking about your work

    ✳ Negotiate when in conflict

    ✳ Pace and balance yourself

BACKGROUND

The classic symptoms of work burnout include pessimism, increased dissatisfaction, absenteeism, and inefficiency at the job. While you may not be on the verge of work burnout, you may be one of the growing majority of Americans who report that their work causes them stress. Job stress accounts for a tremendous amount of personal misery and billions of dollars lost annually in productivity, wages, and medical bills. Americans are waking up to the fact that work-stress management makes personal and financial sense.

WHAT CAUSES WORK BURNOUT?

Every job includes some built-in difficulties that the worker is paid to adjust to. Job difficulties alone do not cause burnout. Rather, it is the worker's lack of control over his or her work situation that leads to uncertainty, frustration, reduced motivation, fatigue, reduced productivity, and eventually burnout. Here are some other factors that can lead to work burnout:

- Chronic work overload

- Unfair treatment

- Impossible expectations of your boss

- Unsupportive or hostile coworkers

- Inadequate training

- Lack of recognition or rewards

- Your values conflict with those of your company, boss, or coworkers

- Unpleasant work environment

- Lack of clear direction about priorities

Even minor factors beyond your control can have a stressful impact. Consider the many unexpected interruptions in the course of your workday: special meetings, e-mail, phone calls, people dropping in, and equipment breakdowns. Think about having to go through authorized channels and dealing with bureaucratic red tape. Think about the faulty air-conditioning system or the constant din of machines, elevator music, and voices. It's also likely that your daily commute adds to your accumulated stress for the day as well.

It is a common error to associate only excessive stress with lowered productivity. *Stress underload* occurs when a job is too easy or is insufficiently challenging. As early as 1908, Robert Yerkes and John Dodson pointed out that the symptoms of stress underload are quite similar to those of stress overload: reduced efficiency, irritability, a sense of time pressure, diminished motivation, poor judgment, and accidents. We all have a unique "performance zone" within which we experience manageable stress that stimulates our energy, motivation, decision making, and productivity.

Burnout is not caused simply by too much stress in your job. If your job made no demands on you, you would be bored. Job-stress management, like stress management in general, involves finding the right types and amounts of challenge to stimulate your interest and performance without overloading you. It also requires managing those areas of your job that are inevitably distressing. Finally, it includes balancing leisure and work-related activities so that they complement one another. Work-stress management is a dynamic process over which you can exercise personal control.

SYMPTOM-RELIEF EFFECTIVENESS

Work-stress management is effective in increasing your sense of control in the workplace. Increased feelings of personal control can improve job-related symptoms of guilt, irritability, depression, anxiety, and low self-esteem. Job-stress management can also reduce job-related psychosomatic symptoms such as insomnia, fatigue, upset stomach, headaches, eating disorders, and lowered immunity to infection.

TIME TO MASTER

Over the next few days, you will identify how you currently respond to your specific work stressors, and then you can set a few goals for change. Learning how to respond more effectively to job stress will take at least a month. The habits of effective work-stress management may take two to six months to integrate into your daily life.

FIVE STEPS TOWARD MANAGING YOUR WORK STRESS

Step 1: Identify How You Respond to Your Specific Work Stressors

What are your specific work stressors and how do you tend to respond to them? Over the next few days, observe how you respond to both big and little stresses at work. Also, reflect on your recent experiences at work to recall and identify any troublesome responses you may have had to work stressors. In the far left-hand column of the following form called My Response to Specific Work Stressors, list your specific stresses. For each stressful item, write down your feelings the day the stress occurs, what you say to yourself about it, and what you do in response to it.

For example, Patty, a computer programmer, wrote down the specific stressors in her job and her responses to them in the following shorthand manner:

MY RESPONSE TO SPECIFIC WORK STRESSORS

Your Work Stressor	Your Feelings	Your Thoughts	Your Behavior
Programming	Bored, numb	"Nonstop programming makes Patty a dull girl."	Plodding, inefficient; eat sweets, drink coffee
Deadlines	Anxious	"I'll never make it!"	Work faster and longer, make mistakes
Meetings	Annoyed, impatient	"What a waste; I've got work to do."	Critical, resistant to suggestions
Vague supervisor	Insecure, confused, annoyed	"What does it take to please this jerk?"	Guess what he wants, complain
Chatty coworker	Angry	"Why does he keep interrupting me? He's so inconsiderate!"	Respond politely and return to my own work
Uncooperative administrative assistant	Angry, frustrated, dissatisfied	"She's lazy, slow, and utterly useless."	Refuse to talk to her
No privacy	Annoyed	"Hard to focus."	Tense my muscles; neck pain and backache
Working at a terminal	Strained, tired	"I wish I didn't have to do this."	Eyestrain, headache
Downtime	Frustrated, refreshed	"Damn, I lost everything I just wrote!"	Eat, drink coffee, socialize
No raise	Angry, frustrated	"I deserve better than this!"	Complain bitterly

Exercise: Using the following form, list your specific work stressors and describe how you respond to them. Use as little or as much detail as you need.

MY RESPONSE TO SPECIFIC WORK STRESSORS

Your Work Stressor	Your Feelings	Your Thoughts	Your Behavior

Exercise: Now that you have written out your specific job stressors and how you typically respond to them, review your list and see whether any troublesome patterns emerge. Write these patterns down on the My Problematic Responses to Work Stressors form that follows below.

For example, Patty wrote down the following patterns:

My Problematic Responses to Work Stressors

1. I respond to boredom and frustration by eating too much and drinking too much coffee.

2. Working at a computer terminal for long periods of time and having to concentrate in spite of a lack of privacy causes me a variety of physical and emotional symptoms of stress.

3. I waste time because I'm not assertive enough to ask my supervisor questions, say no to my officemate, or request administrative assistant support firmly enough.

4. I tend to be highly critical of myself, others, and my environment, but I rarely do anything constructive to improve my situation. I can see why I feel chronically irritated and tense at work.

My Problematic Responses to Work Stressors

1. _____

   _____

2. _____

   _____

3. _____

   _____

4. _____

   _____

Step 2: Set Goals to Respond More Effectively to Your Work Stressors

Now that you've identified your patterns of stress in your workplace, you can begin to formulate a more effective plan for responding to those stressors you can anticipate. Maybe you can avoid some of them altogether. Perhaps you can be better prepared for them when they happen. The name of the game is taking more control … and this is where you begin to do it.

You will probably want to make changes in one or more of the following general areas:

1. Change the external stressor (quit the job, assertively tell the boss not to overload you, take regular breaks, reorganize your time).

2. Change your thoughts (learn how to turn off work when you go home, alter your perfectionist attitude, stop assuming that you are responsible for others' problems, stop dwelling on vague worries or old injustices).

3. Change physically (relax, exercise, eat properly, get sufficient sleep).

When you are designing goals for yourself, remember the following guidelines. Remember that useful, attainable goals are:

- Specific
- Observable
- Achievable within a certain time frame
- Broken down into small intermediate steps
- Compatible with long-term goals
- Written down in simple self-contract form
- Reevaluated at specified intervals
- Rewarded when achieved

For example, Patty decided to set a new, more effective response to each of her four stress patterns as a goal. To that end, she wrote out the following self-contract:

October 10th

I, Patty Bowers, agree to change my four old patterns of responding to stress in the following ways:

Patterns 1 and 2: Rather than eating or drinking coffee when I am tired, bored, or frustrated, I will take regular breaks once an hour in which I'll either do a brief relaxation exercise or I'll get up and walk around and talk to people. I'll take advantage of flextime and go to an aerobics class three days a week and run personal errands two days a week in the middle of the day. I will eat three nutritious meals a day, rather than snacking on junk food.

Pattern 3: I will enroll in a one-day workshop on assertiveness training and I will ask my supervisor more questions until I am sure I know what he wants. I also will tell my chatty coworker not to interrupt me with small talk, other than when I get up and walk around. I will assertively ask the administrative assistant for help.

Pattern 4: I will take each one of my critical thoughts and turn it into a constructive action thought. For instance, rather than saying about meetings "What a waste, I have work to do," I could say "Whew, a break from programming! I could do a relaxation exercise. I may learn something interesting. Also, I might contribute something to the meeting."

I will reevaluate my progress for each goal on a weekly basis. After one month, I plan to spend a weekend at a local hot springs as my reward for changing these four patterns.

Patty Bowers

Exercise: Using the Self-Contract form on the next page, write out your goals to modify a few of your responses to the specific stresses in your work life.

SELF-CONTRACT

Date: _____

I, _____ , agree to:

1. _____

   _____

2. _____

   _____

3. _____

   _____

4. _____

   _____

I will monitor my progress every _____ (length of time).

I will reward myself with _____ .

Signature: _____

Post this contract in a place where you will see it every day to remind you of what you are to do. If you like, share the contract with a friend or coworker who can encourage and support you to follow through with your plan. You can report back to that person on your progress toward each goal on a weekly basis. Remember to reward yourself when you achieve your objectives.

Step 3: Change Your Thinking

Work stress occurs, in part, because your thoughts trigger a painful emotional reaction. Here are three generic thoughts that can do you in:

1. I've got to do _____ *(a certain task)* _____ *(perfectly) (on time)*
    (so my boss will be pleased) or _____ *(something painful)* will happen.

2. They're doing this to me and it's not fair.

3. I'm trapped here.

The first thought makes you anxious, the second triggers anger, and the third generates depression. You can do something about these thoughts and the work stress they create. Right now, list the things you tell yourself about your job that fit into each of the above three categories.

Category 1:

_____

_____

_____

Category 2:

_____

_____

_____

Category 3:

_____

_____

_____

Here's how you can cope with these stress-producing thoughts:

1. Make a realistic appraisal of what exactly will happen if the task isn't finished on time, absolutely flawless, or totally pleasing to your boss. A realistic appraisal means looking at what happened to you and others in the past when tasks like this one were late, had errors, and so on. "Realistic" also means being specific. It's time to get rid of that vague sense of doom. Exactly what is your boss likely to say to you? What, if anything, is likely to happen to you?

    Example: "If I don't meet Friday's deadline, it's likely that my boss will tell me to come in on the weekend to get this report done for Monday's meeting with the client. I'll have to put off going shopping with my friends. Disappointing, but I can handle that."

Exercise: Now it's your turn. Rewrite each of your vague, catastrophic thoughts by filling in the blanks in the following sentence:

"If _____ isn't _____ (*perfect*), (*on time, totally acceptable*), _____ is likely to happen (*something realistic*). I can handle it."

Mentally repeat this coping statement each time you catch yourself having catastrophic thoughts about vague and dire consequences. Note: If you have no idea what will happen, find out: for example, you could say, "Boss, if I'm a day late with the Crocker report, will that be a problem?"

2. There's absolutely no good that can come from blaming anyone else for your work stress. Blaming maintains your sense of being stuck, helpless, and trapped. Blaming encourages you to see yourself as a victim who has no alternatives and has lost the power of choice. Blaming triggers anger and stress hormones like adrenaline that deplete your energy and, over the long run, damage your health.

As stated in chapter 12, Refuting Irrational Ideas, "The conditions for things or people to be otherwise than they are don't exist. ... They are what they are because of a long series of causal events...." Saying to yourself that your boss or the company president should act differently is like saying former President Bush should never have tried to use the existence of weapons of mass destruction as a reason to invade Iraq. The conditions necessary for Bush to be obsessed with the dangerousness of Saddam Hussein existed. Bush's values, needs, ambitions, advisors, and personal history all pushed him to believe that the weapons existed and constituted a threat to the United States, even though proof was lacking.

No one is supposed to take care of or protect you on your job. Your coworkers and supervisors are all busy taking care of and protecting themselves. This is natural: this is an inescapable fact of working life. So what can you say to yourself to stop wasting anymore of your energy on blaming and anger?

Exercise: To answer this question, ask yourself, "What steps can I take to change the conditions I don't like?"

1. _____

_____

2. _____

_____

3. _____

   _____

If you can't think of a way to change the conditions you don't like at work, you have two rational choices. You must either adapt to and accept the conditions or look for another job.

Exercise: If you decide to accept the current situation, fill in the blanks in the following coping statement: "_____ is acting exactly as he/she should. The conditions necessary for him/her to act this way (his/her needs and the coping strategies to meet those needs, past successes and failures, fears, attitudes toward our relationship) all exist, and this is why he/she did _____ (to) (with) me."

3. You are not trapped. You may have difficult choices, but you aren't trapped. Right now the pain of your job seems less than the pain associated with your other available choices. Is this really true? Here's a chance to explore your options for change and compare them with the option of doing nothing.

   Exercise: What specific steps could you take to change a major stress producer at your job?

   _____

   _____

   _____

   What would you risk in attempting that change?

   _____

   _____

   _____

   What steps could you take to change jobs altogether?

   _____

   _____

   _____

What would you risk in attempting to make that change?

_____

_____

_____

What steps could you take to change your perception of a risk so that you would be willing to try to make a change?

_____

_____

_____

Typically, this involves acquiring additional information so that you feel more confident you can cope with the challenges involved in making a change. For example, if you think that the risk in changing jobs is that you are too old, you might set as a goal asking someone your age who is employed in the type of position you want whether your age will really make a difference. Or, if you believe that you risk blowing an interview for a new position in your present company, you could set taking an interview class as a goal.

If you are not ready to do whatever is necessary to effect change, rather than saying "I'm trapped," the more accurate statement to make to yourself is "I choose to stay with the current conditions on this job because right now it seems less painful than doing

_____

_____

(list the steps necessary to effect change). I may choose differently in the future."

Step 4: When in Conflict, Negotiate

Whether your disagreement is with your boss regarding your salary or with your coworkers about who is supposed to make the coffee, you need to present your position and negotiate a compromise you can all live with.

Read chapter 17, Assertiveness Training, to learn how to express your opinions, feelings, and wants as you negotiate for change. At the very least, read Step 7: Arriving at a Workable Compromise. Here is a four-step model to follow when you want to discuss a specific problem with your supervisor or coworkers with the aim of arriving at a mutually acceptable outcome.

State:

1. The problem (what you perceive to be the cause of your stress)

2. How you feel about the problem

3. How it affects your productivity and motivation

4. A win-win solution (both sides of the conflict get something positive from your solution)

For example, Randy, a creative high school teacher, was refused compensation for the time he spent developing new courses. Randy told his principal, "Ever since I realized I wouldn't receive money for my course development work, my enthusiasm for teaching has deteriorated. I think my students have gained tremendous value from my new, special classes. They're now suffering as a result of my loss of motivation. It's important to me and the school to continue creating new classes and it's important for me to be compensated in some way. Since the money isn't available, I would be satisfied to be reimbursed with time. If I could take one class period each day for an entire semester to develop my new class, that would work for me and the school." The principal's response was "I can't spare you a class hour every day, but I can agree to give you three hours a week." Randy accepted this workable compromise.

Exercise: Negotiating a Mutually Acceptable Outcome

Think of something you want at work that would require you to convince someone else to cooperate with you. Fill in the following blanks:

The problem as I see it is: _____

I feel _____ about this problem.

It affects my productivity or motivation in that _____

_____.

I suggest we try this win-win solution: _____

_____

Change the wording to fit the situation. Memorize your short script and then, look for an appropriate moment to share it with the person whose cooperation you are seeking. Remember to be open to hearing that person's point of view and look for a workable compromise that can benefit the two of you.

Step 5: Pace and Balance Yourself

Do you pace yourself at work? If you are like a sprinter, you can afford to throw everything you've got into the race. That's because at the end of a fast, short run you know you have plenty of time to recover from your intense effort. Most jobs, however, require you to be more like the marathon runner who must pace himself in order to get across the finish line in a timely manner without collapsing. Like the marathon runner, you need to maintain a certain detachment from the immediate demands of your job so that you will remember to reserve enough energy to deal with what you anticipate down the road, as well as with any surprises.

Here are eight tips for pacing and balancing yourself:

1. Pay attention to your natural rhythms to determine when you tend to perform optimally, and schedule your most difficult tasks for that time in your day.

2. Try to set up your day so you shift back and forth between pleasant and more difficult tasks. After finishing a tough assignment, make an effort to schedule something you enjoy.

3. Schedule periods of time into your day for work-related tasks that are pleasurable though not terribly productive. These time periods should be sacrosanct. Try to do this even when you feel rushed.

4. Take advantage of your coffee breaks and lunches to do things that will reverse the stress response. For example, go to a quiet place and do a relaxation exercise. A ten-minute brisk walk will give you as much energy as a cup of coffee. A pleasant conversation with your coworkers will release tension and may be just what you need to get a fresh perspective on a problem that is weighing you down.

5. If you are fortunate enough to have a flexible schedule, consider taking a long break in the middle of the day to do aerobic exercise, a relaxation exercise, or to run personal errands.

6. Take minibreaks throughout your day to reduce or prevent symptoms of tension and stress. These breaks need not take more than a few minutes, and the payoff can be seen in increased mental alertness and productivity. See chapter 10, Brief Combination Techniques, for exercises appropriate for short breaks.

7. Choose leisure activities that balance the unique stresses of your job.

If your job requires:	*Consider a complementary leisure activity such as:*
Much sitting or mental concentration	Aerobic exercise
Mindless repetition	Intellectually challenging hobbies and interests
A controlled environment	Hiking in nature; adventure
Boring tasks or no recognition	Competitive or achievement-oriented activities
Responding to people's demands	Solitary activities
Dealing with conflicts	Peaceful activities
Working alone	Social activities

8. Carefully plan the timing and type of vacations you take to maximize their recuperative effects.

Exercise: List at least three ways that you can better pace yourself at work and create more balance in your life:

1. _____

_____

2. _____

_____

3. _____

_____

FINAL THOUGHTS

It's to be expected that from time to time you will feel stressed by some aspects of your work. This chapter has shown you how you have the power to make positive changes to reduce if not eliminate that stress. Now it is up to you to use your power. In addition to the chapters Assertiveness Training and Refuting Irrational Ideas, the Goal Setting and Time Management chapter can also help you decrease work stress.

FURTHER READING

Arden, J. B. 2002. *Surviving Job Stress: How to Overcome Workday Pressures.* Franklin Lakes, NJ: Career Press.

Bailey, K., and K. Leland. 2006. *Watercooler Wisdom.* Oakland, CA: New Harbinger Publications.

Dolan, S. L. 2006. *Stress, Self-Esteem, Health and Work.* New York: Palgrave Macmillan.

Dunn, G. 1999. *From Making a Living to Having a Life.* Fairfax, CA: Violin Publishing Company.

Maddie, S. R., and D. M. Khoshaba. 2005. *Resilience at Work: How to Succeed No Matter What Life Throws You.* New York: Amacom Books.

Strank, J. 2005. *Stress at Work: Management and Prevention.* Oxford: Elsevier Butterwork-Heinemann Publications.

Yerkes, R. M., and J. D. Dodson. 1908. The relationship of strength of stimulus to rapidity of habit formation. *Journal of Comparative Neurology and Psychology* 18:459-482.

WEBSITE

Job Stress: www.stress.org/job/htm

19

Nutrition and Stress

In this chapter you will learn to:

　❋ Assess your current eating habits

　❋ Eat a balanced diet to optimize health and manage stress

　❋ Eat to prevent or minimize chronic disease

BACKGROUND

Eating is one of the natural joys in life, as well as a wonderful strategy you can use to reduce stress. Preparing and eating well-balanced meals is a delightful way to give yourself pleasure as well as providing good care of your body. Meals can be a time to relax and socialize and, as such, they help to reduce stress. Most cultures celebrate holidays and the passages of life with feasting; these times bring people together and give life meaning. Unfortunately, the foods that people eat for pleasure are not always nutritionally sound. Eating right is a learned skill and not something that "just comes naturally."

The American retail food industry actively promotes convenience and fast foods over fresh foods. Grocery stores now stock four times more convenience foods than they do produce and other fresh foods. People with face-paced, busy lives embrace these convenience foods. However, in so doing they lose out on good nutrition, creativity, and the sense of accomplishment that comes with planning, preparing, and eating their own meals—all activities that help to decrease stress.

America's love affair with snack foods has led some people to joke that the four major food groups are candy, cookies, coke, and chips, but the result of Americans' supersized portions of these foods is not a laughing matter. The average American diet, with its emphasis on large portions and convenience foods, contains too much fat, sugar, and sodium. Adult obesity rates have increased from 15 percent of the total population in 1980 to 33 percent in 2005. Obesity now exceeds 20 percent in all but four states, and has reached epidemic levels (CDC 2005). But obesity is only one of the risks run by physically inactive people who eat a high-fat, high-calorie diet. It is well-known that such a diet contributes to the nation's high rates of degenerative joint disease, high blood pressure, cardiovascular disease, and some cancers.

This chapter will help you assess your present eating habits and provide you with guidelines for a healthy diet. You can compare your current diet with these recommendations and set goals for retraining your eating habits. By taking charge of your nutritional health, you will begin to enjoy healthy eating. You'll find that it isn't hard to eat a balanced diet, even if you're not a chef at heart.

SYMPTOM-RELIEF EFFECTIVENESS

A healthy body responds to the inevitable stresses of life better than an unhealthy one, and good nutrition is an essential building block of good health. Eating well can help prevent or control high blood pressure, heart disease, indigestion, constipation, hypoglycemia, diabetes, and obesity. Good eating habits may also reduce irritability, PMS, headaches, and fatigue.

TIME TO MASTER

Plan to keep track of your food intake for three days. After reading the guidelines for a healthy diet, you will go on to compare them with your own eating habits and then decide what changes you want to make in your diet. You can begin to apply the recommendations in this chapter in a matter of hours. To make lasting changes in your diet, plan on gradually introducing a few changes at a time that you can stick with for a minimum of one month.

TWELVE STEPS TO POSITIVE EATING

These twelve steps to positive eating will help you feel better today and stay healthy for tomorrow. They include the basics of the *Dietary Guidelines for Americans* (2005). The Guidelines provide authoritative advice for people two years and older about how good dietary habits can promote health and reduce risk for major chronic diseases. They serve as the basis for federal food and nutrition education programs. They offer tips on healthful food preparation and making healthy eating a habit.

The 2005 Dietary Guidelines provide suggestions on how to eat to feel better today and to stay healthy for tomorrow. (See website in the Websites section at the end of the chapter.) The five Feel Better Today steps that follow are for actions that produce immediate results. They include making smart choices from all food groups; maximizing nutrition in your calories; eating frequent, calm meals; planning ahead; and finding the right balance between food and physical activity. Our seven Stay Healthy for Tomorrow steps have longer-term effects and suggest changes that impact your health over the long term. Staying healthy may depend on cutting back fats, limiting sodium, attaining your ideal weight, limiting caffeine and alcohol, and taking vitamins.

MyPyramid reinforces the concepts of good eating practices. MyPyramid Food Plans provide personalized food plans. This sample plan on the next page is for Sharon, a 5'7", forty-year-old paralegal who is moderately active and weighs 170 pounds.

MyPyramid provides nutritional guidelines, which now include exercise guidelines. The slices of the pyramid represent the various food groups and provide guidance on a balanced diet.

MyPyramid
STEPS TO A HEALTHIER YOU

Based on the information you provided, this is your daily recommended amount from each food group.

GRAINS 7 ounces	VEGETABLES 3 cups	FRUITS 2 cups	MILK 3 cups	MEAT & BEANS 6 ounces
Make half your grains whole	**Vary your veggies**	**Focus on fruits**	**Get your calcium-rich foods**	**Go lean with protein**
Aim for at least **3 1/2 ounces** of whole grains a day	Aim for these amounts **each week:** **Dark green veggies** = 3 cups **Orange veggies** = 2 cups **Dry beans & peas** = 3 cups **Starchy veggies** = 6 cups **Other veggies** = 7 cups	Eat a variety of fruit Go easy on fruit juices	Go low-fat or fat-free when you choose milk, yogurt, or cheese	Choose low-fat or lean meats and poultry Vary your protein routine— choose more fish, beans, peas, nuts, and seeds

Find your balance between food and physical activity

Be physically active for at least **30 minutes** most days of the week.

Know your limits on fats, sugars, and sodium

Your allowance for oils is **6 teaspoons a day.**

Limit extras—solid fats and sugars—to **290 calories a day.**

Your results are based on a 2200 calorie pattern.

Name: _____

This calorie level is only an estimate of your needs. Monitor your body weight to see if you need to adjust your calorie intake.

Feel Better Today: Make Smart Food Choices by Eating a Variety of Foods

You need over forty nutrients for optimum health. These are classified as *macronutrients* (proteins, carbohydrates, and fats) and *micronutrients* (vitamins and minerals). (As the names suggest, you need the former in larger quantities and the latter in smaller amounts.) Although an excess of macronutrients will lead to weight gain, an excess of micronutrients may actually be toxic for you, or at the least a waste of the money spent on unnecessary vitamin or mineral supplements.

There is no perfect food. Even milk, which provides the cornerstone of a baby's diet, doesn't supply vitamin C or iron, which is why we include juice and cereal among baby's first foods. Even the natural foods favored by many health-conscious individuals can contain naturally toxic components. For instance, potatoes naturally contain over 150 chemicals, including traces of arsenic and solanine—chemicals that are safe in low doses but poisonous at high ones (according to www.acsh.org/news/newsID.184/news _ detail.asp). Varying your diet helps to maximize your nutrients and minimize your exposure to any toxic substance or contaminant. A wide variety of foods supplies a wide variety of nutrients.

When you visit the MyPyramid website (www.mypyramid.gov), you can obtain a personalized eating plan to maintain your weight or reach a healthier weight. The following practices are recommended for an average diet of 2000 calories a day:

- **Make half your grains whole.** Eat six servings of grains daily, including bread, rice, cereal, and pasta products, the proverbial "staff of life." At least three of these choices should be whole grains, such as whole grain breads or pasta, to add fiber to your diet. Enriched grain products restore the known nutrients that may be removed by milling. When you do buy refined foods, be sure they are enriched to restore the B vitamins and iron lost in milling. Six servings may seem like a lot, but it really isn't. Many people eat two servings of cereal at breakfast. A sandwich provides two more servings of bread, and a plate of spaghetti easily provides two more servings of pasta of a half a cup each.

- **Vary your veggies.** Your veggies should total 2½ cups daily. Be sure to select vegetables of different colors to obtain all the nutrients and antioxidants required for optimum health. It is recommended to eat at least 3 cups of dark green veggies, 2 cups of orange veggies, and 3 cups of starchy veggies weekly.

- **Focus on fruits.** Eat fresh fruits rather than drinking fruit juice. Try for a total of 2 cups daily; for example, 1 small banana, 1 large orange, and 6 to 8 dried apricot halves. Dried fruit makes an easy, nutritious snack; just remember the same weight of that dried fruit has the same calories as the fruit had before it was dried, so if you would eat one fresh pear, eat no more than two dried pear halves.

- **Concentrate on calcium-rich foods.** Take the equivalent of 3 cups of low-fat or fat-free milk every day. Substitute 1 ounce of cheese or ½ cup cottage cheese or 1 cup yogurt for 1 glass of milk.

- **Go lean with protein.** Consume 5.5 ounces of protein daily. Read labels and choose meat items that have less than 3 grams of fat per serving. Using beans and legumes liberally in your diet will help keep your protein intake up and your fat content down. A ½ cup of beans, lentils, or soy products is the equivalent of 1 ounce of meat. Choose fish for the omega-3 fatty acids that help to control your LDL cholesterol. Be aware that some fish have more fat than lean red meat, and that red meat contains the iron that most women need. Bake, broil, or barbecue to reduce fat. Remove the skin from chicken before cooking, since just the skin on one chicken breast has 5 grams of fat.

- **Oils and fats.** These should be poly- or monounsaturated. Aim for a maximum of 6 teaspoons of monounsaturated oils and fats daily. Monounsaturated oils include olive oil and canola oil.

- **Discretionary calories.** These are your luxury food choices that add fat and sugar. You will have about 250 daily calories for fun foods of your choice. How about an oatmeal cookie or two?

Eating grains, fruits, and veggies that provide starch add to your sense of well-being. You'll notice that complex carbohydrates and fiber make meals more filling and satisfying. Eating lots of fresh fruits and vegetables is also good for your peace of mind, since these "power foods" contain the fiber, vitamins, minerals, and phytonutrients (natural plant chemicals) that can protect you against chronic illnesses, including diabetes, cancer, and heart disease. Carbohydrates also seem to function as "edible tranquilizers." They contain tryptophan, an amino acid that stimulates the production of serotonin in the brain. Serotonin has a calming effect that eases tension and may cause drowsiness. Is this the explanation for that happy full feeling that a big spaghetti dinner usually seems to create?

Evidence continues to build that dietary fiber (including cellulose, gums, pectin, and lignin) is an essential component of a healthy diet. Fiber helps to prevent or reduce constipation by increasing stool bulk and water absorption to control blood sugar and blood lipids by binding nutrients. It also decreases stool transit time, thus reducing the risk of colon cancer and diverticulitis.

Although the recommended intake of dietary fiber is 25 to 40 grams daily, the average American consumes only 5 to 10 grams. For most of us, fresh fruits and vegetables, whole grains, and legumes are the chief sources of fiber in our diets. You can supplement your fiber intake by increasing your use of legumes and bran products or by adding bran to homemade foods. Plan to increase your fiber intake gradually, as rapid increases can lead to bloating and flatulence.

Dietary Fiber in Common Foods	
Food Group	Dietary Fiber Content
Legumes	5.0–9.5 grams per serving
Bran cereals	2.6–8.8 grams per serving
Fruits and vegetables	2.5–6.5 grams per serving
Grains and starches	2.8–5.0 grams per serving
Nuts	1.0–3.3 grams per ounce

Feel Better Today: Eat Frequent, Calm Meals

Positive eating includes taking the time to prepare and eat frequent meals or snacks and relaxing while we eat them. Our fast-paced society, along with a plethora of fast-food options, encourages eating on the run and denies us the time to relax while we eat. Our bodies run better if we refuel them frequently. Blood sugar is like gasoline for a car, and we all know a car won't run if its fuel tank is empty. Eating three to five small meals a day helps to maintain an even blood-sugar level.

To reduce the daily stress of meal preparation, plan meals and shop weekly. When you cook, prepare enough for additional meals or snacks. It's cheaper, quicker, easier, and healthier to reheat something in the microwave than to run out to buy a fast-food meal. Also, reheated leftovers make tasty lunches to take to work.

At work, take time away from your workstation to sit and relax with your meal or snack. Likewise, take some time alone to relax and reflect during your breaks. Learn to savor the flavors, textures, and colors of your food.

Feel Better Today: Don't Give In to Temptation When You Eat Out or Are on the Go

It's important to have a basic food plan and to make smart choices at the grocery store, at work, at restaurants, and when you are on the go running errands or chauffeuring the children.

- Make a weekly menu and grocery list to save time and ensure that you have the ingredients for simple meals in your cupboard and refrigerator.

- Avoid the convenience foods and impulse items at the ends of the supermarket aisles. For lunch at work, take some healthy leftovers or make a sandwich on whole wheat bread. Drink a sugar-free beverage or a serving of low-fat milk and take a piece of fruit for dessert. This is cheaper and healthier than eating at the deli.

- When running errands, chauffeuring, or commuting, take along some sliced-up fruit, baby carrots, string cheese, or raw almonds.

Feel Better Today: Balance Food and Activity

About one-third of the new MyPyramid is comprised of steps representing the importance of physical activity in our lives. Every day that you eat, you should plan to get some form of exercise. Sixty minutes of moderate intensity exercise is recommended for most days. Our bodies were made to move, and we feel better if we are more active. Find a friend or get a dog to walk with. A dog will get you into the habit of a daily walk and won't let you miss a day. Vary your activities so that you won't become bored with your exercise routine. You'll be surprised when you begin looking forward to your exercise time. If finding time to exercise is a problem, take the stairs at work and park a few blocks away from your workplace. See chapter 20, Exercise, in this workbook for more ideas on this important topic.

The MyPyramid Food Calorie Levels are based on your activity level. *Sedentary* is defined as less than thirty minutes of moderate physical exercise in addition to your daily activities. *Moderately active* is thirty to sixty minutes of daily exercise and *Active* is defined as more than sixty minutes of daily exercise in addition to your daily routines.

Determine your activity level, then select your gender and age to find your recommended calorie level. The numbers that appear under your activity level and across from your age are the recommended daily amounts of calories you should consume for optimal health. After you determine your calorie level, check the MyPyramid Food Intake Patterns chart and note your daily number of food choices from each group. When you've completed these steps, you'll have the information you'll need to evaluate your dietary intake according to your activity level.

MyPyramid Food Calorie Levels							
Males				Females			
Activity Level	Sedentary	Moderately Active	Active	Activity Level	Sedentary	Moderately Active	Active
Age				Age			
18	2400	2800	3200	18	1800	2000	2400
19–20	2600	2800	3000	19–20	2000	2200	2400
21–25	2400	2800	3000	21–25	2000	2200	2400
26–30	2400	2600	3000	26–30	1800	2000	2400
31–35	2400	2600	3000	31–35	1800	2000	2200
36–40	2400	2600	2800	36–40	1800	2000	2200
41–45	2200	2600	2800	41–45	1800	2000	2200
46–50	2200	2400	2800	46–50	1800	2000	2200
51–55	2200	2400	2800	51–55	1600	1800	2200
56–60	2200	2400	2600	56–60	1600	1800	2200
61–65	2000	2400	2600	61–65	1600	1800	2000
66–70	2000	2200	2600	66–70	1600	1800	2000
71–75	2000	2200	2600	71–75	1600	1800	2000
76+	2000	2200	2600	76+	1600	1800	2000

USDA Center for Nutrition Policy and Promotion, April 2005

MyPyramid Food Intake Patterns										
Daily Amount of Food from Each Food Group										
Calories	1000	1200	1400	1600	1800	2000	2200	2400	2600	2800	3000
Fruits	1 cup	1 cup	1.5 cups	1.5 cups	1.5 cups	2 cups	2 cups	2 cups	2.5 cups	2.5 cups	2.5 cups
Veggies	1 cup	1.5 cups	1.5 cups	2 cups	2.5 cups	2.5 cups	3 cups	3 cups	3.5 cups	3.5 cups	4 cups
Grains	3 serv.	4 serv.	5 serv.	6 serv.	6 serv.	7 serv.	8 serv.	9 serv.	10 serv.	10 serv.	10 serv.
Meat and beans	2 oz-eq.	3 oz-eq.	4 oz-eq.	5 oz-eq.	5 oz-eq.	6 oz-eq.	6 oz-eq.	6.5 oz-eq.	6.5 oz eq.	7 oz-eq.	7 oz-eq.
Milk and milk products	2 cups	2 cups	2 cups	3 cups	3 cups	3 cups	3 cups	3 cups	3 cups	3 cups	3 cups
Oils	3 tsp.	4 tsp.	4 tsp.	5 tsp.	5 tsp.	6 tsp.	6 tsp.	7 tsp.	8 tsp.	8 tsp.	10 tsp.
Discretionary calorie allowance	165	171	171	132	195	267	290	362	410	426	512

USDA Center for Nutrition Policy and Promotion, April 2005

Feel Better Today: Maximize the Nutrition in Your Calories

You have just determined your personalized calorie allowance and recommended servings from each food group. It's important to choose a wide variety of nutritionally rich foods each day; foods that are packed with vitamins, minerals, fiber, and other micronutrients. Pick fresh fruits, whole grains, and low-fat dairy products. Look at nutrition labels to make your calories count. Any food item with over 400 calories per serving is too high in calories.

Sugars contribute many calories and few, if any, nutrients to your diet, so use foods low in added sugars. Sugars include sucrose, glucose, fructose, high-fructose corn syrup, corn syrup, honey, and maple syrup. Americans have a sweet tooth. If you've been abroad, you've probably noticed that American desserts tend to be much sweeter than desserts from other parts of the world. Including table sugar, sugar in soft drinks, canned foods, baked goods, and other sweets, the average American eats 130 pounds of sugar and sweeteners annually. These items provide very few nutrients.

As children, we were given sweets to comfort us. So as adults, when we are stressed, we still reach for cookies, candy, or sweets. Women are more likely to seek solace in sweets than men. It is thought that sweets trigger the release of *endorphins*, the natural opiates that create euphoric feelings. Although sugar may provide a temporary "high," it also stimulates the pancreas to secrete insulin to process the sugar. The pancreas sometimes overreacts and secretes excess insulin. The result can be *hypoglycemia*, a condition characterized by dizziness, irritability, nausea, and hunger pangs that may, in turn, prompt a craving for another sweet treat. Cravings for sweets are better satisfied with a piece of fruit. Fruit provides the complex sugars, fiber, and vitamins that sugary foods lack.

Clues for cutting sugar:

- Use less sugar, raw sugar, honey, and corn or maple syrup.

- Eat fewer foods that contain sugar, such as candy, cookies, and soft drinks.

- Select fresh fruit or fruits canned in juice or light syrup rather than heavy syrup.

- Avoid foods with sucrose, glucose, maltose, dextrose, lactose, or fructose listed as first ingredients.

Stay Healthy for Tomorrow: Cut Back on Fats

Despite all the bad press that fat has received in recent years, the average American ingests significantly more of his or her calories from fat (37 to 42 percent) than the 20 to 30 percent or less recommended by the U.S. Dietary Guidelines. We talk about cutting fat, but when we get hungry we still reach for our high-fat favorites, despite the presence of so many alternatives. The food industry has come up with dozens of new lower-fat snack and cookie products to help you make the change, but fruit or vegetable sticks are still the best low-fat snacks. Any bookstore has shelves full of low-fat cookbooks that offer menus full of tasty and creative dishes. Fat-free salad dressings or flavored vinegars provide alternative ways to reduce the fat in your diet. Even those people with no time to cook can fall back on "lean" or "healthy" frozen entree products. Be sure to check the label and select items with 3 grams or fewer of fat per serving.

There are three kinds of fat. *Saturated fat* is solid at room temperature and is usually of animal origin. Examples are visible meat fat, chicken skin, and butter. Crisco is an example of a *trans fat*, or an oil that has been highly saturated, or hydrogenated. U.S. Dietary Guidelines suggest keeping saturated fats under 10 percent of daily caloric intake and trans fats as low as possible. *Polyunsaturated fats*, like corn and safflower oil, remain liquid even when refrigerated. *Unsaturated* or *monounsaturated fat* is liquid at room temperature but solidifies when chilled. Monounsaturated oils, such as canola and olive oil, are now recommended over polyunsaturated oils. Although the exact relation of fats to hypertension and heart disease is still controversial, the most widely accepted theory is that saturated and trans fats contribute to heart disease and strokes by elevating the body's cholesterol level. *The Dietary Guidelines* (2005) recommend total fat intake of 20 to 35 percent of total calories, or 400 to 700 fat and oil calories daily in a 2000 calorie diet.

Dietary products to reduce or modify fat intake are widely available on the market, but there are as yet no long-term studies of their impact on health. Molly McButter is a low-calorie butter substitute. Products containing omega-3 fats are available to assist in reducing triglyceride and cholesterol levels. Fat replacers like olestra (brand name Olean) are chemically altered so that they pass through the body unabsorbed.

PLANT STANOLS AND STEROLS

Plant stanols and sterols are found in cholesterol-lowering spreads. Plant sterols and stanols are *phytosterols*—essential parts of plant membranes that resemble the chemical structure of animal cholesterol and carry out similar cellular functions in plants. *Sterols* are present in small quantities in many fruits, vegetables, nuts, seeds, cereals, legumes, vegetable oils, and other plant sources. *Stanols* occur in even smaller quantities in many of the same sources. Benecol, a brand with stanol esters, can be used both as a spread and for cooking; whereas Take Control, a brand with plant sterols, is recommended for use only as a spread but not recommended for cooking.

How do you score on fat intake? Answer the following questions by circling the number in the column that best describes how often you select or limit the foods listed on the scorecard. Add up the numbers you circled for your total score.

Your fat score: Do you ... ?	Rarely	Often	Almost always
Choose lean meat, chicken, or fish?	1	5	10
Eat high-fat meats like bacon, lunch meats, or sausage?	10	5	1
Limit eggs to four yolks per week?	1	5	10
Read labels and select foods with less than 3 grams of fat per serving?	1	5	10
Choose low-fat or nonfat dairy products?	1	5	10
Limit fried foods?	1	5	10
Choose donuts, croissants, or sweet rolls for breakfast?	10	5	1
Choose reduced-fat or fat-free products when they are available?	1	5	10
Limit margarine, butter, salad dressings, and sauces on foods?	1	5	10
Balance a high-fat dinner with a low-fat breakfast and lunch?	1	5	10

Insert Your Fat Score: _____

Scoring. If you scored 10 to 59 points, you can do better. At 60 to 79 points, you're on your way. If you scored over 80 points, keep up the good work!

Stay Healthy for Tomorrow: Limit Sodium Intake and Increase Your Potassium Intake

Although sodium is an essential mineral, most adults in the United States ingest more than the recommended sodium requirement. The Dietary Reference Intake for recommended daily sodium intake is 1300 to 1500 milligrams (mg) for adults or approximately less than one teaspoon of salt a day. One teaspoon of salt contains 2300 mg of sodium. Generally, adult men average more salt than 4200 mg daily and women average 3300 mg daily (DRI). Sodium regulates body fluids, maintains pH balance, and controls nerve and muscle activities.

Our major sodium sources are table salt (composed of 40 percent sodium and 60 percent chloride) and processed foods, but sodium is also a natural component of milk, cheese, meats, and bread. A single slice of bread contains the minimum daily requirement for salt (230 mg of sodium). Check the label, and if any food serving has more than 500 mg of sodium, the salt content is too high, providing more than 20 percent of your daily total. If hypertension runs in your family, you may want to restrict sodium with the DASH (Dietary Approaches to Stop Hypertension) plan of eating. Information about this plan is available on the Internet or at your bookstore.

A high intake of sodium correlates with high blood pressure and increased risk of stroke. Since stress also aggravates these conditions, you will be wise to reduce your salt intake. Salt also increases edema, an excess accumulation of fluid that adds to the stress of premenstrual syndrome. High potassium intake (lots of fruits and vegetables) counteracts some of the effects of sodium on blood pressure.

Tips for shaking the salt habit:

- Avoid salty snacks like chips, pretzels, and nuts.

- Limit your intake of salty condiments like soy sauce, pickles, and cheese.

- Restrict your use of cured meats, sausages, and bacon.

- Learn to savor food with less salt and to substitute spices and herbs.

- Do not cook with salt and add little or no salt at the table.

- Read labels carefully. Avoid foods with salt or sodium listed in the first three to four ingredients.

Stay Healthy for Tomorrow: Know Your Ideal Weight and Body Mass Index

The body mass index (BMI) is one frequently used technique to assess body weight. BMI is a number based on a weight-height ratio that indicates your weight-related health risks. It doesn't measure body fat, nor does it take gender or age into consideration. A BMI of 18.5 to 24.9 indicates a low risk for weight-related problems. A BMI of 25 to 29.9 indicates some risk for weight-related health problems, and a BMI over 30 indicates a significant risk for weight-related health problems. Look at the BMI Table and determine your BMI and health-risk level. Another way to assess your health risk is waist measurement. If your BMI indicates a health risk and your waist is over 35 inches for women or more than 40 inches for men, your health risks increase as your waist size increases. This is based on research that indicates those with "apple-shaped" bodies

Body Mass Index Table

Body Weight (pounds)

BMI → Height (inches)	Normal						Overweight					Obese										Extreme Obesity														
BMI	19	20	21	22	23	24	25	26	27	28	29	30	31	32	33	34	35	36	37	38	39	40	41	42	43	44	45	46	47	48	49	50	51	52	53	54
58	91	96	100	105	110	115	119	124	129	134	138	143	148	153	158	162	167	172	177	181	186	191	196	201	205	210	215	220	224	229	234	239	244	248	253	258
59	94	99	104	109	114	119	124	128	133	138	143	148	153	158	163	168	173	178	183	188	193	198	203	208	212	217	222	227	232	237	242	247	252	257	262	267
60	97	102	107	112	118	123	128	133	138	143	148	153	158	163	168	174	179	184	189	194	199	204	209	215	220	225	230	235	240	245	250	255	261	266	271	276
61	100	106	111	116	122	127	132	137	143	148	153	158	164	169	174	180	185	190	195	201	206	211	217	222	227	232	238	243	248	254	259	264	269	275	280	285
62	104	109	115	120	126	131	136	142	147	153	158	164	169	175	180	186	191	196	202	207	213	218	224	229	235	240	246	251	256	262	267	273	278	284	289	295
63	107	113	118	124	130	135	141	146	152	158	163	169	175	180	186	191	197	203	208	214	220	225	231	237	242	248	254	259	265	270	278	282	287	293	299	304
64	110	116	122	128	134	140	145	151	157	163	169	174	180	186	192	197	204	209	215	221	227	232	238	244	250	256	262	267	273	279	285	291	296	302	308	314
65	114	120	126	132	138	144	150	156	162	168	174	180	186	192	198	204	210	216	222	228	234	240	246	252	258	264	270	276	282	288	294	300	306	312	318	324
66	118	124	130	136	142	148	155	161	167	173	179	186	192	198	204	210	216	223	229	235	241	247	253	260	266	272	278	284	291	297	303	309	315	322	328	334
67	121	127	134	140	146	153	159	166	172	178	185	191	198	204	211	217	223	230	236	242	249	255	261	268	274	280	287	293	299	306	312	319	325	331	338	344
68	125	131	138	144	151	158	164	171	177	184	190	197	203	210	216	223	230	236	243	249	256	262	269	276	282	289	295	302	308	315	322	328	335	341	348	354
69	128	135	142	149	155	162	169	176	182	189	196	203	209	216	223	230	236	243	250	257	263	270	277	284	291	297	304	311	318	324	331	338	345	351	358	365
70	132	139	146	153	160	167	174	181	188	195	202	209	216	222	229	236	243	250	257	264	271	278	285	292	299	306	313	320	327	334	341	348	355	362	369	376
71	136	143	150	157	165	172	179	186	193	200	208	215	222	229	236	243	250	257	265	272	279	286	293	301	308	315	322	329	338	343	351	358	365	372	379	386
72	140	147	154	162	169	177	184	191	199	206	213	221	228	235	242	250	258	265	272	279	287	294	302	309	316	324	331	338	346	353	361	368	375	383	390	397
73	144	151	159	166	174	182	189	197	204	212	219	227	235	242	250	257	265	272	280	288	295	302	310	318	325	333	340	348	355	363	371	378	386	393	401	408
74	148	155	163	171	179	186	194	202	210	218	225	233	241	249	256	264	272	280	287	295	303	311	319	326	334	342	350	358	365	373	381	389	396	404	412	420
75	152	160	168	176	184	192	200	208	216	224	232	240	248	256	264	272	279	287	295	303	311	319	327	335	343	351	359	367	375	383	391	399	407	415	423	431
76	156	164	172	180	189	197	205	213	221	230	238	246	254	263	271	279	287	295	304	312	320	328	336	344	353	361	369	377	385	394	402	410	418	426	435	443

Source: Adapted from *Clinical Guidelines on the Identification, Evaluation, and Treatment of Overweight and Obesity in Adults: The Evidence Report.* (www.nhlbi.nih.gov/guidelines/obesity/bmi_tbl.htm)

have more health risk factors than those with "pear-shaped" bodies, who carry their weight on their hips and thighs.

Healthy Weights for Men and Women

Height	Men	Women
4'10"		91–119 lbs.
4'11"		94–122 lbs.
5'0"		96–125 lbs.
5'1"		99–128 lbs.
5'2"	112–141 lbs.	102–131 lbs.
5'3"	115–144 lbs.	105–134 lbs.
5'4"	118–148 lbs.	108–138 lbs.
5'5"	121–152 lbs.	111–142 lbs.
5'6"	124–156 lbs.	114–146 lbs.
5'7"	128–161 lbs.	118–150 lbs.
5'8"	132–166 lbs.	122–154 lbs.
5'9"	136–170 lbs.	126–158 lbs.
5'10"	140–174 lbs.	130–163 lbs.
5'11"	144–179 lbs.	134–168 lbs.
6'0"	148–184 lbs.	138–173 lbs.
6'1"	152–189 lbs.	
6'2"	156–194 lbs.	
6'3"	160-199 lbs.	
6'4"	164–204 lbs.	

Stay Healthy for Tomorrow: Attain or Maintain Your Ideal Weight

Although there are thousands of weight-reduction diets, the best weight-control strategy is a lifelong sensible eating plan. Today, we know that diets just don't work. Current research indicates that "yo-yo" dieting damages health and makes each successive attempt to lose weight even harder.

Diets don't work because most dieters don't reach their diet objectives. After all, diets represent food deprivation, which is emotionally difficult for most of us. In addition, your body interprets the diet regime as a famine, and reduces your overall metabolic rate to decrease the impact of deprivation on your body. The more rigorous the diet, the more your body will resist losing weight. For those who do achieve significant weight loss, more than 95 percent of them will not keep the weight off for even one year, and they end up dieting again. This sets the yo-yo spinning, and with each new diet the body lowers the energy required for maintenance a little bit more, making weight control increasingly more difficult.

It is better for you to maintain a moderate weight gain than to diet continually in order to lose the same ten pounds over and over again. The simple math is that you must expend more calories than you eat in order to avoid gaining weight. The ideal combination is to eat a little less and exercise a little more. It is also possible to eat the same quantity of food, or even more, if you cut the fat content of your food.

The best approach to weight control is to reduce your daily food intake by 100 calories and to burn 100 more calories a day by increasing your exercise. This means that by cutting out one slice of bread a day and walking one mile a day more than you do now, you will be twenty pounds lighter one year from now!

Diets are just a temporary quick fix; weight control is a lifelong lifestyle issue. Dealing with this issue means making a commitment to low-fat cooking methods, to choosing low-calorie, low-fat foods consistently, and to being satisfied with smaller portions.

A program that provides good nutrition education and realistic exercise goals can help you make a lifelong commitment. For example, Weight Watchers, one of the most reputable programs, advocates eating lots of vegetables, cutting down on fat, and increasing exercise. It also offers behavior modification programs, and support. There are chapters in most cities; check your phone book or local website for a convenient location. Other organizations that provide educational and support programs include Overeaters Anonymous, the YMCA and YWCA, as well as many health-insurance programs, local colleges, and community centers.

Good weight-control programs emphasize behavioral changes that enhance weight control, such as the following:

- **Eat slowly.** Take small bites and truly enjoy the color, taste, and texture of your food. After you've finished eating a meal, remember that it takes twenty minutes for the hypothalamus—the area in the brain that governs appetite and hunger—to register that you are full and to provide that feedback that you are full to your brain.

- **Concentrate on eating.** Eat mindfully. Don't read or watch TV while eating. Enjoy eating as your primary activity so you can be aware of flavors, colors, and portion size.

- **Eat regularly.** Some studies have shown that people who eat three to five small meals daily are more likely to control their appetite and their weight successfully. This may be because they do not get excessively hungry and overeat. People who eat breakfast consume fewer calories, maintain healthier weights, and have reduced risk of heart disease. Studies also indicate that people who eat a healthy breakfast consume fewer total calories daily (Duyff 2006).

- **Control portion size.** Portions are generally a half a cup. You can eat anything you want so long as the portion fits in a four-ounce Pyrex custard cup.

- **Don't eat when you're bored.** Substitute a different pleasurable activity, such as taking a walk, calling a friend, or engaging in a hobby.

- **Don't eat when you're angry.** Write a letter to the person you're angry with (but don't send it) or go jogging or do some gardening. If you must bite down on something, make sure that something is a carrot or sugarless gum.

- **Don't eat when you're tired.** Go to bed or take a hot bath. You may be surprised to find that a walk or a bike ride may even reenergize you.

- **Don't eat when you're anxious or depressed.** Engage in physical activity, go to a movie, talk to a friend, or find a way to deal with the issues contributing to the anxiety or depression.

Stay Healthy for Tomorrow: Limit or Avoid Caffeine

Coffee, tea, chocolate, colas, and some medications may be high in caffeine, which may contribute to irritability, nervousness, sleep difficulties, and gastrointestinal distress. If you drink regular coffee, that is, not decaffeinated, a daily limit of 200 mg of caffeine, or 1 to 2 cups of percolated coffee, is recommended by the American Medical Association.

Caffeine Content of Beverages and Chocolate		
Beverage or Chocolate	*Serving*	*Caffeine Content*
Regular coffee, brewed	8 oz.	80–135 mg
Decaffeinated coffee, brewed	8 oz.	5–10 mg
Instant coffee	8 oz.	65–100 mg
Black tea, brewed	8 oz.	35–40 mg
Instant tea	8 oz.	15 mg
Green tea	8 oz.	15–30 mg
Canned iced tea	12-16 oz.	9–50 mg
Cola drinks	12 oz.	35–55 mg
Hot chocolate	8 oz.	5–15 mg
Dark chocolate	1 oz.	5–35 mg
Milk chocolate	1 oz.	5–10 mg

Stay Healthy for Tomorrow: Drink in Moderation or Not at All

As a tool for reducing stress, alcohol has the bothersome side effect of reducing one's accurate perceptions of reality as well. Although some research indicates that a drink a day may increase longevity, reliance on alcohol to deal with daily life is a dangerous practice. Alcoholic beverages are high in calories and low in nutrients. Excess alcohol depletes B vitamins, alters blood sugar, elevates blood pressure, and disrupts relationships. If you drink, limit yourself to one to two drinks.

Stay Healthy for Tomorrow: Take a Multivitamin Tablet Daily

In the early 1990s, the Food and Nutrition Board of the National Academy of Sciences undertook the task of revising the Recommended Dietary Allowances (RDAs), and the Dietary Reference Intakes (DRIs) were born. DRIs include the Recommended Dietary Allowance (RDA), the Adequate Intake (AI), and the Tolerable Upper Intake Level (UL). The old Recommended Dietary Allowances (RDAs) are now expressed as Dietary Reference Intakes (DRIs). DRIs are daily nutrient recommendations based on age and gender and are set at levels to meet the needs of healthy individuals. The recommendations include allowances for individual variation. You will also see Daily Values (DV) used on vitamin and nutrition labels, which are based on the RDA.

Vitamins and minerals are necessary in small amounts, and without them metabolism is impaired. Because we do not all eat according to the recommendations every day, a multivitamin tablet may serve as an "insurance policy." However, taking vitamins is not a substitute for eating well. There are undoubtedly compounds in foods that we have not yet identified that are nutritionally important adjuncts to the proper functioning of vitamins and minerals in metabolism.

Multivitamins provide you with extra amounts of the B vitamins, which are linked to stress, and vitamins A, E, and C, which seem to have anticarcinogenic properties. Multivitamins can also supplement any minerals that have been inactivated by fiber in the diet. Vitamins marketed as "stress tabs" or "stress formulations" are meant to be taken for physical stress, rather than psychological stress. Note that more is not better when supplementing vitamins and minerals.

Fat-soluble vitamins may become toxic because they accumulate in the liver. New evidence indicates that an overdose of water-soluble vitamins may also be toxic. We do know that consistent doses of over 3 grams of vitamin C a day increase the risk of kidney stones. Vitamin and mineral function is interrelated: vitamin C enhances iron absorption; vitamin D, calcium, and phosphorus work together in bone metabolism; and B vitamins are necessary for burning glucose as a fuel for the body. As stated, vitamins and minerals are interrelated, so increasing intake of one often causes an imbalance in another. Supplements should not exceed the Tolerable Upper Intake Level (UL) for each element, due to the danger of toxicity.

Dietary Reference Intakes (DRIs) (Recommended Intakes for Individuals)				
	Men		Women	
Age	31–50	51+	31–50	51+
Protein (grams)	63	63	50	50
Fat-Soluble Vitamins				
Vitamin A (μg /d)*	**900**	900	700	700
Vitamin D (μg /d)	5	10	5	10
Vitamin E (μg TE/d)	**15**	15	15	15
Vitamin K (μg/d)	120	120	90	90

Water-Soluble Vitamins				
Vitamin C (mg/d)	90	90	75	75
Thiamine (mg/d)	1.2	1.2	1.1	1.1
Riboflavin (mg/d)	1.3	1.3	1.1	1.1
Niacin (mg/d)	16	16	14	14
Folate (μg/d)	400	400	400	400
Vitamin B$_{12}$ (μg/d)	2.4	2.4	2.4	2.4
*(μg/d) = micrograms a day				
Minerals				
Calcium (mg/d)	1000	1200	1000	1200
Copper (μg/d)	900	900	900	900
Iodine (μg/d)	150	150	150	150
Iron (mg/d)	8	8	18	8
Magnesium (mg/d)	420	420	320	320
Phosphorus (mg/d)	700	700	700	700
Selenium (μg/d)	55	55	55	55
Zinc (mg/d)	11	11	8	8

ł Bold type = RDA, regular type = AI   (National Academy of Sciences 2004)

SELF-ASSESSMENT

Daily Food Diary

If you are interested in making significant changes in your eating habits, it will be worth your while to keep a record of everything you eat and drink for the next three days. Be sure to note the sizes of the portions. By doing this, you will discover exactly how much you neglect certain food groups and overindulge in others. You will be amazed to see how sugars and fats sneak into your diet. You will see important connections between the circumstances in which you eat and drink, your feelings, and your diet. You can compare your food diary records with the guidelines in this chapter to create a plan for a more nutritionally balanced diet. You may want to repeat this exercise periodically to measure your progress.

Before you start, take a look at Sharon's sample diary. Notice that in addition to writing down everything that she ate, she also noted the setting in which she ate and how she felt while she was eating. You should do the same as you record your daily intake.

Refer to Sharon's diary and MyPyramid Plan to fill in the Food Group Servings column of your diary. Sharon's example shows you how to count servings. Here are some specific guidelines to keep in mind:

- Note that low-fat milk counts as one milk serving and one fat serving, because nonfat milk is the recommended milk serving. Use plain or light yogurt to avoid the sugar content of yogurt with added fruit.

- Count all alcohol, cookies, cake, donuts, ice cream, or sweet rolls as discretionary and record their calories. All treats with fat or added sugar count in the discretionary group.

- Note that French fries contain at least three teaspoons of oil (equal to three servings of fat).

- Salad dressing is one fat serving for every 1 to 2 tablespoons of dressing. Use olive oil and vinegar for a healthy dressing.

Now, make some extra copies of the blank Daily Food Diary form and use them to record your food intake for at least three days. Be sure to write down where and when you eat, the setting and the people with you at the time, and your feelings. Eating is often tied to internal and external cues, and keeping track of this information may give you clues as to why you eat the way you do.

Sharon's Daily Food Diary Sample

Meal	Food	Amount	Food Group Servings	Setting	Feelings
Breakfast	Oatmeal Low-fat milk	½ cup 1 cup	1 grains 1 milk + 1 fat	Kitchen, alone	Hungry, hurried
Snack	Crumb donut Coffee w/ sugar	1 2 cups 2 teaspoons	240 calories 2 caffeine sugar: 36 calories	Coffee room	Happy, social
Lunch	Tuna sandwich on whole wheat with mayo Diet coke Apple	3 oz. 2 slices 1 tbsp 12 oz. 5 oz.	2 meat, fish 2 grains 3 fat 1 caffeine 1 fruit	Alone at desk, working	Busy, pressured
Snack	Grapes	Medium bunch	1 fruit	Coffee room	Tense, headache
Dinner	Hamburger on whole wheat bun Lettuce & tomato and mayo French fries	6 oz. 1 bun 2 tsp. 4 oz.	6 meat 2 grains 1 vegetable 2 fat 1 vegetable 3 fat	Home with family	Tired, grumpy
Snack	Rocky road ice cream	½ cup	250 calories	TV, alone	Tired, bored

			Daily Food Diary		
Meal	Food	Amount	Food Group Servings	Setting	Feelings

Sharon's Food Diary Summary

Food Group Servings	Day 1	Day 2	Day 3	Daily Average	MyPyramid Servings for 2000 daily calories
Breads and grains A serving equals 1 slice of bread, ½ cup rice, cereal, or pasta	5 servings	6 servings	7 servings	6 servings	6 servings
Fruit A serving equals ½ cup or one small apple, orange	1 cup	1 cup	2 cups	1.3 servings	2 cups
Vegetables A serving equals ½ cup or one 4 oz. potato	1 cup	3 cups	2 cups	2 cups	2.5 cups
Milk, cheese, yogurt A serving equals 1 cup milk or 1 oz. hard cheese	1	2	3	2 cups	3 cups
Meat, poultry, fish	9 ounces	6 ounces	8 ounces	8 ounces	5.5 ounces
Fats and oils A serving equals 1 tsp. oil or 1 tbsp. salad dressing	7	4	6	5.6 tsp.	6 teaspoons
Caffeine A serving equals 8 oz.	3	2	4	3	0–2 servings
Discretionary calories (includes alcohol)	526	350	450	442	270 calories 0–1 serving

Food Diary Summary

Food Group Servings	Day 1	Day 2	Day 3	Daily Average	MyPyramid Servings for 2000 daily calories
Breads and grains A serving equals 1 slice bread, ½ cup rice, cereal, or pasta					6 servings
Fruit A serving equals ½ cup or one small apple, orange					2 cups
Vegetables A serving equals ½ cup or one 4 oz. potato					2.5 cups
Milk, cheese, yogurt A serving equals 1 cup milk or 1 oz. hard cheese					3 cups
Meat, poultry, fish					5.5 ounces
Fats and oils A serving equals 1 tsp. oil or 1 tbsp. salad dressing					6 teaspoons
Caffeine A serving equals 8 oz.					0–2 servings
Discretionary calories (includes alcohol)					270 calories 0–1 serving

Summarizing Your Food Diary

For each day that you kept your Daily Food Diary, add up the total number of servings in each food group and write that number in the appropriate box on your Food Diary Summary. Average the result for each food group for the three days. Write this number in the Daily Average column for each food group. You will then be able to compare your daily averages for each food group with the ideal servings listed in the sixth column of the summary form. Refer to Sharon's Food Diary Summary as an example and then go on to fill out the blank Food Diary Summary using the personal data in your Daily Food Diary forms.

TAKING CHARGE OF YOUR NUTRITIONAL WELL-BEING

The food guide pyramid provides a goal for daily food choices. Review your Food Diary Summary and compare your average servings per food group against the ideal servings. Put a check in the margin of the groups in which you were below the recommendation. Put a star in the margin next to the groups in which you exceeded the recommendation.

After reviewing the facts presented in this chapter, is your diet more like the typical American diet or the MyPyramid recommendations? Chances are good that your diet is generous in fats and sugars and skimpy on fruits, vegetables, grains, bread, and cereals.

After Sharon had reviewed her own summary, she sat down and filled out her goal-setting chart. The solutions she developed may suggest some positive steps that you can take.

Sharon's Goal-Setting Chart

Food Group	Problem	Solution
Fruit	A little short of goal	Eat fruit instead of ice cream at night.
Vegetables	I hate veggies, so I did not meet 3-cup goal, and I did not choose any green or brightly colored veggies.	Eat more salads and add one new veggie each month.
Meat, fish	Portions too large	Weigh or measure portions for 1 week.
Caffeine	Too much caffeine	Switch to herbal teas, or walk during breaks.
Discretionary calories	Too many calories	Eat fruit or light yogurt at A.M. break.

Now it's time to fill in your own positive eating goals below. After completing your goals, go back to your Daily Food Diary again and review the settings in which you ate. Note anything about the settings in which you ate that might contribute to unhealthy eating behavior. For example, it's clear from Sharon's sample diary that eating alone at her desk provided no break from work and may have made her less efficient as her tension level grew in the afternoon.

Having lunch with friends or, at least, in a different locale would have provided a change of scene. She takes her breaks in the coffee room, where high-fat, high-sugar snacks are a constant temptation. If she plans ahead and takes a piece of fruit or some light yogurt to the coffee room, she can still have the benefits of socializing, and will markedly improve the nutritional value of her break.

SET YOUR PERSONAL POSITIVE EATING GOALS NOW

What changes or improvements would you make regarding the setting in which you eat?

_____

_____

_____

Now review the feelings that you recorded in your Daily Food Diary. Note any feelings that contributed to unhealthy eating behavior. For instance, looking at Sharon's food diary, you can see that she uses comfort food to try to feel better when she has negative feelings and sensations (tension, headaches, boredom, fatigue). Aerobic exercise, socializing, or a relaxation exercise might have been more effective for symptom reduction. She can also plan ahead to have a favorite low-calorie substitute available for those times when she knows she is likely to feel down. Going to bed earlier might prevent her need to snack when she feels bored or tired at night. If an earlier bedtime led to getting up earlier in the morning, she would also have time for a less hurried breakfast. How do your feelings contribute to your dietary intake? What changes can you make?

_____

_____

_____

Changing your eating habits will take some time. Concentrate on no more than one to two goals at a time for a minimum of one month. When you have integrated these new eating habits into your daily life, set one to two more goals. Depending on how many habits you wish to change, you should be enjoying a healthier lifestyle in one to six months. Making too many changes at a time can be stressful, so ensure your success by going slowly. Note that the changes you make to your diet also need to be tasty ones, otherwise you will feel deprived and have difficulty sticking with your plan.

FINAL THOUGHTS

You have the power to take charge of your eating habits, and taking charge will make a positive difference. Just keep the twelve steps of positive eating in mind and gradually make changes in your food selections. Put a copy of MyPyramid on the refrigerator as a reminder and keep it in mind when you shop. Go to your local bookstore and check the cookbook section for a new low-fat cookbook or magazine to inspire you. If you need a personalized nutrition plan, consult a registered dietitian at your medical clinic or check the yellow pages of the phone book. If you have questions about nutrition, try the American Dietetic Association website. Food is a necessity and a pleasure in life, so make positive, healthy choices!

FURTHER READING

Cain, A. A. 2006. *Cooking Light Cookbook*. Birmingham, AL: Oxmoor House Inc., Subsidiary of Southern Progress Corp.

Centers for Disease Control (CDC). 2005. *Behavioral Risk Factor Surveillance System*. www.cdc.gov/brfss

The Copenhagen Heart Study. 2000. *European Heart Journal* 24:567–576.

Dietary Guidelines for Americans. 2005. Published jointly by the Department of Health and Human Services (HHS) and the Department of Agriculture (USDA).

Duyff, R. 2006. *The American Dietetic Association's Complete Food and Nutrition Guide*. 3rd ed. Hoboken, NJ: John Wiley & Sons.

OTHER RESOURCE

Weight Watchers Program: (800) 651-6000.

WEBSITES

American Dietetic Association: www.eatright.org

DASH diet: www.nhlbi.nih.gov/health/public/heart/hbp/dash/new _ dash.pdf

Dietary Guidelines for Americans (2005): http://www.health.gov/dietaryguidelines/dga2005

Dietary Reference Intakes (2004): www.iom.edu/CMS/3788/3969/18495.aspx

Eating Healthy with Ethnic Food: www.nhlbi.nih.gov/health/public/heart/obesity/lose _ wt /eth _ dine.htm

Eating Healthy When Dining Out: www.nhlbi.nih.gov/health/public/heart/obesity/lose _ wt /dine _ out.htm

Food Intake Patterns: www.mypyramid.gov/downloads/MyPyramid _ Food _ Intake _ Patterns.pdf

Food Pyramid: www.mypyramid.gov

Food Pyramid Calorie Intake Levels: www.mypyramid.gov/downloads/MyPyramid _ Calorie _ Levels.pdf

Food Pyramid Personal Diet Tracking: www.mypyramidtracker.gov

Just Enough for You (About Food Portions): http://win.niddk.nih.gov/publications/just _ enough.htm

Low-Fat, Low-Cal Alternatives: www.nhlbi.nih.gov/health/public/heart/obesity/lose _ wt/lcal _ fat.htm

Mayo Clinic: www.mayoclinic.com

Exercise

In this chapter you will learn to:

* Use exercise to decrease the stress response

* Apply three categories of exercise to create a balanced program

* Monitor your response to exercise

* Motivate yourself to get started and stay committed to your exercise program

BACKGROUND

Exercise is one of the simplest and most effective means of stress management. The human body is designed for movement so we need to remain physically active if we want to keep our life in balance. Any form of exercise can counteract your body's natural stress response.

HOW DOES EXERCISE REDUCE STRESS?

Exercise returns your body to its normal equilibrium by releasing natural chemicals that build up during the stress response. Exercise can improve your resilience to stress in various ways. Some of its benefits are listed below. Exercise performs the following functions:

- Releases endorphins into your bloodstream creating a sense of well-being. (Some people call this the body's "natural high.")

- Decreases muscle tension caused by emotional stress and produces a relaxation response in your mind as well as in your body.

- Increases alpha-wave activity in the brain, thus allowing you to clear your mind so you can focus and concentrate more easily.

- Rids your body of toxins.

- Improves your overall flexibility and posture, thus decreasing any spinal stiffness or pain caused by stress.

- Relieves indigestion and chronic constipation caused by stress.

- Lessens fatigue and improves overall energy level.

- Combats insomnia caused by stress and produces more restful sleep.

- Provides a natural outlet for your daily pressures and enables you to better cope with the stress of modern-day busy life.

- Strengthens your heart and lungs, thus improving your overall physical fitness level and health.

- Increases your resting metabolism or energy expenditure and can help you to lose weight; thus, you both look and feel good and can shed a negative self-image caused by stress.

- Helps you realize that if you can change your attitude and behavior toward exercise, then you can change your ability to manage the stress in your life.

- Improves blood flow to the brain that nourishes it with needed oxygen and helps eliminate waste products.

- Reduces risk for those with stress-related medical conditions. "The evidence is growing and is more convincing than ever! People of all ages who are generally inactive can improve their health and well-being by becoming active at a moderate intensity on a regular basis" (CDC website: http://www.cdc.gov/nccdphp/dnpa/physical/importance).

This last statement alone should be enough to motivate you to choose exercise as a primary way to reduce the stress in your life.

WHAT IS THE EVIDENCE?

Evidence-based medicine (EBM)—you've probably heard this phrase. Your primary care practitioner probably cites evidence-based medicine when discussing options for your health care. But you don't have to be a health care practitioner to appreciate the evidence that exercise reduces stress. Some studies go as far as saying that physical exercise not only reduces stress, but that it also prolongs life. Exercise has been likened to the fountain of youth. Here is just a small sample of some of the evidence that's been gathered over the past ten years:

1. In the Winter 1996 *Journal of Behavioral Medicine*, an article by M. H. Anshel et al. investigated the effects of a ten-week aerobic exercise and progressive relaxation training program on responses to acute stress. They concluded that aerobic exercise is an effective strategy for dealing with acute stress because it helps reduce *task heart rate* and *systolic* blood pressure with the added advantage of producing superior performance on the target motor task.

2. A 1997 article on exercise and relaxation by R. J. Shephard concluded that acute stress may suppress immune function, and chronic stress may predispose people to a number of ailments that can "cause a substantial shortening of life expectancy." The article recommends choosing an exercise that is noncompetitive, moderate in intensity, and done in pleasant surroundings to achieve an optimum relaxation response.

3. Another article's results suggested that both physical and social activities are needed to buffer the effects of functional decline in the elderly (Unger, Johnson, and Marks 1997).

4. It was suggested that high-intensity aerobic exercise can increase vigor while decreasing tension, depression, fatigue, and anger (Kennedy and Newton 1997).

5. A study at Duke University Medical Center (Surwit et al. 2002) showed conclusively that stress increases blood glucose levels in diabetics, thus creating more susceptibility to the long-term physical complications of diabetes.

6. The ancient Chinese form of exercise called "tai chi" has been shown to combat a negative side effect of stress by reducing blood pressure (Science Daily 1998).

TYPES OF EXERCISE

There are three categories of exercise: aerobic/cardiovascular; stretching/flexibility; and toning/strengthening. If you want to achieve a fully balanced exercise program, all three categories must play a role.

Aerobic or Cardiovascular Exercises

Aerobic exercises are repetitive and rhythmic. They involve sustained use of the large muscles in the body, especially in your legs and arms. The goals of aerobic exercise are to strengthen your cardiovascular system and to increase your overall stamina. Aerobic exercise can improve the composition of your body by causing you to develop more lean body mass, thereby making you healthier. To produce this effect, you need to choose an activity that will allow you to reach your target heart rate. Instructions for determining your target heart rate are given below in the section called Sample Exercise Program.

Popular aerobic exercises include running, jogging, brisk walking, swimming, bicycling, and dancing. The wide array of choices offers alternatives to suit every lifestyle and range of physical conditions. You probably get a certain amount of exercise each day in activities such as walking, climbing stairs, housecleaning, shopping, and gardening. To find out how much activity you get in a day, use a pedometer. This device clips to your clothing and records the number of steps you take in a day. Wear it for one week, removing it when you do aerobic exercises, and record how many steps you do in a day. Approximately 2,000 steps is the equivalent to one mile. If you walk less than two miles per day, you should consider yourself an inactive person and begin your exercise program slowly. To round out your exercise program, be sure to include both stretching and toning exercises.

Prescription for Aerobic Exercise

Frequency: Most days of the week

Duration: Thirty minutes of uninterrupted, continuous exercise

Intensity: 60 to 75 percent of your maximum heart rate

Stretching and Toning Exercises

Stretching and toning exercises are neither vigorous nor prolonged enough to produce the cardiovascular strengthening that results from aerobic exercise. Instead, they are used to increase muscle strength and flexibility and to maintain healthy joints. If you lead a sedentary life or if you are in poor physical condition, stretching and toning exercises will help prepare you for aerobic exercise with a minimal risk of cardiovascular strain.

Stretching exercises are slow, sustained, and relaxing. To be effective, a stretch needs to be held steady for at least thirty seconds. Stretching exercises are convenient to do, because you don't need special clothing or equipment and they can easily be done indoors as well as outdoors. Stretching decreases muscle tension, improves circulation, and helps prevent injury when used during the warm-up and cool-down periods before and after aerobic exercise. The slow sustained movements of stretching help you relax and feel good as you focus and center your thoughts on the activity of the moment; you'll find that the worries of the day just drift away. You may even find that stretching before going to bed helps prepare you for a good night's sleep. Yoga is an example of a well-balanced stretching program.

Prescription for Stretching Exercises

Frequency: Stretch both before and after aerobic exercises, that is, during your warm-up and cool-down periods. You can also stretch whenever you're feeling stressed, tense, stiff, or tired.

Duration: Begin by holding the stretch position for thirty seconds. Do not bounce in and out of the stretch. Gradually increase the stretch to two minutes over a period of a few weeks. Breathe rhythmically and observe how your body relaxes.

Toning exercises utilize higher repetitions and lower weights to target muscles that need firming. Some good examples of toning exercises are crunches for stomach muscles, squats for thigh muscles, heel raises for calf muscles, and push-ups for arm and chest muscles. *Muscle strengthening* is a step beyond muscle toning. You strengthen your muscles by overcoming a resistance by using a greater weight and a fewer number of repetitions. There are three ways to strengthen muscles: concentrically, isometrically, and eccentrically.

1. *Concentrics* involve the *shortening* of muscles against resistance through a range of movement. Free weights, resistance bands, or the use of resistive weight machines are the most popular forms of concentric exercise. Concentric strengthening can be used to increase the size of the muscle or simply to tone it. Bigger muscles can provide more power, endurance, and speed. Toned muscles yield a firmer-looking body and are important for protecting joints. Concentric strengthening is a good way to gain and maintain the lean body mass that helps your body to withstand the stresses of daily life.

2. *Isometrics* involve the contraction of muscles against resistance, without any change in the length of the muscle fibers. For example, you can push your two hands together at chest level and feel your chest muscles tighten. Isometrics do not make muscles larger, but they do increase muscle strength.

3. *Eccentrics* involve the *lengthening* of muscles against resistance through a range of movement. For example, walking down stairs requires eccentric lengthening of the quadriceps (front thigh) muscles, whereas these same muscles must be concentrically shortened in order to walk up stairs.

Prescription for Toning Exercises

To tone muscles, rather than increase muscle size, use less resistance and do more repetitions. Doing three sets of ten repetitions with moderate weight is a good rule of thumb.

To increase muscle size, use more resistance and do fewer repetitions. One set of eight to twelve repetitions with heavy weight is a good rule of thumb.

Prescription for an Overall Exercise Program

Recommendations of the 2006 President's Council on Physical Fitness & Sports

(www.fitness.gov/challenge/stayactiveandbefit.pdf)

Phase 1: Begin doing something every day by increasing your physical activity as part of your daily routine.

Phase 2: Start walking, or any other low-impact activity, to build your endurance.

Phase 3: Exercise at the right intensity and duration for your age and health.

- Stretching and some light aerobic activity 30 or more minutes most days of the week
- Vigorous-intensity aerobic activity 20–30 minutes, 3–4 days per week
- Strengthening (1–2 sets of 8–15 repetitions) of all major muscle groups, 2 days per week

Phase 4: Enjoy a variety of sports.

SYMPTOM-RELIEF EFFECTIVENESS

Regular exercise is the best choice for relieving chronic muscle tension caused by stress. As stated above, the greater flexibility and better posture gained through exercise can relieve lower back pain caused by stress. Also, improved metabolism is a benefit of regular exercise that can relieve indigestion and chronic constipation caused by stress. In addition, exercise fights chronic fatigue and insomnia caused by stress. And, last but not least, exercise is one of the best ways to get relief from emotions like irritability, depression, and anxiety because when you are focused on your workout routine, your emotional concerns take an automatic backseat.

TIME TO MASTER

Set up a schedule of at least three exercise sessions per week over the next eight weeks. Make a commitment to yourself to stick with this schedule. Keeping a diary similar to the one described later in this chapter will provide you with a picture of the progress you are making during this initial period. You'll be surprised by how much better you'll feel at the end of these eight weeks!

DEVELOPING YOUR OWN EXERCISE PROGRAM

Hopefully, by now you appreciate the numerous benefits of exercise. If you are ready to start exercising, you can skip this next section. If you aren't, what's standing in your way? Do any of the following reasons sound familiar?

- I'm too tired.

- I don't have enough time.

- My obligations don't leave me enough time.

- I get enough exercise doing my job.

- I'm too out of shape.

- The weather is too bad.

- I'm too embarrassed in front of others.

- I don't want to look like a bodybuilder.

- It will increase my appetite and I'll just gain more weight.

- I'm too old.

- Exercise is boring.

- I'm afraid I'll look silly.

- I have more important things to do.

- I'm too fat to exercise.

- I'm afraid I'll hurt myself.

The reasons you may give yourself for not exercising are powerful. They are so powerful they've succeeded in preventing you from meeting one of your basic needs. Facing up to your excuses is an essential step to overcoming an inactive lifestyle. If stress reduction is an important priority for you, then you can find the time to exercise. Choose an exercise that you consider fun to do and you will be more likely to stay motivated to remain physically active. Begin by keeping a daily Diary of Opportunities to Exercise, which will help you discover the times in your schedule when you can exercise regularly. Make a note in your diary each time you have at least ten minutes free to take a walk or do some other kind of exercise. Also, write down the things you say to yourself that hold you back or give you an excuse for not exercising. Continue to write about your excuses for not exercising in your diary and when they arise, describe how you'll deal with those excuses.

Here is a sample Diary of Opportunities to Exercise:

ANGELA'S DIARY OF OPPORTUNITIES TO EXERCISE

Time	Opportunity to Exercise	Reasons For and Against Exercising
7:45	Let dog out to run in the yard.	I'm running late, so I can't walk the dog this morning.
8:15	Drive to work.	It's too far to walk, and my bike bike has a flat.
10:00	Drive with coworker to a special conference three blocks away.	I would have walked, but I couldn't very well say no to a friend offering a ride.
12:00	Drive to lunch.	I want to save time. Besides, it looks like rain.
1:00	Make calls to people who work on different floors of my building.	It's more efficient to phone.
3:00	Walk to post office.	I need to stretch my legs.
5:00	Collapse on sofa at home.	I could go jogging, but I'm exhausted and too out of shape since gaining those five pounds at Christmas.
7:30	Back on the sofa.	I could walk the dog, but it's dark and this isn't a safe neighborhood. Also, I have a headache. Maybe tomorrow …

Make a minimum of three copies of the following form to fill out over the next few days:

DIARY OF OPPORTUNITIES TO EXERCISE

Time	Opportunity to Exercise	Reasons For and Against Exercising
_____	_____	_____
_____	_____	_____
_____	_____	_____
_____	_____	_____
_____	_____	_____
_____	_____	_____
_____	_____	_____
_____	_____	_____
_____	_____	_____
_____	_____	_____
_____	_____	_____
_____	_____	_____
_____	_____	_____
_____	_____	_____
_____	_____	_____

- Look over your diary and examine the statements that you made to yourself. Are they really valid reasons for not doing something that is essential to your health and well-being?

- If exercise is really important to you, then you will create a space for it in your life. Remember that for a busy person, exercise is an especially important outlet for daily pressures. Without exercise, your ability to cope with the everyday stresses of your busy life is jeopardized. Exercise will give you energy and help keep your body fit, strong, and capable of handling any stress that comes your way.

- Even though you recognize the advantages of exercise, you may persist in a sedentary lifestyle because you see yourself in a negative light. Such beliefs can make it hard for you to initiate an exercise program on your own. To counter such a negative view, you could take a class, join an exercise group, or get together with a friend who already exercises regularly and who would encourage you to do so as well. Remember that exercise is for all ages and shapes.

You may be afraid of injuring yourself. If such is the case, books, classes, and experienced professionals can provide you with information about how to exercise safely, what to expect as you progress, and how to cope with any difficulties you encounter.

When Angela reviewed her exercise diary, she took a very close look at the reasons she was choosing not to exercise. Because she knew that these reasons were a barrier to doing something that she needed and wanted to do, she took the time to write out ways of overcoming these obstacles.

ANGELA'S RESPONSES TO REASONS FOR NOT EXERCISING

Reason for Not Exercising	*Response or Solution*
Running late … can't walk the dog.	I rarely have time to walk the dog in the morning because I don't get up early enough to do it. I'll set the alarm fifteen minutes earlier and get up as soon as it goes off.
Can't bike to work … flat tire.	It's not a matter of "can't": I just don't want to bike to work. But I can fix the flat so that I can bike on weekends, when I do enjoy biking in the country.
Can't decline a ride from a friend.	I'm full of "can'ts." Obviously I can say no, but sometimes I choose not to. I'll ask my friend to walk with me to meetings in the future.
Save time by driving to lunch.	An hour is plenty of time to walk to lunch, eat, and walk back.
Drive to lunch because it looks like rain.	This is the dumbest excuse yet! So what if it's cloudy? If I'm so concerned about the weather, I'll carry an umbrella or eat in the cafeteria downstairs.
It's more efficient to phone.	True, but face-to-face contact is valuable. And I do have the time to make the rounds in person.
I'm too exhausted, out of shape, and overweight to jog.	These are all signs of exercise deprivation and the very reasons why I should jog.
The neighborhood is unsafe after dark.	I could ask my husband to walk with me, or do some indoor exercises, or join a health club, or plan my exercises for earlier in the day.
I have a headache.	Another possible sign of exercise deprivation and stress accumulation.
Maybe tomorrow …	My favorite strategy for avoiding exercise! I'll go walk the dog right now!

CHOOSING THE BEST TYPE OF EXERCISE FOR YOURSELF

If you aren't sure which exercises you might like to try, then here are a few key questions that can help you decide. Think carefully about your answers. Be honest with yourself, because the answers to these questions may determine how successful your exercise program will be.

1. How physically fit are you now? 1 means "I'm really out of shape," 5 means "I exercise occasionally," and 10 means "I'm fit as a fiddle." Circle the number that describes your condition and add any comments you would like to make:

   1   2   3   4   5   6   7   8   9   10

   _____

   _____

2. What do you want to achieve with your exercise program?

   _____

   _____

3. How much time are you willing to spend exercising each day? Each week? What time of day do you prefer to exercise? Will this fit into your current schedule? What changes do you need to make to incorporate exercise into your regular routines?

   _____

   _____

4. How far are you willing to travel to exercise?

   _____

   _____

5. How much money are you willing to spend on exercise equipment, classes, or club membership?

   _____

   _____

6. What exercise/activities have you tried and enjoyed versus tried and did not enjoy? What exercise/activities have you thought of trying, for example, competitive sports, structured class versus spontaneous workout, alone versus with others, indoors versus outdoors?

_____

_____

Your answers to these questions will give you a sense of the kinds of activities that are appropriate for you. Walking may be the best way to start if you are middle-aged, somewhat overweight, or have been relatively inactive. Swimming is good for people who are substantially overweight or have bone or joint problems. If you work with people all day, you may prefer exercise that you can do alone such as walking, bicycling, or swimming. On the other hand, if you spend most of your day in solitary preoccupation with your work, you might prefer to make dates with friends to exercise or join a class in a community venue such as the YWCA.

Perhaps tension is a normal part of your daily routine, and you need an exercise that will help you let off steam such as kickboxing or a martial art, or a competitive sport like basketball or tennis. If you feel that "your glass is half empty" by the end of your workday, then a set of centering exercises like yoga or tai chi may be just what you need. The list of exercises below highlights some of the typical advantages and disadvantages of each and will help you select the best form of exercise for yourself.

ESTABLISHING GOALS

You are now ready to set goals and develop a plan to increase the amount of exercise you get during the day. Make sure that the goals you set are specific, measurable, realistic, and achievable, taking into account your overall health, your current level of fitness, your doctor's advice, your age, the resources available to you, your time limitations, and your personal interests. Write your goals down and post them in a place where you'll see them every day.

When establishing goals, you'll want to select the most convenient times for yourself. Once you've determined your optimal time to exercise, be consistent and stick to your schedule. Set one short-term goal for each week and keep the following considerations in mind:

- Morning offers the advantage of cooler weather and fewer people.

- Midday offers warmer weather and more people.

- Evening again offers cooler weather but most likely more people will be out exercising.

- On cold days, be sure to wear several layers of clothing and a hat that will prevent heat loss.

- On hot and humid days, drink lots of water during your exercise session and be aware of the signs of heat stroke: feeling dizzy, weak, light-headed, or excessively tired. On such days, you should sweat a lot. If sweating stops, your body temperature can become dangerously high. That's why you should stay hydrated.

- If your schedule requires you to exercise at night on city streets, be sure to wear reflective clothing, travel on well-lighted streets, and carry identification, a loud whistle, and a cell phone. This is an excellent time to exercise with a friend so that you are not out at night by yourself.

- Plan to exercise before meals or at least two hours after your last meal.

- Make a promise to yourself to stick with your program at least three times a week for two months and tell your friends, family, and coworkers about your exercise plan. They may provide support and encouragement to help you stay on track.

- It's true that "variety is the spice of life," so choose more than one type of exercise activity to minimize the possibility of boredom.

TYPES OF AEROBIC EXERCISES

Exercise	Advantages	Disadvantages
Basketball	Challenging An excellent whole-body exercise	Cannot be done alone Requires a court to play on
Bicycling (outdoors)	Changing scenery makes it interesting Not stressful on bones or joints Good exercise for the legs and heart	Requires a bicycle and a helmet You need to know how to fix a flat Traffic can be dangerous You need an alternative when the weather is bad Your arms don't get exercised
Bicycling (stationary)	Weather or traffic makes no difference No flat tires	Requires access to a stationary bicycle Can be monotonous

Dancing	It's fun, especially if you enjoy music Can be an excellent whole-body exercise	If done on a hard, nonwooden floor, can cause harm to bones and joints
Hiking	Takes you outdoors into the fresh air and lets you experience nature	Requires hiking boots May require other equipment or precautions if hiking in remote or unfamiliar territory
Martial arts	Challenging An excellent whole-body exercise	Requires skill Usually requires a partner or a class Requires space
Racquetball	An excellent whole-body exercise	Requires access to a court Requires some skill Requires a partner May be too strenuous for beginners
Rope jumping	Cheap and convenient Equipment is small and portable Can be done alone Can be done almost anywhere	Requires some skill
Rowing a boat	Can be very relaxing A scull with a sliding seat provides an excellent full-body workout	Requires a boat and access to water
Rowing (stationary)	Can be done indoors	Requires access to equipment Can be monotonous
Running or jogging	You can enjoy changing scenery You only need a pair of running shoes You can do this alone or with others Good exercise for the legs and heart	Can increase wear and tear on joints Can lead to injuries if not properly done May be too difficult for beginners or overweight individuals Takes a longer time to learn to enjoy than other forms of exercise

Skating (roller skates or on ice)	Can be done alone or with others	Can give you skinned knees and elbows Requires some skill Requires equipment and access to facilities
Skiing (cross-country or alpine)	An excellent way to enjoy nature	Requires some skill Requires equipment and access to snow
Skiing (cross-country on a ski machine)	Can be done indoors	Requires some skill and coordination Requires access to equipment
Stair climbing	Requires no skill	Can be very monotonous
Swimming	A good way to stay cool Good for joint pain or muscle weakness Good for large muscles in arms, legs, and chest	Requires an ability to swim and access to a pool Not a good choice if you are sensitive to chlorine
Tai chi	Low impact Increased balance Increased strength and flexibility	Requires a teacher It takes practice to master
Tennis (singles)	A good whole-body workout Can be done with others	Requires some skill Requires equipment and access to a court Cannot be done alone
Walking briskly	Can be done anytime, anywhere Requires only a pair of shoes	It takes longer to reach your target heart rate than other forms of exercise
Weight lifting	Excellent way to develop muscle definition	Requires access to free weights or weight machines
Yoga	Improves strength, balance, and flexibility	Requires a teacher It takes practice to master

SAMPLE EXERCISE PROGRAM

Warm-Up to Prepare Your Body for Exercise

Always start first with gentle warm-up stretches to avoid putting too much sudden stress on your body. Warm-up exercises increase your metabolism and your body temperature by increasing the flow of blood and oxygen to your muscles, heart, and lungs. They prepare your body for more vigorous exercise. They also decrease your chance of injury or cramping and can lessen overall muscle soreness.

- Length of time: Ten minutes of stretching and/or light aerobic activity before you begin your workout

Follow Warm-Ups with Aerobics

The simplest, most readily available form of aerobic exercise is brisk walking or jogging. Accordingly, a walking and jogging program is used in this section to illustrate the principles of aerobic exercise. You can use a similar graduated approach for running, bicycling, swimming, cross-country skiing, jumping rope, or any other aerobic exercise that you choose to do.

As you exercise, your large skeletal muscles rhythmically tense and relax, stimulating the blood flow through your arteries, veins, heart, and lungs. Your heart rate is particularly important. Much like the speedometer in your car tells you how fast you are going, your heart rate tells you how hard you are working. If you are traveling too fast in your car, you slow down; likewise, if you are going too slowly, you speed up.

Just as the speed of your car is measured in miles per hour, the work of your heart is measured in beats per minute. You can find out how fast your heart is going by taking your pulse. Practice taking your pulse while sitting quietly. Wear a watch with a sweep-second hand or digital seconds on your left arm. Turn the palm of your right hand toward your body. Place the fingertips of your left index and middle fingers firmly on your right wrist near the bone that joins your thumb to your wrist. You will feel your pulse. To determine your heart rate for one minute, simply take your pulse for ten seconds and then multiply this number by six. You can also find your heart rate in beats per minute by referring to the following chart. "Length" in the following bulleted list refers to the amount of time that should be spent exercising.

- Easy length: Ten to twenty minutes

- Intermediate length: Twenty to forty minutes

- Advanced length: Forty to sixty minutes

Heart Rate in Beats Per Ten Seconds and Per Minute

If you got this number in ten seconds	10	11	12	13	14	15	16	17	18	19	20	21	22	23	24	25
This is your heart rate in beats per minute	60	66	72	78	84	90	96	102	108	114	120	126	132	138	144	150

A normal resting pulse may range from forty to one hundred beats per minute, depending on your level of physical fitness. In order to benefit from aerobic exercise, your heart must reach and stay within a range known as your *target heart rate* for at least twenty minutes. You reach this range when your heart is beating at a rate of between 60 and 75 percent of its maximum rate. It is the safest exercise range for you, and exercising at this pace stimulates the relaxation response. The following table shows the estimated heart rates for different age groups.

Estimated Heart Rates for Selected Ages

Age (years)	Average Maximum Heart Rate (beats per minute)	Target Heart Rate (60 to 75 percent of maximum rate)
20–24	200	120–150
25–29	195	117–146
30–34	190	114–142
35–39	185	111–138
40–44	180	108–135
45–49	175	105–131
50–54	170	102–127
55–59	165	99–123
60–64	160	96–120
65–69	155	93–116
70+	150	90–113

Exercising at your target heart rate places a moderate stress on your heart, that is, a *positive* stress that strengthens your heart muscle gradually to improve its efficiency. By monitoring your heart rate during exercise and comparing it to your target rate, you'll have immediate feedback about whether you are doing too much or not enough exercise. If your heart rate is greater than your target rate, you slow down; if your heart rate is less than your target rate, you speed up.

If you are out of shape, brisk walking may push your pulse over 60 percent of the maximum heart rate for your age group. As your heart and lungs become better conditioned, you'll have to exert more effort by walking faster or jogging to attain your target rate. Here are three simple tests that you can do to determine how fast you should walk or jog in order to reach your target rate.

Test Number 1 Walk five minutes at a *comfortable pace*. Take your pulse immediately because the rate goes down immediately. If it is less than the target rate for your age group, go on to the second test. If you have already reached your target rate, continue to walk at this pace every other day until your heart rate falls below 60 percent of your maximum rate, and then go on to the second test.

Test Number 2 Walk five minutes at a *vigorous pace*. Again, take your pulse immediately. If you haven't reached 60 percent of your maximum heart rate, go on to the third test. If your pulse is within your target range, continue at this pace with aerobic walks every other day until your pulse falls below your target rate, and then go on to the third test.

Test Number 3 Alternate one minute of *slow* jogging with one minute of *brisk* walking for five minutes, and then take your pulse. If you still haven't reached your target rate, you are ready to continue with slow jogging every other day. If you have reached 60 percent of your maximum heart rate, continue to alternate one minute of jogging with one minute of brisk walking every other day until your pulse falls below the target level. Then increase the amount of time you spend jogging as you decrease your time walking.

You will need to check your pulse frequently until you find a pace that will keep your heart rate within your target range for at least twenty minutes. After that, monitor your pulse once per week to make sure that you are maintaining your target rate.

As you become more conditioned, you'll find that you'll need to gradually spend more time jogging or even running to stay within your target heart rate zone. A good rule of thumb is to continue to jog until you feel winded, and then slow to a brisk walk for about a minute. If you can sing while exercising, you're not exercising hard enough. However, note that you should be able to carry on a conversation while you're jogging without becoming excessively short of breath. If you can't, you're going too fast.

End by Cooling Down: Allow Your Body to Return Safely to Its Pre-Exercise State

A period of cooling down helps decrease your metabolism and body temperature and slows down your heart rate. Likewise, a cooldown period helps prevent muscle soreness. When jogging or running, always end your session with five minutes of slow walking. Take long, exaggerated steps, stretching your legs. Let your arms dangle loosely, and shake your hands. The stretching and toning exercises that you used as warm-ups can be used for cooling down as well.

- Length of time: Ten minutes of stretching or light aerobics after your workout

SPECIAL CONSIDERATIONS

Avoiding Injury

Here are a few suggestions to decrease your chances of injury:

- Have a physical checkup. Get cleared by your doctor or primary health care provider before beginning a regular exercise program. This is especially important if you are older, out of shape, obese, recovering from a serious illness or operation, or if you are taking medications that require regular checkups.

- Follow any special precautions suggested by your doctor or health care provider.

- Start slowly and build up gradually. Progress at a steady pace.

- Set realistic goals and monitor your progress.

- Spread your exercise over the week, rather than exercising only on weekends.

- Exercise within your target heart rate zone. Remember that you should be able to talk comfortably while you are exercising. If you are too breathless, you need to slow down.

- Always warm up before going for your target heart rate and always cool down afterwards.

- Drink plenty of fluids to replace the fluids lost during vigorous exercise.

- Don't exercise if you are feeling sick. Your body needs rest to recover its state of health.

- Don't exercise after a large meal because blood flow to the large muscles is limited.

- Don't use ankle or arm weights if you have low-back pain or knee or ankle problems. Weights place added stress on your back and joints.

- Wear comfortable shoes that offer good support to your feet and ankles. Replace your running shoes every 400 to 600 miles or every six months.

- Wear comfortable, lightweight, loose-fitting layers of clothing. Be prepared to remove clothing as your body temperature increases during the warm-up and aerobic phases and to add clothing as your body temperature decreases when you are cooling down.

- Use any equipment that is recommended for your protection.

- Listen to your body. Although you may experience some soreness after the first few times you exercise, you should not experience acute or sharp pain.

- Contact your doctor or primary health care provider once you have begun your exercise program if you develop any of the following symptoms:

  - Your heart rate becomes irregular and begins to skip beats

  - Your heart rate takes longer than fifteen minutes to slow down

  - You feel a tightness, pressure, or pain in your chest, shoulders, arms, or neck

  - You feel dizzy or nauseated

  - You feel extreme breathlessness after only mild exertion

  - You feel exhausted long after your exercise session is over

  - You experience acute or sharp pain anywhere in your body whenever you exercise

Sticking with It

There are two major obstacles to overcome when starting an exercise program. The first is just getting started. The second is keeping at it. If you have followed the instructions in the preceding sections, you've jumped the first hurdle. The second may be more difficult. Choose exercise activities that you enjoy doing and cross-train so that you have more than one activity from which to choose. Visualize success and stay with your exercise program until it becomes a routine part of your day.

Congratulations! By choosing to exercise on a regular basis, you are taking an important step toward easing the stress in your life.

Make a number of copies of the Exercise Diary and fill them out day by day for several weeks until exercise has become a regular part of your daily life.

EXERCISE DIARY

Week of _____

Target heart rate: _____

Remember to WARM UP and COOL DOWN.

Day	Activity	Location	Distance or Duration	Comments, Thoughts, Feelings
Monday				
Tuesday				
Wednesday				
Thursday				
Friday				
Saturday				
Sunday				

FURTHER READING

American College Sports Medicine. 2003. *ACSM Fitness Book*. Champaign, IL: Human Kinetics.

Anderson, B., and J. Anderson. 2000. *Stretching*. 20th Anniversary ed. Bolinas, CA: Shelter Publications.

Bodger, C. 1998. *Smart Guide to Getting Strong & Fit*. Hoboken, NJ: John Wiley & Sons.

Bonifonte, P. 2004. *Tai Chi for Seniors: How to Gain Flexibility, Strength, and Inner Peace*. Franklin Lakes, NJ: New Page Books.

Dworkis, S., and P. Moline. 1994. *ExTension: The 20-Minute-a-Day, Yoga-Based Program to Relax, Release, and Rejuvenate the Average Stressed-Out Over-35-Year-Old Body*. New York: Poseidon Press.

Finger, A., and A. Bingham. 2000. *Yoga Zone Introduction to Yoga: A Beginner's Guide to Health, Fitness & Relaxation*. New York: Three Rivers Press.

Gerrish, M. 1999. *When Working Out Isn't Working Out: A Mind/Body Guide to Conquering Unidentified Fitness Obstacles*. New York: St. Martin's Griffin.

Katz, J. 1993. *Swimming for Total Fitness*. New York: Main Street Books.

Kennedy, M. M., and M. Newton. 1997. Effect of exercise intensity on mood in step aerobics. *Journal of Sports Medicine & Physical Fitness* 37(3):200-204.

Meyers, C. 1992. *Walking: A Complete Guide to the Complete Exercise*. New York: Random House.

Rones, R., and D. Silver. 2007. *Sunrise Tai Chi: Simplified Tai Chi for Health and Longevity*. Boston: YMAA Publication Center, Inc.

Science Daily. March, 20, 1998. Tai Chi Lowers Blood Pressure for Older Adults.

Shephard, R. J. 1997. Exercise and relaxation in health promotion. *Journal of Sports Medicine* 23(4):211-217.

Sobel, D., and R. Ornstein. 1997. *The Healthy Mind, Healthy Body Handbook*. New York: Time Life Medical.

Surwit, R. S., M. A. L. van Tilburg, N. Zucker, C. C. McCaskill, P. Parekh, M. N. Feinglos, et al. 2002. Stress management improves long-term glycemic control in type 2 diabetes. *Diabetes Care* 25:30-34.

Unger, J. G., C. A., Johnson, and G. Marks. 1997. Functional decline in the elderly: Evidence for direct and stress-buffering protective effects of social interactions and physical activity. *Annals of Behavioral Medicine* 19(2):152-160.

TELEVISION PROGRAMS, VIDEOS, AND DVDS

Check your local TV listings for channel and times:

Sit & Be Fit, mornings

Stretch, mornings

Yoga, mornings

Chair Dancing. A series of exercise videos and DVDs that you do in the comfort of your chair at home. Call (800) 551-4386 or visit www.chairdancing.com

Collage Video's *Guide to Exercise Videos.* Call (800) 433-6769 or visit www.collagevideo.com to view their extensive catalog of home fitness videos and DVDs. Descriptions and ordering information available online.

WEBSITES

American Association of Retired Persons
www.aarp.org/health/staying _ healthy/stress/a2003-03-12-stressresources.html
www.aarp.org/health/fitness/work _ out

American College of Sports Medicine: www.acsm.org

American Heart Association: www.americanheart.org

Centers for Disease Control: www.cdc.gov/nccdphp/dnpa/physical
www.cdc.gov/nccdphp/dnpa/physical/growing _ stronger

National Center on Physical Activity and Disability: www.ncpad.org

National Institute on Aging: www.niapublications.org/agepages/exercise.asp
www.nia.nih.gov/HealthInformation/Publications/ExerciseGuide/chapter01.htm
www.niapublications.org/exercisebook/ExerciseGuideComplete.pdf

President's Council on Physical Fitness and Sports: www.fitness.gov
www.fitness.gov/challenge/stayactiveandbefit.pdf

Shape Up America: www.shapeup.org

Stretching Software: www.stretchware.com (sells computer software that reminds you to stretch throughout the day)

COMMUNITY RESOURCES

Health Education Centers at local hospitals and medical clinics

Walking Programs at shopping malls

Community Centers

Departments of Parks & Recreation

Senior Centers

TRAINING RESOURCES FOR LONG-DISTANCE ACTIVITIES

Avon Walk for Breast Cancer (walking): (800) 510-WALK, www.avonwalk.org

National AIDS Marathon Training Program: www.aidsmarathon.com

Team in Training, The Leukemia & Lymphoma Society (running, cycling, swimming): (800) 955-4572, www.teamintraining.org

When It Doesn't Come Easy— Getting Unstuck

This book has covered many techniques to reduce stress and tension. Essentially, they provide alternatives to your old stressful habits. You may have found that just practicing the new skills and observing the positive effects has caused you to give up your old habits. For instance, you may have found that practicing slow, deep breaths rather than short, constricted breaths results in a relaxed sense of well-being. This positive feedback from your body may have provided ample motivation for you to give up your old anxiety-provoking shallow breathing habit. However, if you are like most people, at some point you probably encountered some difficulty in exchanging familiar old habits for new ones. This chapter takes a look at why old habits are hard to part with, even when they are obviously contributing to your stress. It also offers some suggestions for how to deal with your own resistance to change.

If you find yourself skipping an exercise session you have contracted with yourself to do, or you are aware that you are just going through the motions of the exercises, ask yourself some of the following questions:

1. Why am I doing these exercises? What outcome do I want?

2. Are these reasons really important to me?

3. What am I doing or would I like to be doing instead of these exercises?

4. Is this alternative activity more important to me than doing the exercises is?

5. Can I schedule my life so that I can do the exercises *and* this alternative activity?

6. If I do not want to do the exercises now, exactly when and where will I do them next?

7. What would I have to give up if I succeeded with my exercises?

8. What or who would I have to confront if I succeeded with my exercises?

Chapter 16, Goal Setting and Time Management, covers many topics that could help you get back on track by: (1) clarifying what is most important to you; (2) setting goals; (3) developing an action plan; (4) evaluating how you spend your time; (5) combating procrastination; (6) organizing and prioritizing your time; and (7) dealing with overstimulation.

TAKING RESPONSIBILITY FOR YOUR DECISIONS

It is difficult to learn new habits on your own when, at first, the rewards for your efforts may be minimal. When distractions occur, decide whether you want to be detoured or to continue on your chosen route. If you decide to take the detour, do so with full awareness after weighing the pros and cons. Before going off on the detour, make an appointment with yourself for when and where you are next going to do your exercises. In this way you take responsibility for your decision. In addition, you are less likely to feel bad about yourself for not following through on your original plan, if that is your conscious choice.

What are the reasons you give yourself for skipping your exercises? Typical reasons are: "I'm too busy today," "I'm too tired," "Missing once won't hurt," "David needs my help," "This isn't working," "This is boring," "I feel relaxed and unstressed today, so I don't need to exercise," or "I feel too bad today to do the exercises." These excuses are seductive because they are partially true. That is, you may really feel very busy or tired, somebody may need your help, and missing one session probably won't hurt. The part that isn't true is the implication that because you are busy or tired or someone needs your help, you cannot do the exercise sessions. A more truthful statement would be "I am tired. I could do the exercises, but I choose not to," or "I could do my exercises, but I choose to help David rather than do them." The important point here is that you take responsibility for your decision to choose one activity over another, rather than pretend that you are the passive victim of circumstances such as your fatigue, David's demands, or any other priorities that keep you busy. You are in charge of your own life balance.

CONFRONT YOUR EXCUSES

The excuses you give yourself for not doing your exercises are likely to be the same ones that you've used for years to keep yourself locked into a stressful situation. These excuses are based on faulty premises. For example, a busy executive firmly believed she had no right to relax until all her work was done. She thought that if she ever took some time for herself, her department would not achieve the goals and outcomes she had agreed to meet each year. Over the years, she became anxious and depressed, had difficulty maintaining relationships, and developed a number of physical complaints. Her perfectionist belief that she personally had to oversee all of the work in her department before she could ever have the time to relax had caused a gradual depletion of her energy. Realistically, the work is never done; therefore she could never relax.

But she had overlooked her innate right (some would call it an obligation) to relax and replenish her vital store of energy. This woman had defined her priorities as being "executive first" and "me second," without taking into account the importance of maintaining good mental and physical health by relaxing and getting away from stressful activities for a while. If you, like this woman, say to yourself, "I'm indispensable. Important things won't get done without me and may even fall apart...," consider putting your mental and physical health at the top of your list of priorities. The key to productivity and good health is to create balance in your life.

If you are an energetic person who likes to get things done yesterday, when working with these exercises, slow down your pace. Having to prove yourself or needing to rush can only create stress. Enthusiasm may push you to take on too many exercises at once or to do the sessions for too long a time. When you do too much too fast, you run a high risk of burning out and losing interest. Furthermore, you are likely to feel guilty for not keeping up with the rigorous program you've set for yourself once your early enthusiasm calms down. Soon you will find yourself coming up with excuses to avoid doing your exercises at all ("I'm overextended already in so many areas of my life. Why should I add to my burden?"). In addition, you may feel confused when you begin to experience having more energy as a result of doing the relaxation and stress reduction exercises. Resist the temptation to pour this extra energy back into your work. Rather, use it for further rest and enjoyment.

If you find yourself saying things like "I just don't feel like doing it today, maybe I will tomorrow ..." day after day, give yourself a good mental kick or "talking to." It is simply not true that you must be motivated to do something before you do it. Motivation is often sparked by action. For example, if you take a brisk ten-minute walk, you are likely to feel good from the results and want to continue. Tell yourself that you have to do an activity for only five or ten minutes. Often, once you are into an activity, the momentum of doing it will carry you through to its completion.

At the very least, without feeling an ounce of motivation, you can work on a project five or ten minutes a day until it is done. Sometimes, lack of motivation is a symptom of depression. However, depression often improves when you become more active. Tell yourself, "Of course you don't feel like doing it. So what? Do it anyway!"

CONFRONTING ROADBLOCKS TO STRESS MANAGEMENT AND RELAXATION

If you read this workbook without doing any of the exercises, it's likely that you are only dabbling. Intellectually, you see the value of the exercises, but, somehow, you never get much past the stage of thinking about them; or you may actually do some of the exercises but never apply them to everyday situations. For the dabbler, this is just another book with some interesting ideas, rather than a workbook promoting new ways of experiential learning to deal with stress.

There are some individuals who are frightened by novel experiences, and their fear becomes a roadblock to their success. You might become overwhelmed by some side effect of a relaxation technique, such as tingling in your arms and legs. Unfortunately, you may then stop the exercise instead of going on to find that the tingling isn't harmful and disappears with time. You can get turned off by a single element of an exercise and, rather than changing the exercise to fit your needs, you may drop the entire exercise. Perhaps you don't understand a step in the instructions and rather than ad-lib, you chuck the whole thing. It can be a valuable growth experience to work through these difficulties on your own or to find a friend who would be willing to interpret and do the exercises with you.

WHEN SYMPTOMS PERSIST

Sometimes stress symptoms persist in spite of regular relaxation and stress reduction work. If you are a conscientious person and have been practicing regularly, this can be disheartening. Below, you will find just a few of the most common reasons why this might be happening to you.

Are You Suggestible?

Some people are highly suggestible and once they learn about symptoms, they begin to experience every one they hear about. For example, one very tense policeman joined a relaxation group to overcome his tendency to hyperventilate when under stress. He began to experience all of the physical symptoms described by the other group members: migraines, lower back pain, rapid heartbeat, and so forth. Doing deep breathing or using his coping skills training helped him to combat these tendencies.

Do You Receive Some Benefit from Your Symptoms?

A surprising number of people are attached to their symptoms, which often serve a very definite purpose for them. For example, your headaches may get you out of interpersonal situations you want to avoid without having to take the responsibility of disappointing others. You can find out soon whether your symptoms rescue you from more unpleasant experiences by keeping a log noting when your symptoms first appear and the activities (or would-be activities) that surround them. If you suspect that your symptoms provide you with a "secondary gain" in this manner, refer to chapter 17, Assertiveness Training. It should provide you with the incentive and the tools to learn to be more direct in saying no, rather than having to resort to the discomfort of stress symptoms.

Are Your Symptoms a Reminder That You Need to Change Something?

Your symptoms of tension may be a signal that you are not dealing effectively with something in your life and that you are covering up your feelings. For example, you may be angry with your family but not sharing this fact with them. You might be putting off talking about a particular conflict because you don't see any way to improve matters. For example, a nurse was visited every other weekend by her very spoiled, demanding stepdaughter. The nurse had agreed to the arrangement when she married and now she felt trapped by it. Over the course of three years, the visits from her stepdaughter invariably produced a migraine headache. To counteract this symptom, she finally negotiated a new contract with her husband that allowed her to spend Sundays on her own, away from home, while he spent the day with his daughter.

The people around you may very well be aware that you are withholding stressful feelings and that something is wrong. Nevertheless, they cannot read your mind and are unlikely to come to your rescue. You know best what you need. Letting others know your feelings and what you want opens the way to engaging them in helping you make a change.

Can You Find Other Ways to Take Care of Yourself?

Your symptoms may be your way of getting others to take care of you when you feel you cannot directly ask for help or for extra consideration. If you are tired and have a bad backache, someone else will have to do the cooking, cleaning, and keeping the house quiet. Ask yourself when your symptoms first began. What was going on in your life that might have contributed to them? One retired woman who had suffered from periodic colitis since early childhood recalled that her abdominal cramping had begun when her younger twin brothers were born. She remembered that the only time her busy mother ever had to hold and rock her was when she was suffering from the early symptoms of colitis. As an adult, she noted that she tended to get colitis symptoms only when her husband was away and left her alone in the evenings.

Does Your Way of Dealing with Stress Remind You of Someone Else in Your Life?

It is possible that you've developed a stress symptom similar to that of an important person in your life as a part of your identification with that person. For example, you may have learned not only to be hardworking and successful from your father, but also to deal with stress in a manner similar to the way he does. For example, carrying your tension in your jaw, you may come to the point of grinding your teeth just like your father. Since characteristic ways of responding to stress are generally learned, ask yourself who in your family shares your symptoms. It's often easier to see how your relatives are not dealing effectively with the stress in their lives than to see it in yourself. The next step is to observe and see if the same is true for you.

If you continue having difficulty reducing the stress in your life, consider consulting a professional. You may be interested in one-on-one psychotherapy sessions, or in joining a relaxation and stress reduction group. Your doctor, company health plan, community health organization, local community college, and adult education programs are all good places to start looking for professional help.

PERSISTENCE PAYS

Finally, don't give up. Your ability to relax, learn to handle stress, and heal yourself can be tremendously empowering. Change might not always come easy—you may feel stuck in your old stressful habits—but you can do it. All it takes is patience, persistence, a commitment to yourself ... and time.

Index

RET. *See* rational emotive therapy

risk assessment, 160, 163-166; form used for, 165-166; outcome predictions and, 163-164

S

salt intake, 309-310

Salter, Andrew, 249

saturated fats, 307

Schedule of Recent Experience, 4-7

Schultz, Johannes H., 99

Scientific American Mind, 224

scripts: for assertiveness, 262-270; for self-hypnosis, 87-89

seeing meditation, 61

self-contract, 286, 287

self-hypnosis, 83-98; abbreviated inductions for, 89-90; books for further reading on, 98; coming out of, 87; contraindications for, 84; deepening of, 86-87; effectiveness of, 84; general explanation of, 83-84; personalized inductions for, 85-87, 95-96; posthypnotic suggestions and, 87; power of suggestion and, 84-85; self-induction script for, 87-89; special considerations about, 97; specific problems and, 94-96; suggestions given in, 90-94; time needed to master, 84. *See also* autogenic training

self-talk, irrational, 135-137, 142-146

Selye, Hans, 2

short-term goals, 232

Siegel, Bernie, 66

sighing, 36

Simonton, O. Carl, 66

sitting meditation, 54

social stressors, 1

social support, 10

sodium intake, 309-310

softening around pain/discomfort, 62-63

special place visualization, 69-70; self-hypnosis and, 86

spoiled-child syndrome, 143

stanols and sterols, 308

Staudacher, Carol, 94

Stay Healthy for Tomorrow steps, 299, 307-317

strengthening muscles, 333

stress: aging and, 3-4; disease and, 3-4; fight-or-flight response to, 2; life changes and, 4-7; sources of, 1-2; symptoms related to, 8-9; tactics for coping with, 9-12

stress management: anger inoculation and, 205-221; anxiety reduction and, 157-186; applied relaxation training and, 75-82; assertiveness training and, 249-278; autogenic training and, 99-108; body awareness and, 19-25; breathing and, 27-40; combination techniques and, 109-115; confronting your excuses about, 356-357; coping skills training and, 187-203; effectiveness of techniques for, 13-16; exercise and, 329-353; Focusing and, 117-133; goal of, 12; meditation and, 47-64; need for persistence in, 360; nutrition and, 297-327; overcoming roadblocks in, 357-358; progressive relaxation and, 41-46; rational emotive therapy and, 135-156; self-hypnosis and, 83-98; taking responsibility for decisions about, 356; time management skills and, 223-248; visualization and, 65-73; work- stress management and, 279-295

stress underload, 280

stress-awareness diary, 21-23

stress-coping thoughts: anger and, 209-212; anxiety and, 193-198; creating your own, 195-198; examples of, 194-195, 209-212;

situations for using, 193-194; worksheet for, 214

stressful-events hierarchy: for anger, 215-217; for anxiety, 189-192

stress-hardy individuals, 10

stressors: goal-setting for changing responses to, 285-287; identifying your responses to, 281-284

stretch-and-relax technique, 110-111

stretching exercises, 332-333

Stuart, Eileen, 10

subjective units of distress (SUDs), 190

sugar consumption, 306-307

suggestibility, 87, 106, 358

suggestions, hypnotic, 84-85, 86-87, 90-94

Symptom-Relief Effectiveness Chart, 14-16

symptoms of stress: anger inoculation and, 206; anxiety reduction and, 159; applied relaxation training and, 75-76; assertiveness training and, 254; autogenic training and, 100-101; breathing exercises and, 28, 37-40; checklist for rating, 8-9; combination techniques and, 110; coping skills training and, 188; effectiveness of techniques for relieving, 13-16; exercise and, 334; Focusing and, 118, 129; meditation and, 49; nutrition and, 298; progressive relaxation and, 42; rational emotive therapy and, 137-138; reasons for persistence of, 358-360; self-hypnosis and, 84; time- management skills and, 226; visualization and, 66; work-stress management and, 280

synergistic effect, 109

T

Tactics for Coping with Stress Inventory, 11-12

taking control technique, 114

Taylor, Shelley E., 10

televised exercise programs, 352

Tending Instinct, The (Taylor), 10

tension. *See* muscular tension

tension cutter technique, 113-114

thoughts: anger-triggering, 207-209; autogenic quieting of, 105; catastrophic, 163; irrational, 135-137, 142-146; letting go of, 63; as source of stress, 1; stress-coping, 193-198, 209-212; work stress and, 287-291

threshold tensing, 43

time log, 236-242; evaluating, 240-242; sample of, 238-240

time-management skills, 223-248; action plan development, 233-236; audio recordings on, 248; books for further reading on, 247-248; combating procrastination, 243-244; daily use of, 246-247; effectiveness of, 226; 80-20 principle and, 225; goal setting, 229-232; keeping a time log, 236-242; managing interruptions, 247; multitasking and, 224-225; organizing your time, 244-246; overview of, 223-224; tactics related to, 225-226; time needed to master, 226; values clarification, 227-229

toning exercises, 333-334

trans fats, 307

type A personality, 9-10

type D personality, 10

U

unsaturated fats, 307

V

values clarification, 227-229; daily time log and, 240-242; identifying your priorities, 227-228; ordering your values, 228-229

vasoconstriction, 23

Martha Davis, Ph.D., worked as a psychologist at the Kaiser Permanente Medical Center Department of Psychiatry in Santa Clara, CA, where she did individual, couple, and group psychotherapy. She is now retired and living in northern California with her family. She has co-authored *Thoughts & Feelings, Messages,* and *The Messages Workbook.*

Elizabeth Robbins Eshelman, MSW, is a licensed clinical social worker who worked as a staff operations consultant for the marketing and internet services group of the Kaiser Foundation Health Plan. She is now retired and lives in the San Francisco Bay Area. She is preparing to become a certified coach for executives and other individuals and plans to use skills and techniques from this book in her practice.

Matthew McKay, Ph.D., is a professor at the Wright Institute in Berkeley, CA. He has authored more than twenty-five books, including *When Anger Hurts, Self-Esteem,* and *ACT on Life Not on Anger.* In private practice, McKay specializes in the cognitive behavioral treatment of anxiety, anger, and depression.

Find more help online at <u>cbt-self-help-therapy.com</u>. **CBT Self-Help Therapy** offers web-based treatment for stress based on the book *The Relaxation & Stress Reduction Workbook.* This interactive program can be used by clients working on their own, or their therapists can monitor their work on the secure server. Other modules in **CBT Self-Help Therapy** offer treatment for anxiety, depression, anger, and emotion dysregulation.

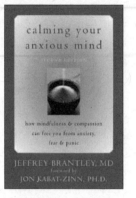